PRECARIOUS JAPAN

ANNE ALLISON

PRECARIOUS JAPAN

Duke University Press Durham and London 2013

Library of Congress Cataloging-in-Publication Data
Allison, Anne, 1950–
Precarious Japan / Anne Allison.
pages cm
Includes bibliographical references and index.
ISBN 978-0-8223-5548-9 (cloth : alk. paper)
ISBN 978-0-8223-5562-5 (pbk. : alk. paper)
1. Japan—Economic conditions—1989– 2. Japan—Social conditions—1989– I. Title.
HC462.95.A45 2013
952.05′1—dc23   2013018903

CONTENTS

ACKNOWLEDGMENTS

This book—on pain and precariousness, struggle and hope—has been as hard as it has been soulful for me to write. I am particularly grateful therefore to those who have given me advice, support, and help along the way.

Ken Wissoker has been in dialogue with me about this project from its inception. As my editor at Duke University Press and, more importantly, as a friend, he has helped germinate and sustain the entire project. For his guidance and belief in me, a deep thanks. Orin Starn has read everything—multiple times—and advised, supported, and prodded as only he can. I can't imagine having completed this without him. David Slater has been quite literally in the trenches with me in Japan, giving extraordinary assistance and wisdom of every stripe and iteration. For his generosity and smarts, I am deeply grateful. Yoshiko Kuga is a friend who has helped me in every possible way during fieldtrips to Japan. She is savvy and kind, resourceful and fun, and my debt to her runs deep. Keiko Nishimura has been a wonderfully resourceful research assistant in both Tokyo and Durham. I thank her for helping me in so many ways.

I have learned much from the many with whom I have shared my work or engaged in conversations on shared topics of interest. In particular, I wish to thank: Brian Goldstone (for all those amazing chats and suggestions), Claudia Koontz (for being my writing partner), Lauren Berlant (for her stunning work and our conversations on attachment, precarity, and sensing), Larry Grossberg (for his friendship and our ponderings about affect, precarity, and the political), Kathy Rudy (for her support and our wonderful talks about everything), Harry Harootunian (for being such an inspiration and now friend for such a long time), Arne Kalleberg and Joe Bongiovi (for the stimulation of our precarious reading group), Kathi Weeks (for walking and talking about work, hope, and precarity), Ian Baucom (for his brilliant class on precarity), Tomiko Yoda (for our lovely outings in Japan and for being such a good colleague), Michael Hardt (for his advice about this project and the bounty of his work), Tomas Matza (for all our delicious chats and for our class on "Anthropology of Precarity and Affect"), and Beth Povinelli (for the utter rush of her work that has been such an inspiration for my own). For their support in soliciting or encouraging my work I also thank: Andrea Muehlebach, Nitzan Shosan, Nick Long, Henrietta Moore, Shiho Satsuka, Clara Han, and Veena Das. For involving me in the Meridian 180 network I thank Annelise Riles and Hiro Miyazaki, and for their organization of the *Possible Futures of Japan* project, Frank Baldwin and Tak Ozaki as well as all the participants. And a very special thanks to the two reviewers of *Precarious Japan*. The attentiveness and care they gave to their task was incredible, making the effort to get what I was doing and to push me further in doing it better. One of my reviewers revealed herself after writing what was the most extraordinary review I have ever read in my life: a poetic re-rendering of the book. To Katie Stewart, thank you for this gift.

I also wish to thank my colleagues in the Department of Cultural Anthropology at Duke for their everyday collegiality, intellectual dynamism, and support; and to our exceptional graduate students, and particularly those who have shared interests and chats around precarity, temporality, and hope: Lia Haro, Yakein Abdelmagid, Juni Kwon, Samuel Shearer, Yasmin Cho, and Alyssa Miller. As at home, I have been grateful for those who extended opportunities for me to speak elsewhere, and for the many engaged interactions I've received while there. These include (Departments of Anthropology or Departments and Institutes of East Asian Studies at): Middlebury College, Reishchauer Institute, Harvard University, William and Mary College, University of Toronto, Tufts University, University of Capetown, University of Pittsburgh, Cambridge University, New York University, Indiana University, Temple University of Japan, Sophia University in Tokyo, University of North Carolina Pembroke, Chao Center at Rice University, University of Alberta, University of Colorado at Boulder, Institute of Ethnology at Academia Sinica, National University of Singapore, Brandeis University, University of California at Berkeley, and Università Ca'Foscari.

Given the nature of my project—on precarity in daily struggles that can lead to death but also friendship and hope—fieldwork was jagged in constantly sniffing things out on the ground rather than following a systematic grid or pre-ordained plan. I was seeking out "hardship in life"—something people aren't necessarily keen to share about their own lives or to have an outsider poke her nose into. And yet many generously helped me, and those who gave interviews, or invited me into their spheres of activity (of activism, protests, public speaking, everyday life), typically did so in the midst of horrendously busy schedules. Particular thanks to Yuasa Makoto—who allowed me into his NPO, Moyai, and made time for an extensive interview, Kimura Naoki—who took me into the temporary shelters of Sumita and opened up the world to me there, Suzuki Takayuki—for introducing me to his NPO and youth support center in Niigata and leading me to the *chiiki no cha no ma* scene, Kawada Keiko for her warmth at *Uchi no jikka*—Genda Yūji, Uno Shigeki and to all the other participants of the "Hopology" research group at Tokyo University for their wonderful work on hope, Dohi Masato—for welcoming me into his activist design seminar and involvement with the Setagaya Trust Fund, Tsukino Kōji and all the members of the *Kowaremono* performance group, Ochi Toshi and Shikimura Yoshiko—for their friendship and hospitality in Nīgata, Kyle Cleveland—for all his help and support for multiple summers in Tokyo, Kuse Keiko—for her continued friendship, Ueno Chizuko—for inviting me into her home, on her birthday, for an interview. In addition I would like to thank: Amamiya Karin, Miyamoto Michiko, Osawa Machiko, Tsurumi Wataru, Yoshimi Shunya, Mori Yoshitoshi, Rebecca Jacobsen, Tsutomi Hiroshi, Numazaki Chieko, Sugawara Yukie, Tamada Tomoko, and Kotani Mari.

Finally, in a book about a precariousness that extends to family and home, I return to my own. To my two sons, Adam and David Platzer, who are finding their way away from home, I am so lucky to have them in my life and to be engaged in a worlding of their own. To my siblings and their partners, I feel lucky to have their warmth and to share care-giving with one another, and our mom. To my mother, I delight in our evening chats and admire the strength and resilience she has carried to this stage of her life. And to Charlie, I thank for everything: for reading every word, for being smart about even dumb things, and for keeping my life less precarious than it would be without him.

ONE. PAIN OF LIFE

The story grabbed the nation's attention. The body of a fifty-two-year-old man, "mummifying" already, was discovered one month after starving to death. Not yet old and a former public official, the man was ordinary. But he died from lack of food in the apartment building he'd called home for twenty years. A welfare recipient ever since disease kept him from work, he was suddenly told funds would be cut off. With no one to turn to, the man was dead in three months. All alone, he kept a diary, pondering—page after page—what the country was doing for citizens like him who, struggling to live, have no recourse but to die. By the end, though, his thoughts were only on food. This last entry was what shocked people the most— "[All] I want is to eat a rice ball" (*onigiri tabetai*) (Yuasa 2008a).

A man dies alone craving the crudest of Japanese meals—a plain rice ball, a symbol of life and the cultural soul of Japan or, when lacking, of death, desertion, the utter soullessness of the times. The story was chilling. But, occurring in July 2007, it came at a moment surging with news similarly pinned to the collapse of mundane everydayness—of lives at once obsessed with and then left unfulfilled by food, human connection, home. Only one year earlier, for example, another case of a mummified body had been reported in the same city—Kita Kyūshū City. The circumstances were similar: a middle-aged man starved to death all alone at home. This man had also been denied welfare but, in his case, had never been granted it on the grounds that he had family—two adult sons—who could feed him. But familial relations were strained and only one son, who worked at a convenience store, gave his father food. And this, as the media reported it, never amounted to more than an occasional bread roll. Unable to work and (twice) denied welfare, the man lived in an apartment he couldn't maintain; all utilities had been cut off and rent hadn't been paid for months when he died (Yuasa 2008a, 43).

Life, tenuous and raw, disconnected from others and surviving or dying alone; such stories cycle through the news these days and through the circuitry of information, communication, and affect that so limn everydayness for people in a postindustrial society like Japan. A memoir about a homeless junior high school student (*Hōmuresu chūgakusei*) became a national bestseller when released in December 2007. Written by a famous comedian (Tamura Hiroshi),[1] it told of how, at age twelve and after having already lost his mother to cancer, a boy comes home one day to a boarded-up apartment and a father who tells his children simply to "scat" (*kaisan*). Deciding to fend for himself rather than burden his siblings, Tamura heads to his neighborhood park (nicknamed "shit park") and lives, as he says, like an animal: sleeping inside playground equipment, scavenging for coins near vending machines, eating cardboard and pigeon food (Tamura 2007). What readers (in chat rooms and on talk shows and websites) remarked upon most were the corporeal details of a "normal kid" reduced to scraping by in a park. That, along with the tragic story of family dissolution and fatherly abandonment: what made this, as Tamura's editor called it, an entertaining story of poverty (Shimizu 2008:29). Comic book, television, and movie versions followed in 2008 and Tamura's so-called "shit park" is now a tourist site. As one commentator put it, "we couldn't imagine a story like this ten years ago, but now, in every Japanese family, there is some unhappiness (Shimizu 2008:112).

The anguish of everyday life for those who have "socially withdrawn"—

a condition said to affect at least one million Japanese today—has been taken up by pop culture. These individuals, called *hikikomori*, often withdraw and remain in a single room they rarely, if ever, leave. Hikikomori are socially disconnected and detached from human contact: "homeless at home," as one hikikomori described it (Tsukino 2004). More often male than female and most commonly young adults, this is the depiction given to hikikimori in NHK *ni yōkoso*—the story of a university dropout who is entering his fourth year of isolation. Written by a self-avowed hikikomori as a way to make money by never leaving home, NHK *ni yōkoso*[2] is vividly brutal. Zooming in, as does Tamura, on the graphic details of a tortured existence, the story is said to be realistic in capturing the everyday rituals, nagging obsessions, and paralyzing delusions of a hikikomori. At the same time, this too—first as a novel (2002) and even more in the manga (2004–7) and anime (2006) versions[3]—has been heralded as edgy entertainment. With a storyline that jags between netgames, erotic websites, suicide pacts, and pyramid schemes, NHK *ni yōkoso* was promoted, rather oxymoronically, as "non-stop hikikomori action."

The contraction of life into a tenuous existence spurred action of a different kind in the summer of 2008. A string of violent attacks, all random and conspicuously public, plagued Tokyo starting in June. The first took place in Akihabara (Tokyo's electronics and *otaku* [fandom] district) on a Sunday at noon when the streets had been closed for pedestrians. Driving his truck into the crossing and then jumping out to stab more victims, a twenty-five-year-old man killed seven people within minutes. A temporary worker who feared he had lost his job, Katō Tomohiro lived a solitary, unstable life estranged from his parents and lacking—as he complained in the long trail of postings he left on a website—everything of human worth, including a girlfriend. Without anything to live for and no place to call home (*ibasho*), Katō went to Akihabara to randomly kill. His act triggered a series of copycat attacks in public settings like malls. The perpetrators shared certain life circumstances with Katō: solitude, job insecurity, familial estrangement, precarious existence. And while most were young, the last attack of the summer was committed by a seventy-nine-year-old homeless woman who, stabbing two women in Shibuya train station, said her motive was to be carted to prison where she would find shelter and food.

This violence was notable for how impersonal it was. Random attacks on strangers by people desperately disconnected themselves. But stories of more intimate violence are common as well. Those most spectacu-larly newsworthy have taken place within families — that unit assigned, by society and the state, the responsibility of routine caregiving and even sociality itself. In the same month of the Akihabara killings a seventy-seven-year-old man in Tokyo entered his kitchen and killed his wife with a hammer. Apparently enraged that she had called him a nuisance, the man then proceeded to kill the rest of his household — a son, daughter-in-law, and grandchild: his entire orbit for not only care but human con-tact. As it was reported, this "dangerous old man" (*abunai ojīchan*) thought he'd be happy once his family was dead. It was immediately after she had come to visit, cooked him a meal, and cleaned his apartment that a teen-age boy killed his mother a year earlier in May. In what has been the more persistent trend in familial attacks — children against parents and par-ticularly mothers — this one was especially gruesome. Decapitating her, the seventeen-year-old then carried his mother's head with him to a ka-raoke club and later an internet café. Hours later — and still carrying the head — the boy confessed to the police but could give no motive for kill-ing a mother he claimed to bear no grudge against. As the media reported it, the youth had stopped going to school about a month before and was taking medication for anxiety for which he had been briefly hospitalized. Before that, however, he had been a good student. In fact, it was in order to attend a highly ranked high school that both the boy and his younger brother were living together in an apartment away from home.

STORIES FROM THE everyday where death stalks daily life. Unease crimps the familiar and routine. A disquiet brushing the surface where the all too normal can turn deadly. Mothers beheaded, strangers killed, children abandoned, adults starved. These cautionary tales get told, and retold, at a moment of mounting insecurity — material, social, existential. But what precisely do they caution against? And, more to the point, (how) does one gain protection?

THE JAPANESE ARE certainly not alone in experiencing precarity these days. This condition has become ever more familiar and widespread in the world of the twenty-first century. I write in the aftermath of Arab Spring, in the face of Greece leaning ever closer to leaving the EU, and in the midst of a never-ending economic crisis that has only exacerbated what was al-ready a rising demographic of global citizens at risk — from poverty, disease, unemployment, war. Everywhere people are suffering, caught by the instabilities and inequities of neoliberal globalism run amok. In the acceleration, and spread, of a market logic that has privatized more and more of life and deregulated more and more of capitalism's engine for extracting profits, the struggle—and often failure—of everyday life has become an all too common story for all too many people around the world.

Given the extremity of deprivation experienced by so many of the world's inhabitants today, Japan would seem more notable for its vast wealth and what some say is the most advanced consumer culture in the world. Even today, almost two decades after the bursting of its highly engorged bubble economy, Japan boasts the third strongest economy in the world (having lost the second position recently to China). And any visitor who has recently been to Japan will know that department stores still do a brisk business even for pricey brand-name goods. Yet Japan also has the second highest level of poverty among the Organisation for Economic Co-operation and Development (OECD) member countries. Calculated as the number of people who fall below half of the mean income, Japan—with a rate of 15.3 percent—is second only to the United States, which has a rate of 17.1 percent. In 2007 this constituted twenty million Japanese: one out of six. (This compares with an average of 10.7 percent in OECD member countries and 4.5 percent for welfare countries like Norway.) Further, for a country that once prided itself on lifelong employment, one-third of all workers today are only irregularly employed. Holding jobs that are part time, temporary, or contract labor, irregular workers lack job security, benefits, or decent wages. A surprising 77 percent earn less than the poverty level, qualifying them—by the government's own calibration—as "working poor." The situation is even worse for women and youths; one-half of all young workers (between the ages of fifteen and twenty-four) and 70 percent of all female workers are irregularly employed (Yuasa 2008a).

Poverty, a word seldom spoken in Japan since the country's "miraculous" recovery after its devastating defeat in the Second World War, has returned. Not across the board, of course. But the ranks of the poor are growing (14.6 percent of children; 20.1 percent of elderly), as is an awareness that they actually exist. Few deny that a seismic change in the body politic has taken place in recent years: from a society with a vast (and materially secure) middle class to one that is now, as it's variously called, downstreaming, bipolarized, and riddled by class difference. As activist Yuasa Makoto (2008c) puts it, the reserves (*tame*)[4] that people were once able to count on—whether savings in the bank, families one could turn to in time of need, or educational credentials—are drying up. Japan is a society no longer of winners and losers, just of losers. But, as Yuasa points out, poverty (*hinkon*) is more than material deprivation alone. It also is a state of desperation, of panic over debt collectors and rent, a life lived on the edge. And, by this definition, Japan is becoming an impoverished country. A society where hope has turned scarce and the future has become bleak or inconceivable altogether.

Oddly, or not perhaps, the mood was strikingly different in the years of deprivation following the war. Then, as novelist Murakami Ryū has noted, no one had anything but hope. Today, by contrast, hope is the only thing people don't have, as Murakami wrote of the boom years of the bubble economy in his bestselling book *Kibō no kuni no ekusodasu* (The Exodus of a Country of Hope, 2002). People had become so consumed by materialism by the 1980s that drive and hope for anything beyond private acquisition was ebbing away. But things only worsened. When the bubble burst in 1991, triggering a recession that lingered on (and on), people began to lose not only their ability to consume but their jobs, homes, and future plans. For better or worse, the materialist dreams of postwar Japan are coming undone.

PRECARITY IS A WORD of the times. Picked up first by European social and labor movements in the 1970s,[5] *precarité* indexes shifted in late stage capitalism toward more flexible, contingent, and irregular work. At its base, precarity refers to conditions of work that are precarious; precarious work is "employment that is uncertain, unpredictable, and risky from the point of view of the worker" (Kalleberg 2009, 2). By this definition, most work for most workers around the world has been historically precarious, which makes precarity less the exception than the rule (Neilson and Rossiter 2008). Half of all workers in the world today work in the informal economy that is, by definition, precarious (Standing 2011). And in the United States most jobs were precarious and most wages unstable until the end of the Great Depression. But, in the case of the United States, the government stepped in, bolstering social protections and creating jobs with the New Deal. And as Fordism took hold and unions (and workers' rights to collectively bargain) strengthened, regular full-time jobs—and access to the middle class—became the norm by the 1950s (Kalleberg 2011).[6] In those developed countries that, like the United States, enjoyed a period of postwar Fordism that accorded its worker citizens (in the core workforce at least) secure employment, it is the deviation from this norm that the term *precarity* (and the "precariat" as the precarious proletariat of irregular workers) in large part refers. Precarity references a particular notion of, and social contract around, work. Work that is secure; work that secures not only income and job but identity and lifestyle,[7] linking capitalism and intimacy in an affective desire for security itself (Berlant 2011). Precarity marks the loss of this—the loss of something that only certain countries, at certain historical periods, and certain workers ever had in the first place.

Japan was one of those places. What it had before, and what has become of this in the precaritization of labor and life in the last two decades, is the subject of this book. Precarious Japan, a country struck by a radical change—in socioeconomic relations in post-postwar times—that conveys, and gets commonly interpreted as, a national disaster. And this even before the Great East Japan Earthquake and accompanying tsunami pounded the northeast coast of the country on March 11, 2011, rendering it a gooey wasteland of death and debris. This crisis oozed mud that literalized a muddiness existing already. But not only mud. The tsunami triggered a meltdown in the Daiichi Nuclear Plant in Fukushima that spewed radiation. It was a nuclear disaster reminiscent of the dropping of the atomic bombs that ended the Second World War and killed upwards of one hundred forty thousand at Hiroshima and eighty thousand at Nagasaki in August 1945—a reminder of Japan's unique history as the first, and only, country to be the victim of nuclear warfare. Atomic bombs left an unbearable wound but also ended Japan's militarist ambitions to render East Asia its imperial domain. And in "embracing defeat" under the occupation of Allied (mainly American) forces,[8] Japan entered its postwar period of astounding reconstruction, achieving high economic growth and astronomical productivity in record time.

Nuclear radiation and mud. A strange combination that mixes histories as well as metaphors. For if the disaster at the Daiichi nuclear reactor in Fukushima provoked memories of Japan's victimization and vulnerability at the end of the Pacific War—and the eerie risk of an unknowable, invisible contamination—the sea of mud that pummeled what had been solid on the coastline signaled something else: a liquidization in socioeconomic relations that started in the mid-1990s (but actually before) with the turn to flexible employment and its transformation of work and the workplace. This is called *ryūdōka* in Japanese—the liquidization or flexibilization of work and life. In liquefied Japan a change in the logic of work seeps into everyday relationality: relations once valued for their sturdiness in space (staying in the same company or neighborhood for decades) and durability over time (lifelong marriages, group memberships, and jobs). Sociality today has become more punctuated and unhinged. Along with replaceable work and workers is the rhythm of social impermanence: relationships that instantaneously connect, disconnect, or never start up in the first place. One-third of all Japanese live alone these days and the phenomena of both NEET (not in education, employment, or training) and hikikomori (social withdrawal) are well known among youths. As I've learned in the process of fieldwork in summers since 2008, many Japanese feel lonely, that they don't belong (anywhere), and are struggling to get by. A recent special on public television encapsulated current conditions of social life with the label "*muen shakai*" — the relationless society. Social precarity. Liquified Japan.

Japan had been rumbling long before the recent disaster of earthquake, tsunami, and nuclear reactor accident. Tremors underfoot, a sense of imbalance, the premonition of water turning everything into mud. The events of 3/11 spawned a crisis of unimaginable intensity. Over eighteen thousand are missing or dead; three hundred fifty thousand displaced; almost unimaginable and ongoing damage to businesses, property, livestock, and everyday life; and trillions of yen in clean up, reconstruction, and compensation. Beyond those killed, it has made life even less safe than it was before for so many: precarity intensified. It has also thrown into relief aspects of life that were precarious already; the fact, for example, that so many of the workers in the Fukushima nuclear plants were, both before and after 3/11, part of the precariat (close to 88 percent) — disposable workers for whom the safety of other Japanese (as in cleaning up and containing the spread and exposure of radiation) are now so intimately intertwined. News reports on precarious employment (dispatch, contract, day labor) are much more common these days, and the precariat have assumed greater recognition and sympathy in the public eye. Sensibilities of the Japanese across the country have also been raised to the politics of the "nuclear village": to the location of so many nuclear reactors in the region of Tōhoku where — because of its depressed economy and aging population — residents had accepted the dangers in order to secure revenues and jobs. Sentiments against nuclear energy and the nuclear industry have soared (I protested alongside of fifteen thousand in June 2011, but another protest staged in

Tokyo three months later drew sixty thousand), as have disgust and suspicion against the owners of the nuclear plants and the government for their collusion of interest, and for their mismanagement of safety regulations, clean up, and withholding, even lying about, information regarding radiation exposure.

In pre- and now post-3/11 Japan, multiple precarities — of work, of sociality, of life (and death), as the recent crisis has both exacerbated and exposed — overlap and run together like mud. But that doesn't mean that everyone is situated similarly or affected the same way. Certain workers are more prone to belong to the precariat, for example: those without post-secondary education and who come from households that are single parent and working class (or working poor). And, even during the boom period of the bubble economy, women were overly representative in the peripheral workforce as part-time workers (which they remain today with 70 percent of female workers employed in irregular jobs and with 80 percent of temp workers being female) (Gottfried 2009). That precarity is differentially distributed is seen in the aftermath of 3/11 as well. Those up north, already living in a region economically depressed and overly populated by elderly, have been hardest hit by both the damage of the Great East Japan Earthquake (and tsunami) and the deadly threat of radiation — a threat that has forced thousands to evacuate their homes with no assurance of ever being able to return. Those who have lost everything — family members, the boats or tractors used to make a living, the very village one has lived in since birth — straddle the precarity of life in a particular dance with death. An early story emerging from Fukushima reported how a farmer who had lost his wife and home was happy to see that his cabbages, at least, had survived. When these were then banned from sale because the radiation level was found to be dangerously high, the man committed suicide.

Though it may start in one place, precarity soon slips into other dimensions of life. Insecurity at work, for example, spreads to insecurity when paying bills, trying to keep food on the table, maintaining honor and pride (in one's community or head of household), finding the energy to keep going. It is not only a condition of precarious labor but a more general existential state — a state where one's human condition has become precarious as well (Lazzarato 2004). But the relationship between labor and life, job security and everyday security, depends on where one lives and where one is situated in the socioeconomic landscape of nation, workplace, and home. Workers in countries with good social protections are less vulnerable to labor market insecurity than they would be otherwise. In Denmark, for example, workers' security in life is not tied to a specific job; if a worker loses a job he can either find another one or expect support (in maintaining a basically decent life) from the state. Even with increased precarity in the labor market, local politics—or workers' relative power—can produce "post-market security": what is called "flexicurity" when flexible hiring and firing for workers is combined with a robust social security system for workers (Kalleberg 2011, 15). How to balance flexibility (for business, industry, employers) against security (for citizens, residents, employees) is a perennial problem for modern, industrial states. Different states, at different historical times, resolve it differently—through socialism, corporate capitalism, neoliberalism, state welfare, neoliberalist socialism (China's "neoliberalism as exception" [Ong 2006]). And, according to Polanyi, countries have swung historically in the nineteenth and twentieth centuries from one end of the spectrum to the other in a "double movement" between privileging market and economic growth to—when destitution and unemployment spike, spurring worker protests and populist rage—attending more to the needs (for security) of its citizens (Polanyi 2001).

During the 1970s and 1980s, Japan achieved a remarkable balance between high economic growth and a high level of job security for (male) workers. Under "Japan, Inc.," the country was considered a "super stable society" (*chō antei shakai*): one with a low crime rate, no war or military engagement, and an environment of long-lasting jobs, marriages, and social connections. Security—of a kind—was at once expected and desired: what one traded for diligence and compliance in a social contract that registered as the norm. Different from the post-market security of flexicurity, when workers are protected less by a specific workplace or job than by the state-sponsored social security system, Japan, Inc. operated through the market. Or, more precisely, it ran by collapsing the market into the workplace, which collapsed into the social factory of the family and home. Japan wasn't a welfare state and the government allocated little in the way of social provisions (which is still true today). Rather, it was the corporation and the family that figured as the de facto welfare institutions. Given a family wage to have and support a family, workers were taken care of but also wedded to the workplace—a dynamic that extracted labor from male workers and also their unpaid wives in managing the household, the children, and any attached elderly so that the breadwinner could give all to his job. Japan's "super stable society" depended on this knot of dependencies, labors, and attachments. And, as it unraveled in post-postwar Japan, a very particular kind of precarity and precariat has emerged in its place.

NINE MONTHS AFTER the earthquake and tsunami that crashed the cooling systems at the Fukushima Daiichi nuclear reactors, causing a meltdown at three units, it was announced that the threat had been contained. The reactors had been put into "cold shutdown," Prime Minister Noda Yoshihiko declared on December 15, using a technical term that indicates normalcy: intact reactors with fuel cores in safe condition. In this case "cold shutdown" meant that the temperatures at the bottom of the pressure vessels of reactor numbers 1, 2, and 3 had been stabilized at 100 degrees, stemming the release of radioactive materials. Pledging to restore the plant's cooling system by year's end, the government had lived up to its promise — or so it said. It now declared control over the damaged reactors; national safety was restored (Fackler 2011, A6).

But not everyone believed this assertion. Suspicious that the government was falsely declaring success to appease peoples' fears and anger over its incompetency, many voiced doubt about the accuracy and timing of this claim. Upon hearing the news, the governor of Fukushima Prefecture immediately challenged it. "The accident has not been brought under control" he told reporters, pointing out the myriad of dangers still threatening his contingency, including contaminated water (*Asahi Shimbun* 12/17/2011). And while some experts praised the government and the Tokyo Electric Power Company (TEPCO), the owners of the Fukushima nuclear reactors, for effectively cooling the reactors down, others dismissed the illusion of safety implied by the term "cold shutdown." Given that at least three reactors went into meltdown and have leaked radiation, the next (very delicate) stage of removing fuel from the reactors will be riskier, harder, and more time consuming than usual. Cold shutdown "is a term that has been trotted out to give the impression we are reaching some kind of closure," Koide Hiroaki, a professor at the Research Reactor Institute at Kyoto University, lamented, noting how even according to government predictions it would take at least four decades to fully dismantle the plants: "We still face a long battle of epic proportions and by the time it is really over most of us will be long dead" (Tabuchi 2011, A8).

Deathliness, as Koide suggested, should be faced rather than contained under false illusions by a government whose promises, and infrastructure, of safety can no longer be trusted. But he also spoke of a "battle," of fighting to survive in efforts that may require new tactics, alliances, and maps. A politics of survival; a dance with death that demands a different orientation toward life. What this means for residents of the affected areas now that the nuclear crisis is declared to be officially over and evacuation orders will start to lift is that some refuse to return. Unconvinced that they can be safe here, many are leaving (or breaking up the family, leaving the husband behind) to take their chances as "nuclear refugees" (*genpatsu nanmin*) elsewhere in the country — an elsewhere that means not only forsaking one's community, home, and (former) livelihood but also entering into what can be an alien and inhospitable terrain. Stories of discrimination against Fukushima evacuees floated almost immediately in the aftermath of 3/11. Reminiscent of the stigma that was attached to the atomic bomb survivors (*hibakusha*) of Hiroshima and Nagasaki, those who were living in Fukushima at the time of the disaster harbor a contamination that can render them socially polluting (Douglas 2002).

One news story I heard in July 2011 reported on a woman who left Fukushima Prefecture immediately following 3/11 but never found a home anywhere else to live and was now returning to Minami Sōma, which is thirteen kilometers from the Daiichi Nuclear Plant and close to, but not inside, the evacuation zone imposed after 3/11. But at eight months pregnant, the woman was high risk, a relief worker in town tried to tell her. Yet she was returning precisely because life was too risky elsewhere, the woman replied. Here, at least, she had both a home and a job. Riskiness defined by what and by whom?

But also in Minami Sōma a deputy principal of a high school dismissed the claims made by the government that, with the "cold shutdown" announced on December 15, the nuclear crisis was now over. Though his school had reopened in October when declared safe following a fast-paced cleanup, the principal was not convinced: "This does not ring true for us at all." By December, only 350 of 705 students had returned. Speaking of the Daiichi Nuclear Plant, but also his town and the country too perhaps, he said "the plant is like a black box, and we don't know what is really happening. I feel no relief" (Tabuchi 2011, A8).

And then, rumbling potentially underfoot, is the threat of another large-scale earthquake with the possibility of another tsunami. With its jury-rigged cooling system, the recent repairs on the Daiichi Nuclear Plant have not been made to withstand a major earthquake or high-flowing tsunami: a deficiency in the original plant as well, of course.[9] But geologists have announced that another major quake (somewhere in the region of Japan, sometime soon) is not only a possibility but a certainty. These are facts I was told myself when standing in the ruins of Ishinomaki, the town worst hit by 3/11, suited up in rubber and ready to embark upon shoveling mud in early July. The leader of the volunteer operation I had joined, Peace Boat, stood in front of us, also in boots. It came at the end of his speech about how to work hard, greet any residents, and be respectful of the area and people who had suffered so much. Then, not mincing words, he told us to be prepared because another earthquake would come one day soon. Pointing his finger to the hill behind him, he gestured to where we should run if a tsunami hit: "Run up the hill. And run fast."

This condition of uncertainty, of rumbling instability, a terrain muddied—by debris, contamination, death—is what Japanese face as their country moves forward in this second decade of the twenty-first century. As the recent crisis has shown, the country is on a fault line. No longer a "super stable society" and not (yet) one that has contained the damage and threat of its nuclear accident. Rather, it is one facing the challenge of precarity of multiple kinds. "Can we really call this precarious situation a cold shutdown?," asked Kudo Kazuhiko, a professor of nuclear engineering at Kyoto University, upon hearing the government claim that its nuclear crisis was now under control (Fackler 2011, A11).

Almost certainly not. But just asking the question, as so many (more) Japanese are doing these days, is a sign of something new. It speaks of an emerging and spreading skepticism—toward the government, its proclamations of safety and control, and social institutions that have been running on certain expectations and logics (hierarchy and dependency) that may no longer make sense. And, in some cases at least, trying out new tactics (and resistances) to survive precarious times. Uncertainty is unsettling. But contending with it, going into the mud, is a different response than gripping onto familiar securities or the authorities that pronounce them. This is one of the themes of the book. Asking in what sense, along what lines, and with what effects and affects precarity is engendering a politics of survival: a "representation of politics oriented toward the question of survival" (Abélès 2010, 10).

PRECARITY, JUDITH BUTLER has argued, demands something more than recognition alone: "we ought not to think that the recognition of precariousness masters or captures or even fully cognizes what it recognizes" (2009, 13). She advocates instead what I take to be a politics of social life (and social survival) premised upon the shared condition of precariousness and the grievability of all life and lives.

> Precariousness implies living socially, that is, the fact that one's life is always in some sense in the hands of the other. . . . It implies exposure both to those we know and to those we do not know; a dependency on people we know, and to those we do not know . . . these are not necessarily relations of love or even of care, but constitute obligations towards others, most of whom we cannot name and do not know, and who may or may not bear traits of familiarity to an established sense of who "we" are. . . . There can be no celebration [of a person's life] without an implicit understanding that the life is grievable, that it would be grieved if it were lost, and that this future anterior is installed as the condition of its life. . . . Without grievability, there is no life or, rather, there is something living that is other than life. (2009, 14–15)

Speaking about war and the U.S. invasion of Iraq and Afghanistan, Butler writes that Americans are "recruited" into seeing only a particular reality framed as it is by war reports through the news media ("frames of war" — the title of her book). A central feature in this reportage is the government's figures for casualties based on a selective counting system; certain deaths count, others do not. This official version leaves particular lives and elements out; it also tames people's affective response to the violence by distancing and diluting it in various ways. In order to be "responsible citizens," according to Butler, we must resist "that daily effort at conscription" (2009, xiv). But such a resistance cannot be at the level of image making alone. While the shock of horrific images, as with Abu Ghraib, might cause outrage, that doesn't suffice for political resistance or "utopian excitement" in itself (Butler 2009, xiv). Rather, as Butler enjoins us, we must seek new ways to "act upon the senses, or to act from them" (ix), that evokes an affective reaction with a greater potential for radical change.

It is the way that insecurity or precariousness registers on the senses in the first place — as a sense of being out of place, out of sorts, disconnected (*fuan, fuantei, ibasho ga nai*) — that I take to be the sign, and symptom, of a widespread precarity in twenty-first-century Japan. What people then do with this — with both the sense of precarity they are living themselves and how, or how not, they are able to sense and act upon the precarity of others—is what I track in *Precarious Japan*. Sensing precarity.[10] The sense of an insecure life and the sense that it could, and sometimes does, turn quickly to death. Precarity that registers deeply in the social senses: of an affective turn to desociality that, for many, feels painfully bad. A place (*muen shakai*, a relationless society) where it is difficult to survive and difficult to muster up the kind of civic responsibility to sense beyond one's own pain to that shared by others (whose deaths are grievable), as advocated by Butler. And this then is part of the pain of being precarious and part of the precariat: having a life that no one grieves upon death and living a precariousness that no one cares to share with you in the here and now.

Ikizurasa—the pains or difficulties of life—is the word activist Amamiya Karin uses to capture the sensory nature of precarious living in contemporary Japan. She activates particularly for the precariat, workers who are un- and underemployed in irregular jobs (*hiseikikoyō*), for whom—as she knows from the time spent as one herself—it is not only the material insecurities of uncertain work but the existential nature of social living that is every bit as, if not more, painful. In Amamiya's case, it was the uncertainty of labor and life rhythms (never sure whether she could find work or keep a job even if she found one) and the estrangement from ongoing human relations and recognition (*shōnin*) (not called by name at work and treated as disposable labor) that crippled her sense of self. What Amamiya describes fits what the Italian autonomist Franco "Bifo" Berardi calls the alienation of the soul—what he sees as the very particular kind of alienation affecting the precariat today. Defining alienation as "the relationship between human time and capitalist value, that is to say . . . the reification of both body and soul" (2009, 22), he argues that it offers an opportunity that, while numbingly painful (panic and depression are the two soul pains he views as most symptomatic of the times), positions the worker to resist—and reconnect to other humans—in a radically new way. The precariat is seen as a radically new political subject, and "alienation is then considered not as the loss of human authenticity, but as estrangement from capitalistic interest, and therefore as a necessary condition for the construction—in a space estranged from and hostile to labor relations—of an ultimately human relationship" (2009, 23).

Particularly interested in what he calls the cognitive work of late-stage capitalism and the cognitariat (the cognitive proletariat, many of whom are part of the precariat), who are the new flexible laborers of this capitalist regime, Berardi points to how it is less (likely or merely) the body or set hours from which value is extracted on the job. Rather, labor is now continual and merges with life—that is to say the soul (the meanings, desires, affects of social living)—which is mined for doing the work of capital. Thus, for Berardi, "the entire lived day becomes subject to a semiotic activation which becomes directly productive only when necessary" (2009, 90).

While Berardi is focused on cognitive labor and the cognitariat in late-stage capitalism, I apply what he argues about soul, alienation, and resistance ("the soul on strike," as I call it) to the condition of precarity and the precariat in twenty-first-century Japan. A condition I see in not only the post-postwar but the postwar as well: of a relationship between labor and soul that, if differently assembled (or disassembled) today, stems (at least in part) from the family-corporate system that started in the late 1950s. If Berardi's cognitariat have jobs that eat into their everydayness (of whom they text, what they share online, how they spend all their time wired for work and life), this was certainly true of the *sararīman* who rarely got home for all the late nights, weekends, and trips spent in the company of his company. And of the "education mama" whose motherly routines had to splice discipline into the academic performances she prodded from her kids. When so much (of the self and soul) gets absorbed into work, the loss of not having that work (and longing for it) can be all-absorbing as well. In *ikizurasa* (the pain of life), Amamiya produces a word to signify a condition that has spread in recessionary Japan over the past two decades that overtly stems from un- and underemployment and the social malaise it incurs. But ikizurasa also indexes a particular relationship, and alienation, between "human time and capitalist value" (Berardi 2009, 22)—one that predates the current (post-bubble) moment and spreads beyond those precaritized by irregular work. In the terrain of social living, this indicates a strain: straining to fit human time, energy, and relationships into a calculus of capitalist value. What doesn't fit gets strained or dumped out.

This social and human garbage pit is precarity. And, as the sensory nature of precarious living, it is pain and unease. Life that doesn't measure up: a future, and everydayness, as secure as a black box.

ON JULY 24, 2011, I was heading home after six weeks in Japan. This time, I hadn't gone to do fieldwork per se. The manuscript was done and I'd handed it over to my editor the day before leaving in June. But, just shy of finishing this book, the Great East Japan Earthquake took place, catapulting the country and its people into whole other dimensions of precarity I knew little about. What I did know something about, and had been getting a sense of over three summers of fieldwork since 2008, was of a widely shared uneasiness over an instability and insecurity in life; not having a place that feels steady, not being in a temporality that makes sense. One word given to this was pain: pain in life (*ikizurasa*) and the pain of social loneliness and disbelonging (*muen shakai*).

A pain in life symptomatic not only of economic decline but of a capitalism that had attached so much to, and was now festering around, a complex of belonging to work, family, and state, what is called *mai-hōmushugi* ("my-home-ism" or a family-oriented way of life). A pain bred from an understanding of human living that, now strained for many, felt strangled for the nation at large. I heard Japan referred to as lacking a future and failing to generate hope in its citizens (let alone noncitizens), particularly its youth. And Japanese, I was told, were losing—for better or worse—that sticky relationality of human ties that had been the earmark of not only traditional culture but the country's own brand of Toyota-ist capitalism once deemed so successful to be called a "miracle economy."

The (mainly pre-3/11) story I tell here—of precarity, those suffering it, and a particular variant of its manifestation in, and around, social living that I call social precarity—I picked up primarily through stories of peoples' lives. These stories, often in fragments or pieces or lines of flight that run into (or away from) others, are the center of this book. And because they involve persons more fractured than grounded by precariousness and because of the nature of precarity itself—of uneasiness, uncertainty, risks, or retreat in sociality with others—I try to maintain, rather than weed out, these senses of my precarious subjects. The book is short and not intended to be either exhaustive or linear. Rather, I am more interested in entering the pain—messy, murky, and meandering as it may be—and touching the circumstances, the conditions, and the everyday effects and affects of how precarity gets lived. This is the ethnography I do, gathering stories from not only encounters, conversations, interviews, or events that I was party to but also news accounts, books, movies, television specials, manga and anime, and stories passed on from others.

Much of what I track about precarity involves pain, but this is not all I have learned or come to understand about precarious Japan. For, if hope is the vision of the future in a state of becoming, I see signs of not only hopelessness but also of people struggling to make Japan a place where fewer will fall prey to precarious lives (and ungrievable deaths). Few of these people care for the word *hope*, I discovered. But in trying to survive a condition of precarity that is increasingly shared, one can see a glimmer in these attempts of something new: different alliances and attachments, new forms of togetherness, DIY ways of (social) living and revaluing life. One can sense, if one senses optimistically, an emergent potential in attempts to humanly and collectively survive precarity: a new form of commonwealth (commonly remaking the wealth of sociality), a biopolitics from below. This social and political possibility I call the soul on strike in precarious Japan.

THIS LAST SENTENCE is where I had left things (in the manuscript I handed my editor) before heading to Japan three months after its triple crisis of the worst earthquake in its recorded history, a tsunami with waves over forty meters tall, and the nuclear reactor accident in Fukushima. And after six weeks of being there (about which I write in the last chapter and have used to reshape the entire book, if mainly at both ends), I was headed home late July. The then prime minister Kan Naoto would be out of office the following month (after assuming office only in June); news about contamination (of beef that had sold all over the country, rice that was now banned from Miyagi, soil on the school playgrounds in Fukushima, water pouring into the Pacific Ocean) was spreading as fast as the radiation itself; the politics and cost of reconstruction as well as the future of the nuclear industry were getting heavily debated and contested by just about everyone; and the human stories of what people had faced, were still facing, or had already succumbed to as a result of 3/11 (death, evacuation, suicide, loss) were almost too much to bear for even an outsider going home after a mere six weeks of getting exposed to the mud. On the plane that day—July 24—I felt shaken, a bit shattered, confused about all the different strands and edges to this newest wave of precariousness hitting Japan. The vast majority of Japanese now reported to be against nuclear energy, even joining protests (some for the first time) to demonstrate support for cutbacks in energy production (on which the neon-generated lifestyle of postwar Japan has been so heavily dependent) in favor of a more environmentally safe well-being for the population. But, if this could be read as progressive, far more reactionary responses were in evidence as well. There were charges of "un-Japaneseness," for example, against those in

Fukushima who (not otherwise evacuated) chose to flee homes or make lunches for their children so they wouldn't have to be exposed to the food made at school.

Pulling out the newspaper I had brought with me on the plane, I read an article on the front page: "Country of Lonely Families: No One to Grieve Deaths From the Crisis" ("*Shinsai shi itamu miuchi nashi kozoku no kuni*"). In an ongoing series on what it called Japan's country of solitude, *Asahi Shimbun* was reporting on "the change in people's connections to one another and the rise of those isolated from society altogether" (July 24, 2011: 1). As with the Hanshin earthquake in Kobe in 1995 (when police reported more than nine hundred suicides from those living in temporary shelters), one of the biggest dangers of 3/11 will be heightened solitude, the article surmised: "pushing over the edge," those who are there or close already. But, as it continued, this is hardly a phenomenon unique to the current crisis; in Tokyo alone ten people die from "lonely death" (*kodokushi*) every day. In a society where 31 percent of the population lives alone, 23.1 percent are over sixty-five years old, and one-third of all workers are irregularly employed, the crisis of 3/11 exposes "weaknesses" in the rapidly aging, single living, precariously employed disparities in the social order. A fault line opened up that was deepened, but not created, by the disaster.

The article moves into a juxtaposition of two human stories. The first is of a forty-four-year-old man found sitting alone on a bench in a municipal city park in Sendai (Miyagi Prefecture) close to midnight, staring at the sky. A small day pack by his side, he's a laborer from Nagoya seeking work. As if drawn by the earthquake, many visit the site where it hit. For this one, the earthquake represents an opportunity. He'd been working temp (*haken*) jobs but had been on unemployment (welfare) since last year. In Sendai he hoped to do rubble removal (*gareki shori*) but found work dismantling houses instead. Pay was 7,000 yen per day (US$74) but he'd quit halfway through the contract; this was the fifth day he'd slept in net cafés or the park. Next he aimed to head to Fukushima to join reconstruction work (*fukkyū sagyō*) in the area of the nuclear reactors. Pay there would be much higher, 40,000 yen a day (US$425) for a twenty day contract. But they had all the workers they needed right now, he'd been told. So he'd try for the next slot. The reporter said he'd call the next day. But when he did, there was no answer.

The next story takes place in the center of town, Ishinomaki, Miyagi Prefecture in a wooden one-story house where a couple in their seventies had been living for ten years. They had no contact (*kōryū*) with their neighbors, not even their landlord knew anything about them except that they were on welfare. On 3/11 two meters of water flooded their house from the tsunami. A few days later their bodies were carted away in blue vinyl sheets. Unable to find the names of any relatives (*miuchi*) in their belongings, the police couldn't contact next of kin or even confirm the couple's identities. In April police contacted the landlord seeking his help in verifying their names,[11] but he couldn't help them. Four months later, with the publication of this newspaper article, the names had finally been tracked down and the deaths of these victims of 3/11 were getting announced and grieved for the first time. At last the names of these victims are getting recognized.

Following these two stories, the article mentions a recent survey, conducted online with ten thousand respondents living in Japan in June. Results from the survey were telling: 80 percent responded that they felt insecure (*fuan*) about the future of this country, and 70 percent responded that they felt that the one-to-one connections (*tsunagari*) between people are very important. Summing up, the article concludes that it's up to us. The earthquake has keenly revealed problems in Japanese society. Will a new course be taken? Can we choose to do so? This is the crossroads for a country of solitude.

A crossroads. The earthquake as an opportunity. Of quite different kinds. For the precariat it is the "opportunity" to work in the nuclear cleanup business, where they court danger, possibly death, but more money than other precarious employment. And for "us" it is an opportunity to open up the networks of social connection to make the lives of those who have nobody else to give them recognition (no family, no company, no town) grievable upon death.

These are the issues—sensing precarity—I take up in *Precarious Japan*.

TWO. FROM LIFELONG TO LIQUID JAPAN

Postwar Japan was an era and nation-state of incredible successes: high-paced economic growth, sustained industrial output, creative genius in new-age consumer electronics, global acclaim as a rising postindustrial power, and, at the heart, was a system of lifelong attachments for the Japanese. Starting at school, this system carried over into work and marriage and was clearly mapped by a gendered division of labor: women were to be managers of the family and home, and men were to give their all to the workplace. Postwar Japan is sometimes nicknamed "Japan, Inc." for the corporatization of its social economy and the "marriage" between the social factory at home and the postindustrial factory at work that fueled its off-the-charts productivity.

This marriage is now falling apart, and the lifelong temporality of belonging has fallen into rhythms of a very different sort. In this chapter I briefly lay out this shift: from Japan, Inc. to liquefied Japan in terms of the social ecology of home and work.

The Postwar: High Economic Growth, Corporate Familism, "My-Home-ism"

After its failures at militarism in the Second World War, Japan replaced empire building overseas with a social economy of high growth and material prosperity at home. Rebuilding itself as an industrial producer of high-tech manufacturing, Japan succeeded by becoming a world economic power by the 1970s. The state organized its "enterprise society" around the three pillars of family, corporation, and school (which echoed the three sacred imperial regalia of mirror, sword, and jewel), a structure that was rewarded and enforced by the mass-consumer culture emerging at the same time. This edifice not only fed Japan's economy as an industrial producer and global power but also supplied Japan's middle class with secure jobs, steady incomes, and high-priced consumer lifestyles. Indeed, by the end of the 1970s, a vast majority of citizens self-identified as middle class, sharing a vision of a good life that seemed reachable to a great many people. A designation closely linked to heteronormative family and an increasingly nuclearized one, a good life (and success at it) was calibrated in large part by familial roles. For a man, this meant providing for family; for a woman, it meant raising children and running the home; and for a child, it meant studying hard, excelling academically, and acquiring a job and family of one's own as an adult.

But family, in the postwar buildup of corporate capitalism, became not only the seat of hard work and high performance, but it also fed consumption as the site of a new kind of home: a privatized, domestic space filled with consumer electronics—washing machines, electric fans, and a family car parked outside.[1] Called "my-home-ism" (mai-hōmushugi), this operated as at once a consumer dream and social contract—what people came to desire and what they received in return for working hard, for sticking to a normative life course, and for staying focused on the small picture (versus political protest, for example, which had all but evaporated by the mid-1970s). It also operated according to strict gender roles; the financial running of the household depended on the male wage, while the domestic management of its everydayness—from making food to balancing the budget—fell to the woman. The enterprise society ran similarly on gender performance; core workers were hired for life or long term (*shūshi koyō*), and their tenure was rewarded with calibrated salary increases (*nenkō jore-tsu*) intended to support the families they were (supposed to be) having. This meant that core workers, given a "family wage," were primarily men. This also meant that corporate capitalism, nestled with the family, consti-tuted a "family corporate system" (*kazoku kigyō kan kankei*; Kimoto 2008, 35) that benefited from the pool of cheap labor provided by women—confined, when they did work, to low-paid, mainly part-time jobs.

The feeling of moving forward and progressively improving (as a na-tion, a family, an individual) infused the national ethos and hopes of the times. Certainly, not everyone had a job with lifetime employment or was married to someone who did; no more than about 30 percent of working men had these mainly white-collar positions in middle- to large-sized cor-porations. Yet by 1970, 75 percent of household heads identified as *sararī-man* (Roberson and Suzuki 2003), a term for salaried worker that carries, and underscores, the ideological centrality of the middle-class, hetero-sexual citizen worker in postwar Japan (Gottfried 2000). These jobs in or close to corporate Japan signaled a sense of accomplishment and identifi-cation even with the state. I recall a sararīman telling me in the early 1980s about the stretch of long hours of overtime he was then putting in at the office. Sometimes he stayed up all night or slept at his desk. But no, he wasn't getting extra pay, he told me. And no, this didn't make him resent his company. As he explained to me, the American, naïve about Japanese work culture, "I am doing this for my company. And for Japan." The sac-rifice signaled both duty and honor and also was just part of the job. Be-cause, as the cliché goes about the sararīman, he didn't work for Toyota, he belonged to Toyota. And belonging gave the male worker his location in social place; having a job became his identity—the affiliation stamped on *meishi* (business cards) acquired so voraciously when meeting some-one new. The affiliation also consumed ever more of his actual life. Aspira-tionally, middle-class workers bought "my-homes" in the suburbs, which meant long commutes to the workplace and less time for family, neigh-bors, or anything not related to work itself.

The family-corporate system linked a particular structure of work to one of family and home, operating on a principle of what Lee Edelman has called "reproductive futurism." At the heart of the modern polity, this is the notion that hard work today yields a better tomorrow: the modernist belief in progress staked on "the child as the obligatory token of futurity"

(Edelman 2004, 12). In postwar Japan this was corporate familism operating as blueprint for the nation-state — economic productivity driving and driven by (re)productivity at home, futures made for children, and the child as familial and national investment. As Edelman notes, such an ideology undergirds those in the normative center but consigns those who fail to measure up — those insufficiently productive or unwilling or unable to have children — to the social dustbin. When the child embodies the telos of the social order, the very logic "within which the political itself must be thought" (Edelman 2004, 2), then the refusal or failure to reproduce gets read as "no future" (the title of Edelman's book).

The prospect of no futurity for a shrinking nation-state will have resonance later when we consider how the complicity of family and corporation has imploded in recent times in such precarious forms as *hikikomori*: youths who, failing to be (re)productive outside the home, withdraw into solitary existences that would seem the ultimate perversion of "Japan, Inc." With the hikikomori the home has failed to produce a productive child who — by becoming a sararīman or "education mama" — takes part in the national contract of economic growth. Whoever or whatever is to blame (the corporation, the family, the nation-state, Japanese youths), the specter of "no future" Japan provokes anxiety, some of which is intentionally and ideologically provoked.

When it "worked," though, the family-corporate system drove the social economy. It accompanied Japan's rapid urbanization and postindustrialization in the second half of the twentieth century. This is when, following the war that devastated and emptied the cities, the Japanese soon returned in ever higher numbers, leaving the land for jobs and life in urban centers. By 1970, 72 percent had become wage laborers, 70 percent lived in big cities, and only 9 percent remained farmers (a reduction by half since the 1950s). Incomes rapidly increased; in urban households they rose more than sixteen times between 1955 and 1989. With the demand for a highly educated workforce, raising children revolved around having fewer children and schooling them well. By 1955 family size had decreased to five and went to 3.19 by 1987 (foreshadowing the low birthrate that has become exacerbated today), and the extended family had become a nuclear one (60.5 percent of households in 1987). Division of labor was gendered. Men worked and brought home the paycheck — their primary responsibility as breadwinners. This meant that a wife, much as a boss, expected men to make work their primary commitment — of time, energy, and affective investment. Women, in turn, stayed home and managed the household, the children, and caregiving—their "reproductive bargain" (Gottfried 2009). Though the number of working women increased over time (and, by 1989, more wives of white-collar workers were working than not), it was typically in part-time jobs, particularly after women had resumed work upon leaving it at childbirth or marriage—mandatory practice (except in some professions like schoolteachers) until the law made it illegal in 1986, and one that 80 percent of Japanese women still follow today upon having a child.

In the form it developed following the Second World War, the family not only embedded socioeconomic relations, it served as the "hidden capital of the Japanese economy" (Takeda 2008, 162). Family (along with the corporation) became the basis of Japan's welfare society, assuming this responsibility so the state could cut back on welfare spending, as it did following the oil shock in 1973 (Takeda 2008). Family modeled and fed Japan's emerging enterprise society—work relations that were family-like and allowed men to work long hours, making them virtually nonexistent at home (Yoda 2006). Family also yielded a source of cheap labor in the way of married women who, when returning to the workforce while also raising children, did so in low-paid, peripheral jobs—a locally bred labor force performing the kind of work largely assumed by foreign migrants in other industrialized countries. In all three ways—in terms of Japanese welfare, Japanese management style (*nihonteki keiei*), and a peripheral labor force—the family constituted an important asset to the postwar capitalistic state.

But the family is not what is usually credited for the country's high economic growth and "miracle economy" of the 1970s and 1980s. Rather, it is the "Japanese management style": those industrial practices now iconic of post-Fordist Japan—just-in-time production, lean production (Toyotaism), quality circles. But "Japanese management style" also indexes those business strategies intended to foster sticky socio-affective ties between worker and workplace. As mentioned already, these included lifetime employment, wages based on seniority rather than merit, and all-company unions: practices that targeted only certain workers (core, male), shoring up a system less of "lean production" than of "lean and dual," Beverly Silver's (2003) term for Japan, Inc.'s reliance on both the hard work and loyalty of its core workers and the flexibility and disposability of its peripheral workers in contract and part-time jobs. Though historically recent—

initiated in the 1950s and 1960s to contain worker unrest, union activism, and itinerant work patterns—such work strategies became identified as culturally Japanese—the mark of Japan's own brand of capitalism. As Prime Minister Ōhira famously announced at a policy meeting in 1980, Japan's economic system is different because it is founded on its unique culture that, unlike Western modernity, privileges the communal values of *aidagara* (human relations and respect). A survival from traditional culture, this, as Ōhira asserted, is what gives Japan its competitive edge, representing an alternative—more "humane" and advanced—form of capitalism (Harootunian 1989).

Dependency, performance, and affect melded in a very particular architecture in these "Japanese" relationships of nestled (family and corporate) belonging. Men worked at companies ideally for life, creating a bond that extended beyond "work" to the personal and everyday. A company man (*kaisha ningen*) would devote not only long hours to work but also evenings, weekends, and vacations to "leisure" (golf, karaoke, drinking) spent in the company of fellow workers. At once a duty and a perk, such work-sponsored entertainment affectively blurred the boundaries between labor and life (Allison 1994). Such outings also kept a man from home where complementary webs of duty and dependence spun around mother and child(ren). Women gained recognition for producing children who achieved high academic performances by demonstrating extraordinary output and discipline even as toddlers. But for the "education mama," this was a full-time job that seeped into everything from the lunchboxes sent to school to the games played before bed (Allison 2000). Routine caregiving became embedded with this second nature: using and embellishing everyday rituals as a means to extract and reward output. Because a woman's identity, and social capital, merged with that of a husband but also that of a child, mothers worked hard at love. If she succeeded (measured by how well a child did at every stage along the life course), a woman gained recognition. If the child failed, a mother was held accountable.

Just as in the work sphere, the home knitted an affect of care with that of duty and performance. The two spheres played off one another, nestling social relations—of leisure, loyalty, love—with those of capital, labor, and school. As the sociologist Nakane Chie famously claimed in *Tate shakai no ningen kankei* (Human Relations in a Vertical Society), published in the throes of Japan's miraculous recovery economy (1967), the postwar workplace operated just like a family. Cemented by kin-like bonds, (male) workers were married to their companies (and coworkers) for decades. This meant that, like family, the human and "humane" attachments of aidagara oozed stickiness but were anchored by a structure of differentiation as well—what Nakane called *tate* (hierarchy or verticality). This is the difference that defines every relationship (older and younger brother, boss and employee, teacher and student), dictating the appropriate behavior of each party (the inferior obeys and respects the superior, who takes charge but also care of the inferior). According to Francis Fukuyama (1995), who admires it as culturally "Japanese," this dynamic ensures "trust" in the workplace. Modeled on the family, the affect of dependence (*amae*) is transferred to the workplace—a transference that, in the thesis proposed by the psychiatrist Doi Takeo (2001), assumes special saliency and longevity in Japan.

Staging a helplessness and desire to be taken care of modeled on the infant's relationship with the mother, even adults will "amaeru" on authority figures. Whereas Doi posited amae as a cultural principle—and was criticized for endorsing cultural essentialism (*nihonjinron*, or "unique Japaneseness")—he also felt it had spread too deeply in postwar times, making the Japanese overly attached to the caregiving of their intimate authority figures. Worried that the Japanese were growing too insular, too fixated on their own needs, and too compliant in deferring to those in charge, Doi (along with other cultural critics) criticized the excessive "maternal principle" nestled in the familial relations of both workplace and home (Yoda 2006). But goading subjects into hard work by enveloping them in a crucible of dependency, whether through consumer treats for studious kids or company perks for the sararīman in a hostess club, was part and parcel of the policies undertaken by Japan, Inc. And until it was dismantled by the neoliberal restructuring platform of Koizumi in 2001 as an obstacle to economic reform, its embrace has been seen as critical to the country's postwar success and its "Japanese-style" capitalism.

Writing in 1989, critic Asada Akira argued that dependency produces an "infantilization" at the very heart of Japan's capitalist form. In what he called "infantile capitalism," the Japanese are driven to be competitive by remaining docile and perpetually cared for, a type of subjectivity quite at odds with the self-reliance fostered by "mature" capitalisms elsewhere: "in Japan, there are neither tradition-oriented old people adhering to transcendental values nor inner-oriented adults who have internalized their values; instead, the nearly purely relative (or relativistic) competition exhibited by other-oriented children provides the powerful driving force for capitalism" (1989, 275). Rather than viewing dependency as a cultural survival from the past, however, Asada viewed it as the cutting edge of exploitative capitalism—a cutting edge that catapulted Japan to the heights of global prestige as an industrial power. That is, until it didn't cut it anymore.

After the Bubble, a New Era of Japanese Management Style

By the late 1990s Japan's "dependency culture" had lost its expediency. Seeing it as an obstacle to economic growth, neoliberal reformers urged the dismantling of the Japanese management style. But the indictment went deeper, charging that dependency culture created unhealthy "interdependent relationships that hinder individuals from exercising initiative and developing entrepreneurship" (Takeda 2008, 156). Under its new banner of "risk and individual responsibility" (*risuku to jiko sekinin*), the government asked its citizens to remake their subjectivity to become strong and independent individuals "capable of bearing the heavy weight of freedom" (qtd. in Miyazaki 2010, 243). Such a makeover to a leaner cultural style applauds risks. But as the interdependencies that once grounded work and well-being are undone, many people are left in the lurch. Meanwhile, the state has yet to pick up the slack left by the withering of the old family-corporate system—where it shoved responsibility for welfare at the onset of its high-growth economic surge.

By the 1990s the "super stable society" started morphing into something else: its "era of unsafe nationalism" (*fuantei nashyonarizumu no ji-dai*), as the political scientist Takahara Motoaki (2006) describes post-postwar Japan. Labor sits at the heart of this, shifting from one work model (lifelong, family-linked, associated with Japanese Fordism and miraculous economic growth) to another (short-term, individual, associated with flexible labor, decline, and precarity). However, flexible labor wasn't entirely new in the 1990s. At the end of the 1980s—and when the bubble was still strong—taking on short-term, free-floating jobs became something of a lifestyle option even for middle-class youths. Called "*furītā*,"[2] the concept was spurred in part by a clever ad campaign by the temp company Recruit, which promoted it as new-age alternative to the work-for-life trajectory of sararīman. What started off as an individual choice, however, became more economic fiat (particularly for young workers) with the stagnation in the 1990s that worsened the financial situation of companies nationwide. Even before that, however—and before the furītā phenomenon—Japan, Inc. had its own variant of flexible laborer (Slater 2009). These were the ranks of peripheral (versus core) workers who could be activated upon demand, lending the lean production of Toyota-ism a much-valued flexibility for its trademark just-in-time production. Mainly part-time workers (largely women) and contract workers (largely men of a certain class or inclination, such as dropouts of the "academic credentializing society"), this peripheral labor force was strategically important to Japan's miracle economy. But, as David Slater points out, these workers were never called "furītā" nor given the public attention targeted at furītā,[3] by either critics who have blamed them and their laziness for Japan's unproductivity today or activists like Amamiya Karin, who advocate for furītā under the rubric of the precariat (Driscoll 2007). This will be addressed in greater detail later.

The bubble burst in 1991. As stagnation and recession set in, companies began to downsize, restructure, or merge with other companies. Layoffs and unemployment rose, and as the hiring of regular (core) employees fell, that of irregular workers sharply increased. Temporary work (*haken*), sparking in the 1980s—from 87,000 to 317,000 between 1986 and 1989—continued to grow in the 1990s, doubling between 1994 and 2000 (Gottfried 2000). In this "glacial age of hiring," youths were particularly hard hit, becoming the "lost generation" in Japan's "lost decade." When able to do so, companies tended to hold onto their more senior workers rather than hire young ones under the assumption that older men had families to support—and that keeping the primary breadwinner's salary "safe" meant "safety" for the nation.[4] But even this mindset, a holdover of the enterprise society, was derided for burdening business with a rigidity it could no longer afford. Replacing the job-for-life, family-based model of work came one of more flexible, results-based employment. Trying to lay claim for what was a radical transformation, Nikkeiren officially announced in 1995 that these labor shifts constituted a new cultural moment—the "new era in Japanese-style management" (*shinjidai no nihonteki keiei*).[5] Applauding the flexibility of the country's labor force, the government adopted other signature tendencies of neoliberalism: deregulation of labor policies, heightened reliance on the privatization of social services, and an ideological endorsement of individual responsibility (*jiko sekinin*). Under this new regime of labor (nicknamed labor's "big bang," or *rōdō biggu ban*), what is productive of and for capitalism is no longer the family or the long-term employment of company workers. Rather, it is the detached, adaptable, and self-responsible individual—a deterritorialized, decentered, decollectivized subject.

Neoliberal Millennium: Structural Reform in Labor and Home

A decade after the bursting of the bubble, things hadn't yet bounced back. The economy showed no signs of improving and crises on other fronts were multiplying as well. The Liberal Democratic Party (LDP)—the conservative political party that had held power almost nonstop since 1955—started to lose its hold. And, in the wake of a series of scandals involving a number of powerful ministries and compounded by divisive party politics, a mood set in of political chaos that some saw as "political paralysis" (Takeda 2008). A number of social trends stoked fears as well. The low birthrate continued to plummet, as did concern about the strain this placed on the national pension fund, future productivity, and caregiving for the world's fastest-aging population. Kindled by the economic downturn and insecurity over jobs, levels of panic, depression, and anxiety rose nationwide, peaking in a dramatic increase in suicide, starting in 1998, to about 33,300 deaths a year—a number that has remained at this level ever since. A moral panic raged around youths, who tended to be blamed for the precarity of the new economic order and the "nonproductivity" of Japan itself, through news stories of young girls engaged in "compensated dating," youth violence, hedonistic consumer spending, the furītā work pattern, and significant numbers of both hikikomori and NEET (not in education, employment, or training), the lifestyle of young adults who live "parasitically" off parents for years (nicknamed "parasite singles").[6] Punctured by two startling events mid-decade—the sarin gas attacks by the religious cult Aum Shinrikyō on Tokyo's subway system that killed 13 people and the Kobe earthquake two months earlier with 6,434 casualties—the very fabric of everyday life at the turn of the twenty-first century seemed to be getting ripped asunder (Allison 2006).

It was also a time when a chasm opened up in the ontology of place—where and to whom people connect and what attachments accord recognition and identity. In a society where "the family is the place where people live" (*kazoku wa hitobito no seikatsu no ba desu*), as the sociologist Yamada Masahiro observed about postwar Japan, this dynamic is shifting to one where the family is less of a safeguard from risks than risky itself (the subject of his book, *Kazoku toiu Risuku* [Family Risk], 2001). As the family disarticulates from work, and both become riddled by insecurity, the "contradiction" (*mujun*) between the former family system and the current economic system strains the social placeness of family and work (Yamada and Shirakawa 2008, 12). This produces what Yamada takes to be precarious social deformations, neither good for society nor for the individual, such as the young furītā who don't marry and the rising ranks of NEET who don't find (or even look for) work (Yamada 2003). As he observes, all of this was exacerbated by the structural reforms that Prime Minister Koizumi Jun'ichirō put into effect upon assuming office in 2001.

Japanese workers were already facing a downward wage pressure due to a number of factors in the market (and the fact that companies were relying increasingly on irregular workers and automation to save costs): market competition from the newly industrialized economies in Asia, growing pressure from external shareholders, and low (or zero) interest rates (Chatani 2008). To secure the economy and shock it out of its malaise, the country was asked to cut back further. Adopting neoliberalist rhetoric (and appointing the neoliberal economist Takenaka Heizō as minister in charge), Koizumi presented his "structural reform." Launching further measures to deregulate labor (allowing contract work, for example, to be extended from one to three years and into areas of work once limited to regular employees), to impose "results"-based employment (*seika shugi*), which, overturning seniority-based employment, had been adopted by 77.7 percent of companies by 2003, and to "diversify" the life and work styles of the population by deregulating ever more in the way of public service, Koizumi acknowledged that structural reform would involve "pain." But this was the price the nation needed to pay to streamline and stimulate the economy.

And pay it did as higher levels of precarity hit the Japanese at once. Yet, as noted by the activist Yuasa Makoto, much of this was initially hidden by making certain segments of the population shoulder the burden. Those most at risk—and most likely to become irregular workers—are youths, women, those with less academic credentials (and relatedly, those from lower-class backgrounds and from single-parent households), foreign migrants, and, increasingly, men in their fifties. In 2012 one-third of all workers but half of all youths were irregular workers, a significant shift even from the end of the 1990s. Irregular workers are prey to precarity, needless to say. The wage disparity between regular and irregular employment rose sharply after 1992 (Miyamoto 2008): the average hourly wage for part-time work is 1085 yen (US$11.50) for men and 962 yen (US$10.22) for women,[7] and it should be noted that Japan and the United States have the two lowest minimum wages of all industrialized countries (Tachibanaki 2008). Annual wages for irregular workers average 1,950,000 yen (US$20,712) for men and 1,730,000 yen (US$18,375) for women, which is below the poverty line (Kamuro 2008). This accounts for the fact that 70.4 percent of the homeless in 2007 reportedly had jobs,[8] although 90.7 percent of them earned less than 100,000 yen (US$1,062) per month (Matsumoto 2008). Deregulation has also allowed companies to hire workers to do what is essentially the work of regular employees, paying them significantly less (part-time workers typically make only 50–60 percent what regular workers make doing the same work) (Tachibanaki 2008). Given that contract work can now be extended for three years (without pay raise or insurance), irregular workers are kept on in lieu of hiring permanent workers.

Stuck at a low pay level, irregular workers are often unprotected at the workplace as well; easily replaced and fired, their rights are minimal at best.[9] This is particularly true for female workers, who experience the worst gendered wage disparity of all industrialized countries.[10] Women make up 70 percent of irregular workers, and their treatment is not much better even in regular employment where — based on the premise of the male breadwinner — they make only 67.1 percent of men's salaries.[11] Approximately 80 percent of working women receive less than 3,000,000 yen (US$31,864) a year, 44 percent were paid less than the minimum wage in 2010, and the numbers of professional women remain disturbingly low.[12] It is also still the case that, unless they have a well-paying job or parents willing to support them, women without (working) husbands are particularly disadvantaged. And working mothers who leave the job market to raise children (80 percent of whom do so upon the birth of their first child) are penalized by both the national pension system, which only kicks in after twenty-five years of contributions by a worker, and the social security system, into which a worker and company each contribute half but only, in the case of part-timers, if they are working three-fourths time (Kamuro 2008). Needless to say, single households are one of the poorest contingencies today (despite the fact that 87.3 percent of single mothers work part time). Notable as well is the fact that only 2 percent of children in Japan are born out of wedlock.

Oddly, the government does not keep its own statistics on the number of poor. When confronted by news reporters about such troubling signs as rising unemployment, homelessness, and citizens' angst in his country, Koizumi was dismissive. Attributing poverty to two groups—foreign migrants and Japanese lacking in "self-responsibility"—he found no reason to find fault with anything his government was or was not doing. Similarly curt was Koizumi's reply when asked in the Diet (Japan's national legislature) about the "downturn" of Japan's middle class and its transformation into a polarized society of socioeconomic difference (*kakusa shakai*). "Difference?," he asked, "What's so bad about that?" Admitting to a big disparity between poverty and wealth in Japan after the turn of the century, he attributed this to a differential in the degree of industriousness (*ganbaru*) that people are willing to expend (Tachibanaki 2008, 10). But socioeconomic disparity is critical to something the government, and certainly the public, is deeply interested in: social reproduction. For, as is evident from the work of reverse-poverty activists like Yuasa Makoto and scholars of the family, labor, and the economy such as Miyamoto Michiko and Yamada Masahiro, those on the lower end of the job and life security spectrum today are far less likely to marry, have children, or be in a position to either give or receive care when old or in need. In short, while the overall social trends are away from marriage and family (divorce is up, childbirth is down, and more are marrying later or not at all), all of this is particularly true for those in the least secure jobs today.

Studies show that, due to economic insecurity, women are loathe to marry furītā, and male irregular workers are half as likely as regular workers to get married. Those in a position to have what once constituted the social contract of postwar Japan—hard work today tied to marriage, home, and progressive prosperity for children tomorrow—tend to be limited to those with regular employment. What was such an "ordinary lifestyle" (*hitonami no seikatsu*) has now become a privilege of a diminishing minority (who, even then, often need both spouses to work, which poses its own problems of balancing work and life with kids if there are any). But my-home-ism still signifies belonging and place, the comforts of "being somewhere" and being normal—a utopianism all its own, as Berlant (2011) notes, about the longing for aspirational normativity, particularly when the chance of achieving this is ebbing fast. Such a home evokes "hope," according to Yamada (2003), and as home eludes the grasp of more and more Japanese, so does the capacity to be hopeful—what he calls in his book by the same title "a differential hope society" (or "a society of hope disparity," *kibō kakusa shakai*). Japan is becoming a place where hope has become a privilege of the socioeconomically secure. For the rest of them—the widening pool of "losers"—even the wherewithal to imagine a different there and then beyond the precarious here and now stretches thin.

To Make Live or Let Die

... I think that one of the greatest transformations the political right underwent in the nineteenth century was precisely that, I wouldn't say exactly that sovereignty's old right—to take life or let live—was replaced, but it came to be complemented by a new right which does not erase the old right but which does penetrate it, permeate it. This is the right, or rather precisely, the opposite right. It is the power to "make" live and "let" die. The right of the sovereignty was the right to take life or let live. And then this new right is established: the right to make live and to let die—Foucault 2003, 241

What does this new technology of power, this biopolitics, this biopower that is beginning to establish itself, involve? ... a set of processes such as the ratio of births to deaths, the rate of reproduction, the fertility of a population and so on ...—Foucault 2003, 243

Complicit in its troubled social condition are its demographics: Japan's shift to a *shōshikōreika* (*shōshika*, low birthrate; *kōreika*, fast-aging) society. At both ends of the spectrum the population is getting stretched: stretched thin by a low birthrate and stretched tight by the care needs of its elderly, more and more of whom are living longer. The birthrate, low for twenty years, is the lowest yet today: 7.64 births per 1,000 people (1.34 percent), which makes Japan 192 in the UN list of sovereign states (and above only Hong Kong, which ranks at the bottom with 7.42 births per 1,000). Fertility—the births women average—is low as well; the all-time low was 1.26 births in 2005, and though a bit higher today at 1.37 births, it still falls far below 2.1 percent, the rate considered necessary for developed countries to sustain their population. The population, 127,704,000 people today, which started to fall in absolute terms in 2005, is expected to shrink by one-third by 2050. Additionally, the segment of those working who are between fifteen and sixty-four is expected to decrease to half by 2055. The decline of the real numbers and increase in age of the population put both the productivity and economic growth of the country at risk. As is commonly voiced in the mass media and by public officials, shōshikōreika is threatening the country with the loss of its competitive edge in the global economy.

As striking as its low birthrate (lower than any other country except one) is Japan's life expectancy rate (the highest in the world); for men the average is 78.6 years, and for women it is 85.6 years. Even with one of the lowest infant mortality rates (the third lowest in the world), human life in the biological sense has a harder time actually coming into existence than surviving into old age in the country. Human life is dying slowly, and just as slowly, getting (re)born—a reality that confounds reproductive futurism (and makes Japan's shrinking population a state that is perceived by many as one of "slow death" [Berlant 2011, 35]). For if staking national vitality in the image of the child was once plotted as the horizon of futurity, that investment now conjures up "no future": a specter raised by the sea of old people and scarcity of newborns in twenty-first-century Japan. At 28 million, the elderly (aged sixty-five or above) are currently one-fourth (22.1 percent) of the population but are predicted to reach 33.7 percent by 2035; by 2055 one in every 2.5 people will be old. Meanwhile, old people themselves are getting older; those over seventy-five are expected to outnumber those between the ages of sixty-five and seventy-four by the year 2017, and to account for 65 percent of the total elderly population by 2055. While other countries (such as the United Kingdom, China, Singapore, and South Korea) are facing similar demographics, Japan is graying faster than any of these. It also has the dubious distinction of making the transition from an "aging society" (a population with 8 percent elderly) to an "aged society" (14 percent elderly), as defined by the UN, in record time: twenty-four years compared to 47 years for the United Kingdom, 85 years for Sweden, and 115 years for France (Economist Intelligence Unit 2011).

Amassing population at the upper, rather than lower, end of the age demographic chart puts obvious strains on the economy in terms of both productive output (a shrinking workforce and decrease in those contributing taxes) and social reproductivity (a rise in those needing care in comparison to those who can, or are willing, to give it). As the labor force shifts—a decrease in "core" workers to more flexible and irregular employment (one-third of all workers and one-half of young workers), it is declining in size as well—and predicted to decline much more in the near future. This means that less money is entering the coffers for pensions and social security: a huge issue in the mass media already and one generating a high degree of anxiety, particularly given the mismanagement of the pension funds in 2009 and the raising of the official age at which one can start withdrawing welfare pension insurance—from 60 to 61 in 2013, which will rise to 65 by the year 2025. There are fewer workers today to support the elderly: a decrease in what is called the "dependency ratio." Predicted to be only 1.3 workers supporting every elderly person in 2055, this is down from 3.3 in 2005 and 11.2 in 1964—the years leading up to double-digit high economy growth and the "miracle economy" of Japan, Inc.

As the labor force shrinks, its shape and composition are morphing as well, not only to more flexible and irregular jobs but also to a later retirement age (officially, the retirement age is now sixty, and 20 percent of those over the age of sixty-five work—high for many developed countries) and to attempts made to incorporate more women (under 50 percent of the labor force, which is low compared to Organisation for Economic Co-operation and Development [OECD] member countries). Liberalizing labor and residency policies to accommodate foreign migrants would seem an obvious, even necessary, option to relieve labor and care needs in the future. Yet even when immigration laws were relaxed in 1990 and efforts made to target foreigners of Japanese descent (*nikkei*; particularly from Brazil), the attempt has largely failed: a failure spectacularized by the government's follow-up campaign to pay for the airfare (and a bonus) to send nikkei workers back to their countries of origin upon losing their jobs—a move found insulting by those ("not-quite" Japanese) it targeted.[13] Today, foreign workers constitute a mere 1.7 percent of the population. And in the field of care, the situation is stranger yet. In a country with a care deficit that is worsening by the minute, the government initiated bilateral agreements with both the Philippines and Indonesia in 2008 to bring over nurses and nursing care workers. Yet it imposed such stringent restrictions—to pass, within three years of entering the country, a difficult qualifying exam in Japanese that only 1.2 percent of foreign applicants have ever passed—that many have left, by force or choice.[14]

Tending to the health and health care of the nation increasingly means shifting focus from a red-cheeked newborn to aging flesh. The implications in terms of outlay (of national resources) and output (of productive yield) are tremendous. If the child signifies potential—a forthcoming of growth, productivity, and futurity—the elderly signals deficit, the progressive decline of vitality whose fullness is past. Not only does the temporality of life differ here, so does its economics: what one requires and extracts in order to live and what one produces or yields in the course of living itself. Despite comprising only 20 percent of the population at the time, medical costs for those aged sixty-five and older were five times what younger Japanese spent in 2007 and amounted to half the total health care spending in the country (Suzuki 2007). The drain on the national economy from a contingency that is past (or close to) retirement, in need of more health care (paid largely by the state), and whose numbers are only rising (and quickly) is obvious—what Foucault might call an "endemic" in the biopower of late capitalist Japan. National coffers are getting eaten up by the costs of keeping so many elderly alive, a slow (economic) death brought on, at least in part, by the country's slowly dying elderly, and so many of them. The dilemma has prompted the government to reassess its national health care system, which, created at the onset of the flush period of the postwar economy in 1961, provided universal access (with a sliding payment scale) to national health insurance and, over time, free access for citizens over seventy. With the state underwriting so much coverage, the system has promoted gross inefficiencies. Affordable treatment invited overuse, payment structures for doctors encouraged over-prescriptions and extended hospital stays, and the introduction of expensive medical technologies contributed to skyrocketing medical costs (Economist Intelligence Unit 2011).

In what has become a culture of medicalization and prescription popping, successive administrations have tried to contain health costs and institute reform. Through endless campaigns (such as the Gold Plan in 1989 and the New Gold Plan in 1994, where "gold" indexed money as much as old age), the government has shifted more responsibility to the individual (in the way of copayments even for the elderly) and introduced measures to restructure care away from doctors and hospitals to more home-based care—with subsidiary facilities and services to accommodate this. Couched in a rhetoric of "quality of life" and "living independently," this turn to individual responsibility (*jiko sekinin*) and return to family or household is the signature of governmental attempts to privatize care and cut back on state spending. In the face of state retreat and increased burden placed on individuals, more and more Japanese find payment of health premiums along with those of social security and pension installments to be beyond their means. In 2008, 20 percent of all households failed to pay insurance premiums and lost full insurance coverage.[15] Under a massive deregulation and restructuring platform, then Prime Minister Koizumi instituted further cuts in 2002. By drastically slashing social security spending (70 percent of which is expended on the elderly) and putting a cap on how much the spending could increase each year, this marked the beginning of a new era in Japan: *iryō hōkai*, the fall of the health care system. Meanwhile, in the wake of a new insurance scheme that incentivized the private health care industry the same year, the care market is taking off. Immediately, 130,000 new companies materialized seeking to service a consumer demand that is certain to only increase (Economist Intelligence Unit 2011).

Yet in a business plagued by poor working conditions and low service fees as mandated by the government, the turn to privatization has only piqued citizens' concerns over the quality and availability of affordable health care. Troubling images—of lonely elderly, relationless subjects, overstressed mothers who kill or abandon their children—fill the airwaves. Meanwhile the government calls to retract federal funding and to shift health care away from doctors, hospitals, and medicine to the everyday lifestyles and personal households of the individual. So, back to home, and to making health and care more homelike. This was one of the major proposals to emerge out of a 2008 special task force conducted by the prime minister's cabinet: to devise a bold plan to implement more efficiency in the system and to improve available health care. Suggestions included building more home-life facilities (*kyojyūkei shisetsu*) and investing in research and development (such as care robotics) that would enable elderly people greater autonomy in living alone. A year later Hatoyama, along with his new party, the Democratic Party of Japan (DPJ), entered office on a platform of progressive social policies and made a "health power strategy" the center of his overall growth strategy. Under the pledge to "eliminate the anxiety of the elderly about the future, and induce a change from savings for uncertainty to expenditures for an enjoyable life" (Economist Intelligence Unit 2011, 15), the plan works on two tracks. It intends to assure access to high-quality health care for the people and to also strip inefficiencies from the national system, and budget, to pay for it.

Reportedly based on innovative research and creative development (in such arenas as nursing care technologies and regenerative medicines), the "health power strategy" advocates what is the new buzzword for twenty-first-century living in Japan: self-sustainability. Self-sustainability means the capacity to live ever longer in a state of sufficient well-being maintained (as largely as possibly) by oneself. Linked to this "health power strategy," about a human ecology premised on a sociality of self-responsibility, is one of aging in place: staying out of the hospital (or other health facilities) as long as possible to grow old (and die?) at home (Economist Intelligence Unit 2011). From these new goals emerges a new form of "my-home-ism" for the elderly, where national health care is to be driven by a biopower of "aging in place" and "self-sustainability."

The current "health power strategy" encodes and reflects the new subjectivity of twenty-first-century Japan: the self-sustainable individual (even, or particularly, when this involves the elderly). A strategy for national health intended to not only trim costs from the federal budget but produce a population of self-reliant individuals capable of living alone, this is a different my-home-ist social order from the family-corporate system of postwar Japan, Inc. In its most upbeat iteration self-sustainability generates popular appeal, as can be seen by the recent *ohitori-sama* ("being single") fad. The bestseller *Ohitori-sama no rōgo* (Aging Alone) by the feminist scholar Ueno Chizuko—full of helpful strategies, information, and models for aging robustly alone—sold 750,000 copies in the first ten months of its publication in 2007. A follow-up book targeted expressly to elderly men followed in 2009, as did a popular television drama by TBS, *Ohitori-sama*, featuring stories of single young(er) people.[16] But such a principle—of happy and healthy living alone—also presumes a degree of health, wealth, and human capital that is not the privilege of all. Though praised, Ueno's *Ohitori-sama* has also been critiqued for depicting independence as a lifestyle choice when living alone, or stranded from others, has a far different connotation for so many struggling in Japan today such as the working poor, single mothers, the homeless, the sick, and the disabled. In terms of the elderly and the biology of sustainability alone, for example, the fact of increased longevity in Japan means that people are living longer, and more of them, in a state of physical diminishment if not incapacity altogether. According to Matsushita Hiro, an expert in aging at Hitotsubashi University, the difference between life expectancy and healthy life expectancy is considerable (85.6 versus 77.7 years old for women, 78.6 versus 72.3 for men) and, on average, men will be bedridden for 6.3 years at end of life and women for 7.9 years.[17] Facing these shifts to the body at a time when the state—and social welfare—retreats and human relationality retrofits to an ethics of "self-sustainability" incites panic in the aging population. According to statistics put out by the Ministry of Health, Labor, and Welfare, "life satisfaction" (*seikatsu manzoku do*) has been ebbing—and ebbs as one gets older—along with the increase in rates of depression, suicide, and stress. The demographic most severely hit appears to be the elderly, among whom depression is the highest in the population.[18]

Care Deficit

Given the pressures, it's not surprising that the burdens of caregiving that fall so disproportionately on the family often explode not only the myth of filial piety once at the heart of Japanese culture but also the seeming capacity for people to give or get care at all. For, if not the family, and not much the state, where does care come from today in Japan? Sitting next to Yuasa one afternoon at Moyai, the nonprofit organization he co-runs, listening to one person after another seeking help from the destitution they'd fallen into, I noticed how always, at some point, he asks about family: "What's the situation with your family? Is there anyone there who can help? Do they have money they can send you?"[19] Family is as much the last resource (*tame*) as the first resource people turn to in Japan. Family begins life and once sustained it from birth until death.[20] When family as a source of life and a life resource dissolves, it is not only the country's low birthrate but its slow death of humanism—of people dying from abandonment, lack of care, simple "disinterest"—that feeds a collective sense of a dwindling soul. Bleak stories pepper the news and public imagination, of old people who are dying alone, go missing or get stranded in homes where, after utilities have been cut off and food dries up, they starve to death, leaving remains that get discovered days or months later.

Just as common, though, are stories of the not yet elderly who, struggling with life difficulties, stumble on the new ethos of self-sustainability. For example, a homeless man who saw himself as "already disappeared" was the front-page story in the *Asahi Shimbun* on August 31, 2010—the same month the news broke of the "disappeared centenarians."[21] In this case, the man was in his early fifties and living alongside the Sumida River in Tokyo. Referring to himself as "in the reserves" of the "missing elderly," he told the reporter that, though he'd once had a certificate of residency in Shizuoka Prefecture, his existence wasn't recorded anywhere today. The man no longer hears from his wife and daughter whom he left twelve years ago and, without work or insurance (presumably the reasons he left home in the first place), he can barely survive. A sister, contacted for the article, said she has no interest in him; the money she once gave has now been exhausted. He'd be surprised if he lives another five years, figuring that, even when he dies, no one will notice. Comparing himself to the ungrieved and unnoticed elderly these days, the man wonders, "Will I, too, be an unrecorded Buddha in the end?" (*Asahi Shimbum* 2010, 1).

Without job, residency, or even family to help him out, this man was existing socially and existentially all alone. Without anyone, whether the state, the city, a workplace, or family members, to give him place and recognition, he was "unrecorded"—ungrieved, unseen, not (really) alive, waste of the *muen shakai* (relationless society).

While death hovers nearby for those in the "reserves" of the "missing elderly," it came even quicker for the two children of a single mother who lacked what it takes to keep kids alive, as reported in the news just a week earlier (*Asahi* 2010, 22). Shimomura Sanae was identified as twenty-three years old and a hostess in a cabaret club in Osaka. Raised by her father after her mother left, she and her sister grew up largely alone; their father worked long hours as a rugby coach at high school and Shimomura often stayed away as a teenager when, as the paper reported, she also started smoking and dyeing her hair. After graduating from a vocational high school, she married at the age of nineteen. Giving birth one year later, she found the baby cute and herself "no longer alone." Two years later, in 2009, she'd had another child but was also divorced. Working at a vocational school that provided childcare facilities, she was a devoted mom who even rented a car one weekend to take her kids to the zoo, according to an acquaintance. But she also had to manage entirely on her own and, after moving and starting a new job without childcare, struggled even more. In January she once called her father and asked him to help out with the kids when they had the flu but he'd refused because of his own work. When, after rearranging his schedule he'd called back, Shimomura told him it was a false call and not to worry. She didn't want to bother anyone.

Shimomura gave the same answer when local officials, checking on the fact she hadn't registered her apartment, heard crying children. She was "fine" when asked if she needed help. But her occasions away from home apparently increased—whether for work, "play," or nights with men. Child services returned five times but failed to intervene. Posting on a social networking site on June 10 that there were so many things in life she still wanted to do ("*mada yaritai koto yaranakya dame na koto ippai annenmon*"), Shimomura also reported feeding her children what turned out to be their last meal on the day she left home for good. Nineteen days later, she posted a photo of herself in a soccer uniform holding a vuvuzela during the World Cup.[22] On July 19, a photo of the sea at Kobe during a visit there. On July 28, a photo of the sky at dawn with the greeting "*genki desuka*" ("is everyone okay?") underneath. Two days later the corpses of her two children, aged one and three, were found in the apartment. When taken in by the police, Shimomura admitted to understanding that, without leaving them food or water, she had willingly left her children to die—a slow death—home alone.

But the pressures on family to provide care spill out not only in stories of desertion, estrangement, or severing of familial bonds. Tales of implosion occur as well. Such was that of popular singer and actress Shimizu Yukiko, who, exhausted from taking care of her invalid mother, attempted to kill her mother and herself in a would-be double suicide. An eerie family drama, it became even more so by being staged at the father's graveside in a gesture of filial piety or atonement for the daughter's inability to carry out her responsibilities. Pushing her mother in her wheelchair to the cemetery at dusk, she opened a bottle of hydrogen sulfide she'd concocted and brought there to kill them both. But while the daughter died, the mother survived albeit in a far worsened condition, having spent the night in a blinding rain before being discovered the following morning. In the account she wrote of the event, *Kaigo utsu* (The depression of caregiving, 2009), Yukiko's sister, Yoshiko, recounts how stunned she was upon hearing the news. Never complaining nor letting on that she'd sunk into such despair, Yukiko had seemed the consummate caregiver: selfless, cheerful, compassionate—the perfect daughter. Too good to be true until the goodness wore (her) out. To memorialize not only the life of a beloved sister but also the tragedy that befell her and their family in caring for an aging mother, Shimizu Yoshiko wrote *Kaigo utsu*. The story was meant to end in a double suicide, an act resonant in Japanese history with doomed love affairs—affairs of the heart that can't be fulfilled or contained by social norms. How symptomatic of the times that the family drama, imploded around care, ends here as a love affair that is tragically doomed.

THREE. ORDINARY REFUGEEISM
POVERTY, PRECARITY, YOUTH

War is in the business of producing and reproducing precarity.
—Butler 2009, xviii

In January 2007 a documentary on a new form of homelessness—people who take up residence in net cafés—aired on Japanese TV. Just back after a decade covering warzones from Yugoslavia to Rwanda abroad, the reporter had been surprised to discover something crisis-like in Japan as well. What struck him immediately were the stories of destitution and destruction literally at home: of a single mother who killed her child, a jobless youth his father, a couple in debt their entire family, a middle-aged man his elderly mother (whom he'd been tending to all alone). Shockingly, he realized, poverty had come to Japan. And as shocking to him was how little attention the subject was being given by the public or the press. Further, what commentary there was—as in the news coverage of the above killings—assigned blame to the individual rather than to any underlying set of conditions such as economic or domestic stress (Mizushima 2007).

It was to expose Japanese to the rise of poverty at home that the reporter Mizushima Hiroaki made his documentary. Titled *Netto kafe nanmin—hyōryūsuru hinkonshatachi* (Net Café Refugees—The Drifting Poor), it honed in on a relatively new phenomenon—people who, essentially homeless, take up temporary residence in internet cafés or manga *kissa* (comic book cafés). Such "drifting poor" are mainly flexible or irregular workers who, with unsteady paychecks and no job security, are unable to afford more permanent housing. Indeed, as Mizushima also discovered, many of those who reside temporarily at net cafés are roaming the streets or sleeping in hamburger joints on days when they don't find work. More men than women and most commonly in the two age brackets of the twenties and fifties, café dwellers constitute part of the floating population of flexible workers who have become deterritorialized in post-postwar Japan. At the lower end of flexible labor—usually relying on temp work (*haken*) or day labor (*hiyatoi*)—these workers earn on average 6,000 to 8,000 yen (US$65–85) for one day: a wage that is difficult to live on in Japan. Further, jobs are often transacted one day at a time making the task of job hunting as unpredictable as it is constant—hence the convenience of using the internet at net cafés. According to a government report, 77 percent of irregular workers, whose numbers are rising, fall into the ranks of the working poor (and one-tenth of all households were working poor in 2008) (Yuasa 2009). This means such working poor earn less than half the national mean income and less than they would on welfare.[1]

When first deciding to do his documentary, Mizushima met with Yuasa Makoto, head of the Reverse Poverty Network (*Hanhinkon nettowāku*) and co-director of the nonprofit organization (NPO) Moyai. It was Yuasa who told him that, to understand the "new face" of poverty (away from what had once been an older, mainly single male population) in Japan today, one needed to start with net café dwellers. Following this advice, Mizushima spent two months tracking the lives and socioeconomic conditions of working poor who reside, if anywhere, at net cafés. What he discovered, particularly when it involved young people like the three (aged eighteen, twenty-four, and twenty-eight) profiled in the documentary, was disturbing. This new face of poverty were youth who could pass as the kid next door. They were living out of a rucksack stuffed in a coin locker during the day, never knowing whether they'd find work or not, walking the streets for hours even on nights when they can afford the nighttime pack at a net café, subsisting on bread rolls and instant ramen, working (when they do) at jobs that are degrading and draining, continually worried about what will happen if they get sick, can't find work, fall into debt, get injured on the job, lose the will to keep going. "Home," when they find it in a net café, is decidedly unhomey: a nighttime package for six to eight hours (costing between 1,200 and 2,000 yen [US$13 — $21]) that provides a cubicle or reclining chair, access to a computer, a drink bar with cold and hot drinks, toilets, and — sometimes at the upper end — hot showers. And, for a variety of reasons, those who wind up at net cafés tend to be estranged from their families (two of the three youths profiled had been victims of child abuse) (Mizushima 2007).[2]

Mired in everyday survival, these youths (and the other working poor Mizushima interviewed for his documentary) lived on the edge and, for the most part, all alone. Deprived of a safety net, social support system, or reserves of almost any kind, these net café dwellers were consumed by merely getting through the day. On the day she turned eighteen, one of the three youths featured in the documentary (the only woman) told Mizushima that she had no hopes (kibō) for the future and tried to void desire altogether. When asked how she was coping (gaman), she answered, "by simply blocking out everything beyond survival itself. I am trying to make do with a life absent of desire . . . to be content with just a place to sleep, a job. If I have that, that's enough" (Mizushima 2007, 65–66). Bare life as the limits of existence.

There is no sense of a future here and no expectation that life will or could improve. Even for an eighteen year old, but one stuck in the status of temporary worker, prospects seem dim. Such a youth — floating at work, drifting in life, and halted in time — would seem the inverse of the forward-moving youths who so encapsulated the reproductive futurism of the postwar state. Under its edifice of the family-corporate system, this was a socioeconomic order that counted on children moving through the ranks — school, job, families of their own — but sticking with jobs and marriages for the long term to ensure (re)productivity for the nation-state. Life, by this calculus, was one of place, progression, and productivity: progressing to a place where one then remains productive (and secure) for the long term. But those in irregular (or with no) employment break this mold in every way; there is no movement forward, no long-term placement or security, little productivity (by the calculus it once was figured in, at least). One-third of all workers and one-half of young workers (between the ages of fifteen and twenty-four) fall into the ranks of the flexibly "irregular" (hiseikikoyō) workforce: those with temporary, part-time, short-term, or contract jobs. Not only do these jobs generally fail to provide long-term job security, incremental pay raises, or secure benefits but workers performing them often lack any form of worker's compensation or health insurance. Such risk-inflected work and the workers who perform it (particularly, if not exclusively, youths) are the "precariat"—the precarious proletariat—the word adopted by the activist Amamiya Karin from the Italian autonomist movement. For their indefatigable work on their behalf, both Amamiya (who is a prolific writer, speaker, and activist appearing daily at everything from strikes to demonstrations) and Yuasa Makoto (an activist who assumed a government post in emergency affairs under Prime Minister Hatoyama in 2010) have become the voices for the precariat and working poor; both will appear often throughout this book.

Mizushima's objective was to document the demographic of the precariat as a way of exposing Japan's "new face" of poverty and Japan's "new-era management style" in its turn to the flexibilization of the labor force. His film records the precarity of lives spent not only wandering the streets, scrounging to get by, and crashing in net cafés but also abiding the grinding routine of irregular labor. Scene after scene shows the three profiled youths struggling to find or endure work. Getting picked up for day labor in a van where no one speaks or addresses one another by name, staying glued all day to a cell phone to check in with an employer or seek employment for the next day, never knowing whether a job will materialize or get canceled the minute one shows up, having to arrive way in advance of a pickup and spend excess time merely waiting for a job to start in the first place. Viewers were jolted. Most associated day labor with temporal and spatial otherness: the early postwar years of destitution and poverty when no one had work and those looking for it were rounded up like the haken (temp) workers shown on Mizushima's documentary. This too was the image of Sanya, a remote section of Tokyo where down and out, mainly middle-aged or older men work as day laborers and live in flop houses or on the streets. But here, a typical day laborer appeared as a young adult in a cool tee shirt and fashionable jeans. Someone who could pass as a college student or hip Tokyo youth.

What has happened to Japan, Mizushima asked in his documentary, when the face of its future are young adults who, working temporary jobs, are virtually homeless and devoid of hope or dreams for tomorrow? If this child is Japan's "image of the future," then the country is in crisis, a crisis akin to war. But in this case Japan is not getting attacked by an alien enemy. Rather the country is at war with its own youths,[3] sacrificing them as *refugees* (*nanmin*)—the word Mizushima coined for Japan's "new face" of working poor.[4] The terminology caught on. Sending shockwaves through the country, Mizushima's documentary spurred the Ministry of Health, Labor, and Welfare to do its own study of net café refugees and the working poor the same year. A critically acclaimed series on poverty in Japan by NHK, the national broadcasting service, drew attention to the issue as well.[5] The word *refugee* (*nanmin*) also became part of the national lexicon, referencing—in this country notable for how protectionist its borders and how hostile to foreign migrants—not outsiders but those Japanese who get stranded inside their own country without access to a secure job, stable home, or normal life. Internal exiles, people who could be ordinary youths (like those in Mizushima's documentary) not living how they ordinarily might. This seems to be what Yuasa and Amamiya intended when, taking the word and turning it into a verb, they charged that Japan was at risk of becoming *refugeed* (*nanminka*),[6] raising the curious notion of a country evacuating itself of the homes and land it owes its citizens. Japan was becoming a country displaced (from) itself, a place where the net café refugee could be anyone, an ordinary person.

Japan was slipping into mud.

This is the issue I take up in this chapter. What I call "ordinary refugeeism" in twenty-first-century Japan: the crisis of getting by (human sustainability) and how this registers, in fact and in the imagination, as the dispossession of something as basic as home and land. Not everyone, of course, feels insecure or unstable in the skin of their everydayness. But, as I discovered in doing research on precarity since 2008, it is not simply the working poor who get stricken by unease in facing basic existence. The phrase I kept hearing over and over, and wherever I went, was *"ibasho ga nai"*—without a place or space where one feels comfortable and "at home." It is not just literal homes that are fading from the landscape, though this is true as well. It is also home in the sense "to stay somewhere, over time, in a place to which one can return" (Berlant 2011:162)—the normalcy of being and belonging that often gets associated with the my-home-ism of the postwar social contract. Guided by a principle of reproductive futurism, my-home-ism provided the roadmap for aspirational normativity: working hard, investing in children (who were then expected to invest in caregiving their parents), and building progressively toward a future that included a here and now of material prosperity. The dissolution, if not utter collapse, of reproductive futurism today fuels the fear of "no future" (Edelman 2004) at both a personal and national level. This gets expressed in the longing for a "normative intimacy" (Berlant 2011, 174–5) attached to a time and place that no longer exists. The loss of home and land; the mourning Japanese have for "Japan" (Ivy 1995).

But there is more to the story, which is the issue of human sustainability itself: of a rapid and real decline in the material well-being and social security of many Japanese. This is a time when, even for those who work, a job secures far less in post-postwar Japan than the postwar period that preceded it. A time when annual earnings of workers in their twenties fell 14 percent between 1997 and 2008, when 56 percent of workers between the ages of sixteen and thirty-four need a second source of income to pay for basic living expenses, and when 17 percent of all employed men and women between the ages of twenty and fifty have some form of a side job—and almost half are interested in acquiring one (Standing 2011). And, as the security promised by regular employment diminishes, so do the number of Japanese who can afford what the sociologist Yamada Masahiro (2003, 27) calls an "ordinary lifestyle" (*hitonami no seikatsu*). From a time of mass middle classness, the chasm between incomes is rising rapidly today. For those on the lower end of this "divided society," stability of life is especially at risk. But it is not only job or salary that divides people today. It is also those resources one uses to get a job in the first place or to compensate when times are tight: what Yuasa Makoto (2008a) calls "reserves" (*tame*) such as money in the bank, academic credentials, confidence in oneself, and family and friends.[7] Poverty, as he points out, is not only material but human deprivation: living un- and underemployed, minimally sustained, and often alone without the care or assistance of other humans. What has become of the geometry between labor, life, and well-being when what was once ordinary has become impossible for most ordinary people? And what becomes of those who fall victim to bare life and to the country that fails to shield them? The Japanese are losing their sense of home; Japan is losing its ground, shifting from *Japan as Number One* (Vogel 1979) to a country refugeed from even itself and moving from productive to precarious Japan.

Life on the Edge: War in the Trenches

The following excerpts are all from emails and involve cases of drop-ins at Yuasa Makoto's NPO Moyai (Yuasa 2008b):

A twenty-seven-year-old male *haken* (dispatch worker), sleeping in Shinjuku train station. Still wearing his suit. Work had tapered off lately and his monthly income went from 300,000 to 105,000 yen (from about US$3,189 to US$1,116). Unable to afford housing, he'd been living on the streets (*nojuku*) in Chiba. But now it's gotten cold, and work has dried up altogether.

A nineteen-year-old male who had lived with his father growing up until his father lost his job and couldn't take care of him anymore. He had been *futōko* (not attending school) since middle school; then he became NEET. The father took him to a facility [for deserted kids] but that stopped at age eighteen; he was then kicked out. Now he has no food and wants to die.

A thirty-three-year-old man lost the haken job he'd worked at since graduating from middle school. He'd been living in a capsule hotel, then a net café, while looking for work. When he contacted me, he had four yen in his pocket and had been sleeping on the streets (*nojuku*) for four days.

A thirty-five-year-old female who is trying to find work. But all she has managed is *haken* work that pays 200,000 yen per month (US$2,126). This doesn't give her enough to live on, and she is becoming desperate.

A thirty-one-year-old man is in bad straits. After graduating from vocational school (*senmon gakkō*), he'd been a systems engineer until the company was taken over by a dispatch (haken) company. Reduced to being essentially a dispatch worker, he was uncomfortable at work. Living at home, familial relations were strained as well. Not allowed to use the kitchen, he was constantly hungry. Quitting work, he lived off savings for awhile but now is stranded without a job or a safe home. When he visited Moyai, he hadn't eaten for a week.

A forty-four-year-old male, living with his parents whom, both bedridden, he takes care of single-handedly. He works at Goodwill but only makes an annual salary of 1,000,000 yen (US$10,630). When he called, he didn't have enough money to get to Moyai.

A thirty-five-year-old male with a wife and three kids. Working a *haken* job, he earns 200,000 yen a month and lives with his family in a dorm (where rent plus utilities and rental furniture costs 80,000 yen a month). The oldest child is entering grade school, and he needs 8,000 yen (US$85) to buy her a rucksack.

It is summer 2008. The night is hot, sticky, and wet. Only days before the anniversary of the end of the Pacific War (August 15), which always brings out memories, sometimes protests, of Japan's former militarism, I have come to Kyōgenji temple in the Honkomagome neighborhood of Tokyo for a discussion on "poverty and war" (*hinkon to sensō*). The second of a two night "continued discussion" (the first night's theme was teachers' responsibility regarding war), the sponsors are a teachers' group (not the left-wing Nikkyōso, or teacher's union, my friend, David Slater, tells me as we enter). Tables are set up outside selling pamphlets and books about poverty and war. Inside, where the temple is dimly lit, about fifty people—mainly middle-aged or older—sit on wooden seats and purple *zabuton* (cushions) arranged in the front. At eight, the head of the organization welcomes everyone to the event, then introduces the temple's priest who tells us about the history of the place—how the small temple inside had been the original structure that was reassembled inside upon rebuilding. The main speaker tonight is Yuasa Makoto, cofounder of the Reverse Poverty Network, codirector of Moyai, and future office holder (a position newly created to oversee poverty and precarity) under the Hatoyama administration.[8] Entering from the side and in a state of focused dishevelment—hair flying, eyes tired, but mind sharp as a nail—Yuasa sits Buddha-like on the floor.

Handsome, he looks like a professor. But he also has the sway of a public speaker, comfortable and composed. Once a graduate student in the prestigious department of political science at Tokyo University, Yuasa quit in 1995 to be an activist (involving himself in the plight of Iranian migrants and the homeless in Shibuya).[9] He speaks tonight without jargon or notes in a manner that is fluid and succinct. Yuasa starts in immediately on the complicity between poverty and war:

As in the United States, young people are starting to sign up for the Self-Defense Forces [Japan's equivalent of a military] just for the money.[10] The wages aren't great and there's a time lag between the exam (March) and when new recruits start to work (October or November). Still with wages low and stable jobs hard to find, the *jieitai* is becoming an attractive alternative. Those who sign up are motivated more by economic than patriotic reasons. But wasn't this why Germans were attracted to national socialism, because it offered jobs and economic stability? Like Germany was then, Japan is a weak state now. The line between "winners" (*kachigumi*) and "losers" (*makegumi*) is fading, and the poor today are not merely those who are homeless or on the streets. Ten years ago when I first started activism with homelessness, it was mainly men in their fifties and older. But today more and more young people are becoming homeless and poor. Also, poverty is not just a matter of economics. The situation is different in Japan than, say, in Europe. Here, one can't get married and have kids on low wages or with a wage level that doesn't increase as one gets older. This is true of many jobs now in Japan. The minimum wage is also low for Japan; in Hokkaido, for instance, it is only 660 yen [US$7] an hour.[11]

After half an hour, Yuasa stops. He's been interrupted along the way by questions and is peppered with more now: about the exclusions experienced by ethnic minorities (Okinawans and ethnic Koreans), about the hardship of working under nationalist conditions, about the pressures brought on by what is still Japan's competitive society, and about the risks befalling teachers who refuse to stand during the playing of Japan's national anthem at the start of every school day. The last issue generates the most discussion. A middle-aged man in the audience reminds Yuasa of the high rate of *kyūshoku* (temporary leave) political-minded teachers incur for "disobedience" against the state, a penalty that is accompanied by lost wages. Yuasa listens sympathetically. But then he urges everyone in the room not to respond to such conditions with pity. Our aim here is not to elicit pity, for us or others, no matter how vulnerable we are. Rather, we need to change society. We need to change Japan so it is no longer a society of poverty.

His angry tone and choice of words make it clear that Yuasa sees poverty as a form of war. It is a war that Japan is waging not against external enemies though, as nationalism gets entrenched, more support is being given the reformation of Article 9 (the self-defense and so-called peace clause), which would allow, and possibly encourage, Japan's remilitarization. Rather, it is a war that the state and society is waging by endangering and not fulfilling its commitment to the people—that of ensuring the right to a "healthy and culturally basic existence" that all citizens are entitled to under Article 25 of the constitution. In Yuasa's mind, Article 9 should be a set with Article 25: the defense of the nation alongside the defense, as in the protection, of basic life for the people (Yuasa 2008a). But as the precipitous rise of poverty particularly over the last decade would indicate, the state is not only reneging on its responsibility to ensure "basic life" to all citizens, it is risking (as in making vulnerable) the lives of (too) many. Only one factor in this, as Yuasa sees it, is the nationwide economic decline brought on by the bursting of the bubble and the shift in labor patterns. The government is even more complicit, in his view, with which I agree, in the priorities and policies it has taken. Basically, these are: aligning with (and protecting) big business, privatizing more and more of (what once were) government services under the banner of "individual responsibility" (*jiko sekinin*), and investing too little in social programs, including welfare (for, but not only, the newly flexible labor force with low wages). To wit, the turn of the century, under the deregulation and restructuring policies of the Koizumi administration,[12] was a time when: workers' wages fell by 4 percent, homelessness increased—including for the working poor (70.4 percent of the homeless have jobs [Suzuki 2007]), far too few in the population received welfare (because they were denied it or were too embarrassed to apply in the first place), and all the while profits of corporations doubled, stocks rose in value by close to three times, and the pay of government officials tripled (Makino 2008).

Refugeeization—as in the uprooting, circulation, and insecuritization of people without fixed homelands—is a global phenomenon today in fact. Having gone down in the mid-twentieth century because economies were more closed, today the mobility of people is skyrocketing. In 2010, 3 percent of the global population (214 million) were migrants along with three times that number (714 million) of internal migrants (such as the *dagongmei*, floating rural migrants in China, who give up their rights to residency [*hukou*] when traveling to work in cities or special economic zones like Shenzhen [Ngai 2004]). Those officially declaring themselves refugees and seeking asylum are at a historical high as well; according to the UN refugee agency, there were 15 million refugees in 2009 (mainly from Asia and Africa) and 1 million more waiting decision. Another 27 million people are internally displaced as a result of civil war or conflict. If one includes various kinds of migrancy and refugeeism together (those who, unable to find secure jobs, citizenship, or security at home, either migrate elsewhere or stay stuck and exiled at home), the phenomenon could be seen as not only rising but constitutive of the times. Borrowing a term from the Middle Ages, Guy Standing calls these the new "denizens" of the world: the varieties of migrant ("nomadic, circulatory, illegal, refugee, settler") who are growing along with a migration that is growing and transforming, "intensifying insecurities and putting many more in precarious circumstances" (2011, 93). As in England, a denizen wasn't a citizen but was granted a status similar to resident alien. It is the tendency toward "de-citizenship" of migrants today (a situation different from that in the early twentieth century) that Standing emphasizes in his usage of the word *denizen*. Rather than getting assimilated into citizenship (somewhere else), today's waves of migrants tend to be consigned to (continual or perpetual) de-citizenship instead. At the same time, the new economies (of neoliberal, global, and flexible capitalism) rely ever more on the ranks of irregular laborers: "migrants are the light infantry of global capitalism. Vast numbers vie with each other for jobs. Most have to put up with short-term contracts, with low wages and few benefits. The process is systemic, not accidental. The world is becoming full of denizens" (Standing 2011, 113).

So while capital welcomes migration for the low-cost labor it provides, nation-states and citizens across the globe are far less eager to open their arms. Anti-migrant hostility (and legislation) is rampant all over the world, which means that denizens who are struggling to survive must also contend with a state of disbelonging ("de-citizenship") that may never end. Refugeeism is the new ordinary, as the spread of the nation-state made "belonging to the community into which one is born no longer a matter of course and not belonging no longer a matter of choice" (Arendt 1986, 286; cited in Standing 2011, 113).

The insecurity of life is a worldwide phenomenon today. So is the encroachment of a new stage of transnational capitalism that national governments widely endorse (or have been coerced into). In this "human in/ security on a universal scale" (Bakker, Gill, and DiMuzio 2008, 163), the market is given precedence over the security, even survivability, of people. Well, certain people. For not everyone suffers. The very few who can competitively navigate the system of newly flexibilized, financialized, and virtual capital (what Hardt and Negri [2004] call the immaterial labor of manipulating information, communication, and affect engaged by the new working class of the "cognitariat," using Berardi's [2009] term) can be fabulously wealthy. Today, the world's wealthiest have gotten wealthier and fewer in number. All the while, those below the top ("the 99 percent") have spread (in ranks), declined (in fortunes), and gotten entrenched (stuck in time as well as space). This leads to a new form of classism, what David Harvey (2011, 159) sees as the main substantive effect of neoliberalism: the redistribution of wealth rather than its generation—accumulation by dispossession.[13] Wealth is not being produced anew but getting "dispossessed" by a capitalism that is encroaching ever more insidiously into the life, and lives, of those, the new denizens, for whom everyday security is becoming increasingly precarious as a result. It is the precariatization of daily life. But how long, and with what stakes, can a country survive when inequality, social exclusion, and financial crises compound? This is a question raised for places and populations in the world that would seem much more economically entrenched than Japan: consider the "abjection" faced in Zambia where the country, and its people, have lost hope after the promises of modernity (linked to copper mining) vanished (Ferguson 2006); the local warfare in parts of West Africa facilitated by boy soldiers who (in the absence of any other means of subsistence) grow up to sell their war skills as a form of productive labor (Hoffman 2011); and the case of India where in one of the fastest growing economies in the world a shockingly high percentage of the population has too little to eat (Yardley 2010).

Though different in scale, Japan too has been hit by a "paradox of sustainability" (Brodie 2003, 62). As elsewhere, this entails a tension and a crunch when, as the power of capital extends its reach, the ability of a country to socially reproduce and to protect basic life for its citizens is wrung dry. It is this contradiction between the very wealthy, super secure and what is becoming a majority of insecure everyone elses that angers Yuasa. For the government and industry are making choices—about how (and how not) to allocate resources and who (and who not) deserves an "ordinary lifestyle"—that impact dangerously the rising ranks of poor, working poor, the precariat, and the once (but no longer) middle class. Yuasa admits to being incendiary in his call to turn the tide, "*hanhinkon* may sound too warlike. But this is the meaning I intended: joining together to fight a battle" (Yuasa 2008a, 138). Poverty needs to be reversed, he argues, not only because it is killing people but because it is also killing Japan. Japan needs to be a society where "people can humanely reproduce" (2008: 224)—reproduce sociality and sustain their (and their country's) humanity. That, Yuasa says, is his purpose: "One step by one step. We must gather friends (*nakama*), create places (*ibasho*), and raise our voices. . . . Let's build a strong society that fights poverty and war" (2008a, 224).

A Grievable Life: Apprehending by Sensing Precariousness

> Without grievability, there is no life, or, rather, there is something
> living that is other than life. —Butler 2009, 15

The first day I visit Moyai, I am given a pamphlet. The word *moyai* refers to ropes that are used to tie a boat together and Moyai, an NPO, identifies itself as an "independent life support center": a center that gives support to people so they can lead, or help jump start, an "independent life" (*jiritsu seikatsu*). On the cover of the pamphlet the byline reads: "in order to live inside connectedness" (*tsunagari no naka de ikiru tameni*). Inside the pamphlet "connectedness" is linked to those seeking to start a new life. From finding a job or apartment to applying for welfare.

> In economically poor times, people get lonely even when they have connections with others. Broadly speaking, we're in conditions today of homelessness; finding independence is hard. And in this poverty of human relations (*ningenkankei no hinkon*), it's difficult to find, for example, a guarantor when trying to rent an apartment. We can help with this. Also, it's hard to forge new relationships and to live [as was once commonplace] in a local society (*chīki shakai*). We can help with this too: we can help you make ties so that you're not alone in troubling times. [Humans] don't live alone; we live in the midst of relationships. Let's build a society where we can live safely (*anshin*). This is our philosophy. (Moyai pamphlet)

On July 23, 2008, after reading Yuasa Makoto's book *Hanhinkon* (Reverse Poverty), where he talks so much about the NPO he cofounded and continues to co-run, I decide to go to Moyai myself. The building is a small wooden house, down an alley, twenty minutes from downtown Tokyo in Iidabashi. I'm terrible with directions, and this one is particularly difficult to find. But I manage to locate the place. And, once there, I go up to the second floor, remove my shoes, and introduce myself to the two staff plus Yuasa and his co-director Inaba. It is Tuesday, the day of the week Moyai sponsors its "consultancy room" (*sōdan shitsu*) where volunteers offer assistance with housing, jobs, and welfare to drop-ins between the hours of 10 AM and 10 PM. The room, stacked with pamphlets and memos on the table, gets crowded with the traffic of people. The phone rings and Yuasa deals with the caller in measured efficiency, turning to me when done to extend the same courtesy for the few minutes he can afford. When asked if I can observe the consultancy sessions, he agrees. "Sure," he says, "many people come here to observe. Talk with everyone and stay for lunch!"

Back downstairs, I see people waiting already on benches set outside on the small concrete veranda. Told to join one of the two rooms where consulting has started, I enter the one with tatami mats and sit on the floor next to a big, burly volunteer (a lawyer, he later tells me) just waving in his first consultee for the day. The woman—in her early thirties, plumpish, and sweating profusely—starts off jovially. She had a hard time finding the place. The counselor rejoins that he did too the first time he came to Moyai and, hopelessly lost, stopped to ask a shop clerk who showed him the entire way. They share a hearty laugh, but soon she breaks down in tears. When asked what her situation is, she wonders—where to start?

She's currently living with a friend—not ideal—and has a liver problem that has made her weak. She was doing *haken* (temp) work but it's decreased lately; the last wages she got didn't even come to 50,000 yen a month (US$611). After only a few minutes, the counselor tells her she should apply for welfare (*seikatsu hogo*) and pulls out a huge notebook with forms and information. Ripping out a few pieces, they start going through forms. She says she applied for this before and was twice rejected on the grounds that she was young and could still work. He tells her that being young is not a reason for denying someone welfare and that, this time, he'll help her fill out the form and a caseworker will actually accompany her when she goes (which should be right away, as in the next day).

Back to her condition. She has high blood pressure, dental problems (she's missing a front tooth), and only 2,000 yen (US$21) to her name (though she did have a cell phone). Her family situation is bad; when asked about this in filling out the welfare forms, she doesn't want to give any information (and doesn't want them to be notified, except for her younger brother). When asked how much she paid for the last apartment she rented, she answers 35,000 yen (US$372) a month but adds that the one before that was 100,000 yen (US$1,063) a month. Then she had money because she worked in the *mizu shōbai* (the nightlife) — the reason she's estranged from her family. But life has been hard (*tsurai*) for ten years now; she has no one to turn to, no job prospects, and is in bad health.

The two cover a lot of ground. Securing an apartment (once welfare comes through, which he's assuming it will) may take as much as a month and a half. Meanwhile, she should try to stay with her friend. That might not be possible, she admits. Then, maybe the *ku* (the ward from which she'll be getting welfare) will provide money for her to stay at a *kan'i shukuhakujo* (provisional housing), which might be 1,800 yen a night (US$19). But, given she's a woman, it's probably best for her to try to stay with the friend, the counselor urges her. Then he goes over what the next steps might look like. Under welfare, she'll get a start-up package of 300,000 yen (US$3,189) to find a place to live that will cover the deposit and key money.[14] She won't be given more than 50,000 yen a month (US$532) for rent, so she needs to find something basic. But Moyai will be her official guarantor; this relieves her immensely as she can't imagine who she'd find to do that. Also she will need medical proof for her health problems (which means undergoing an official exam). The woman is paying attention, sitting erect, listening carefully. It's hard to read her affect; is she feeling relief at all, I wonder?

After talking for about an hour and a half, the counselor calls in another volunteer: a woman in her early thirties who is no-nonsense and dressed in jeans and a colorful shirt. This is the person who will accompany her to the welfare office tomorrow. They go over what this will entail and exchange phone numbers and details of where and when to meet. After ten minutes, they're done. "Well, that's about it," the male counselor says, "hang in there and keep your spirits up!" The woman smiles wearily but doesn't immediately get up. He invites her to stay for lunch, but she declines. Getting up, she wonders what to do if she needs help. "You're only open on Tuesdays, right?" "Right," he answers. But handing her his cell phone number, he tells her to call anytime. "Thanks. Now I feel a bit better. Now I am no longer alone."

Moyai was started in 2003 by Yuasa and Inaba Minoru, a fellow graduate student at University of Tokyo who dropped out the same time to do activism with Yuasa. Its funding comes from various sources, but all the labor is volunteer except for two staff. Its main agenda is life support: hands-on help in rebuilding basic life. Those it aims to serve are not only destitute—out of work, without housing, injured or sick—but also have no one else to turn to; they are the socially stranded and humanly bereft. *Tsunagari* (connection) as well as the word *ningenkankei* (human relationships) index those ties between people and with social institutions that anchor identity and provide a safety net in times of need: what workplace and family were once expected to do under the my-home-ist era of postwar Japan. Those severed from social connectedness and human relatedness are truly alone. In some sense they don't exist. Making the lives and circumstances of such people visible in and to the public is part of Yuasa's wider agenda in his reverse poverty (*hanhinkon*, also translated as antipoverty) campaign: putting a face on poverty that, despite its spread over recent years, too often goes unrecognized and unknown (Yuasa 2008a, 2009). In order to "battle" it, poverty must be seen and also owned: owned as a problem facing "us" as a nation and not just othered as befalling those who don't matter (because they don't count). But, as with Judith Butler, who believes "that precariousnss itself cannot be properly recognized" (2009, 13), Yuasa does not trust or rely upon the act of public recognition alone. To apprehend poverty (and precarity), one must sense it, live it, change it as part of the human condition, a part that is shared. This certainly cannot happen when precariousness is framed as an exceptional state or as a state that, by befalling only the exceptional few, exempts everyone else.

This is the part of the battle against poverty that Yuasa wages in the trenches. His work at Moyai is no less political than his work with the antipoverty campaign. But at Moyai, it is more of the flesh. Yuasa is involved in a politics of survival: figuring out ways to make life better for those struggling to get by. This, as I see it, is a politics of sociality. Working together to fill in what Yuasa terms the *hole* plaguing those who struggle the most today: a scarcity in the means of subsistence and a sparseness in human capital and connection. Helping those who have slid deepest is also a way of fighting to change what Yuasa sees as symptomatic of the conditions plaguing Japan's "sliding down society" (*suberidai shakai*): precarity. As he notes, postwar Japan bred its own form of welfare that depended on the corporation and family and organized little public welfare itself. But in the shift to irregularization and lessening of benefits from and at work, more workers are struggling, which puts demands on the family; most *furītā* live at home with their parents, and those estranged from family or with particular needs (handicapped, single-parent households, with elderly in the household) are especially at risk. As with net café refugees, a high number of those who seek out help from Moyai have been abandoned or estranged from their families (Yuasa 2008a; Iwata 2007). Providing a connective tissue of human support for those without any is one of Moyai's missions: a fact of life that is becoming increasingly ordinary in post-welfare, post-family, post-relational Japan.

Yuasa is tireless and fierce in his war against poverty and in the advocacy he mobilizes for people suffering precariousness. His work is tremendous on so many fronts. But I would like to also note a latent tendency even with Yuasa (and shared, I believe, with Amamiya) to, if not memorialize the past, at least treat it as a reference point for the securitization of life so absent today. This reference point haunts post-bubble times with a mapping for normalcy that hinges on a sociality (and social well-being) tied to capitalist value that harbors its own problems and exclusions. And that—as an aspirational normalcy that is as tightly hung onto even or, particularly, when it is so clearly out of reach (Berlant 2011)—can be dangerous in and of itself, as we will see.

War as Hope, Killing as Protest

In the January 2007 issue of *Ronza*, a journal of social criticism, a controversial article titled *"Kibō wa senso"* (Hope is War) appeared. Written by a thirty-one-year-old, self-identified *furītā*, it argued that the hope of his generation is war. Still working a nightshift and living with his parents ten years after entering the labor force, Akagi Tomohiro described his life as "unbearably humiliating" (*kutsujoku*) (2007, 53). With a monthly income of 100,000 yen (US$1,230, well below the poverty line that the government has set at US$22,000 a year for a family of four), Akagi was finding it impossible to acquire even one of the attributes of adulthood: a place of his own, a car to drive, wife and kids. Living as if he were "under house arrest," Akagi despaired of ever becoming unstuck from his dead-end job and the home he had grown up in since being a child. Lucky to have supportive parents, he nevertheless worried that they were aging, fearing his circumstances could get even worse after they die. And yet all he heard from society around him was "get a job and life will be fine." "But where are these jobs society speaks of?," Akagi lamented, and "why are *furītā* criticized for being too weak-willed and lazy to get better jobs? In truth, there are few opportunities for young adults who missed the chance to secure regular employment right out of school."[15] Treated now as a social "parasite," Akagi mourned the existence he and others like him abide "not being humans who can live having hope under these conditions" (*sonna jōtai de kibō o motte ikirareru ningen nado inai*) (2007, 54).

The corrective, as he wrote half-facetiously (though not perhaps), is war. What is needed is something to shake things up and to spur social mobility as occurred after the Pacific War. For despite the new flexibilization (*ryūdōka*) of the economy today, the social order isn't nearly flexible (*ryūdō*) enough.[16] Those in the lower rungs, the precariat like Akagi, are crystallized in what is likely to be an underclass existence that turns permanent.

> During the period of high economic growth after the war, there was temporarily a big opening in class that has since closed up. . . . But, as Japan has acquired stability [*antei suru ni tsurete*], mobility (ryūdōka) has also been lost. . . . It's been more than ten years now since we, low-wage earners, have been thrown out (*hōridasarete kara*) by society. Nonetheless, we don't get any support and we are accused of lacking will and of contributing to the lowering of the GDP. . . . If peace continues, all of this will stay the same. What can break this stalemate and spur mobility again? There's only one possibility: WAR. Economically weak people like myself want relief from our travails, social status, the means to support (our) family, and the possibility of earning respect as independent human beings [*ichininmae no ningen*] from society. Aren't these natural desires? In order for this to happen, unfortunately, we need war. For, without it, social differences will only exacerbate. War is tragic. It's tragic because people who have things will lose something. But, for us who have nothing, it's an OPPORTUNITY. (Akagi 2007, 58).

Peace, with its promise of national stability, security, and a continuance of the status quo, "has a saracastic ring" to Akagi. For none of this brings hope to those low-wage earners who, in this peacetime of "ryūdōka," are mired in a poverty that they have no chance of escaping. Peacetime is the recipe for social stalemate, he argued: a national order that continues to protect those who grew up during the period of high economic growth but has "thrown out" the post-bubble generation who shoulder, disproportionately, the ills of the economy.

Though advocating for national war, Akagi holds quite personal and prosaic desires for the kind of "good life," once the template for postwar my-home-ism, that he feels at once denied and owed by the state. This is how he starts off the article. A scene of basic everydayness: what Lauren Berlant calls the longing to be "nearly normal" with its "nearly utopian" ring (2011, 161). It is a Sunday morning and, after getting off his nightshift at a factory, he has gone to the local shopping mall. While meandering through the aisles, an announcement comes over the loudspeaker: "For the security of your children, surveillance cameras are watching for suspicious persons." Immediately, Akagi feels targeted. A single man without children or spouse stalking the aisles on a Sunday morning in dirty work clothes—a "suspicious man" is precisely how he is (mis)recognized by others. The thought infuriates him for having a wife, kids, and home to shop for is precisely the life he hankers for. And, despite doing everything he was told to—studying hard at school, graduating from a decent college, finding and keeping a job—he is a furīta who lives parasitically off mom and dad. Still a child with no social respect or self-respect, he describes a condition of life akin to death. Indeed, death is often on his mind for he feels deathlike already. And, if this is the reality of many young workers today, then the stakes of war are hardly a leap—his argument about war as the "hope" of his generation.

While Akagi's position here is both polemical and extreme, he is hardly the only young person who sees in the military an attractive alternative to the precarity of work today. As Yuasa noted the evening of the poverty and war discussion, recruitment in the jieitai (Self-Defense Forces) is up: a trend only too familiar from Nazi Germany, Britain in 1941, and history elsewhere. Economic insecurity has long been the driving force of nationalism as well, and Japanese youths are gravitating toward right-wing politics these days. While few young people have taken to social protest, a deep sense of dissatisfaction and victimization plagues the current generation. And although liberals accuse them of being apolitical, their tendency to embrace (right-wing) nationalism is (often) the voice their affect is taking, according to Akagi. The activist Amamiya Karin connects what seems like political apathy to the very thwarting of social identities and daily livelihoods that compels youths to seek out membership in what they may see as the only place where they can find it: right-wing organizations. This is what happened to her when, as a suicidal furīta in her early twenties, she joined rightist associations and felt—for what she says was the first time in her life—a sense of belonging (Amamiya and Kayano 2008). As someone who had been bullied as a schoolchild, failed her university entrance exams, and then got stuck in the humiliating cycle of precarious work, Amamiya felt void of worth. Ontologically empty and socially dead, Amamiya felt hopeless, as so many of her generation still are.

Ghassan Hage (2003) identifies three mechanisms the nation-state has for distributing hope to its citizens: fostering a sense of belonging to the nation (national identification), cultivating investment in and expectations about a progressively better future (social mobility), and recognizing the importance of personal and collective dreams (social hope). When citizens feel plugged into a collective beyond themselves and to a future beyond the here and now, they are more likely to feel hopeful. This, by most accounts, is how people experienced and remember the period of postwar Japan. But when social citizenship or horizons of expectation are blocked, hopelessness sets in, as it has for many today. This also engenders what Hage calls paranoid nationalism: when, feeling excluded from nation or community, one attempts, sometimes violently, to exclude others as well. This is at once an (over)identification with, and disidentification by, the national project: what Arjun Appadurai (2006) sees as a global rash of ethnic cleansing campaigns, marked by a brutal form of ("vivisectionist") violence, from Rwanda to Yugoslavia since the 1990s. Brought on in part by the free flow of finance capital and new inequities of global distribution, the borders of (and membership in) nation-states are getting disturbed in ever new ways. Provoking social uncertainty, particularly for those most vulnerable to economic precarity, people lose clarity and confidence over who they are and where they fit in. As Appadurai notes, such an "anxiety of incompleteness" is often accompanied by a surplus of rage and identitarian violence—as if killing a Tutsi will confirm, and complete, a Hutu's place in the nation-state.

Violence fueled by anxiety of incompleteness characterized the rampage of Katō Tomohiro, a young precariat who, on June 8, 2007, drove a two-ton truck into a crowded intersection then jumped out and stabbed more victims. Seven were left dead, ten injured. Staged as if a publicity event, it took place in Akihabara, Tokyo's electronics district and a hotbed of *otaku* (fandom) culture, on a Sunday at noon when the streets had been closed for pedestrian shoppers. Eliciting high-voltage attention, the act spurred a wave of copycat attacks in public places that lasted all summer—in kiosks, train stations, shopping malls. Katō was a twenty-five-year-old haken (temporary) worker who, having gone from job to job, thought he had been fired from his current one. The young man was deeply troubled, as he admitted on the long trail of postings he left on a phone netsite. An addict of digital chatting, Katō wrote of his despair at being a haken worker with no firm attachments (such as a girlfriend, steady coworkers, or good ties with his parents) that gave him a home base (ibasho) anywhere. Devoid of social status and connectedness, he hated life, as he posted the morning of the killing, "I came to Akihabara because I wanted to kill people. I've come to hate society and am tired of life. Anyone is OK" (Yosensha 2008, 9). In the news reportage that followed, Katō was described as one of the working poor and a member of Japan's sliding-down society who, feeling socially alienated, was suffering from both loneliness (kodoku) and the failure to feel accepted (shōnin). Included were comments about his estrangement from his parents: a mother, whom it was reported, had pushed the high-performing Katō academically, then withdrew her love when his grades declined in high school.[17]

Because of the nature of violence—public, random, impersonal—the attack was considered to be a terrorist act and became known as the "Akiba musabetsu tero jiken" (Akiba, short for Akihabara, indiscriminate terrorist act). But, equally disturbing, was the profile of the so-called terrorist himself, someone not so dissimilar in certain ways from an increasing number of youths: irregularly employed, lonely and disconnected, socially estranged and existentially bereft. If sociality of the new precariat was getting (dis)assembled like this, it was precarious not only for youths but for the population and public at large. These were the terms around much of the voluminous debate over the incident that took place. For example, in a roundtable published in the journal Rosujene (Lost Generation) titled "Who was the enemy in the Akiba terrorist incident?," participants discussed the role society played in creating a killer like Katō. As many noted, youths of the lost generation feel both humiliated and displaced: a sentiment that makes them not only uneasy (fuan) but increasingly dissatisfied (fuman).[18] As the cultural critic Kayano Toshihiko put it, "if only we have hope and respect, we can live. But without a secure means of existence, many today have no place or sense of home at all [ibasho]" (Rosujiene 2008, 34). Youths, as he noted, are driven not only to join right-wing associations for the national belonging they promise but also to the kind of despair and social nihilism that spirals in violence—toward themselves (as in wrist cutting and suicide, both of which are on the rise today) or toward others (as in Katō's attack in Akihabara).

In his own take on what motivated the Akiba attacker, Akagi Tomohiro (author of "Kibō wa sensō") brought it all back to quotidian desires: "His act was not really about leftist or rightist politics. It was more that his private desires were thwarted: his desires for private relationships (*ningenkankei*) and toward society. All he wanted was [normalcy]: to work normally, to be able to live with normal independence, and to have normal relations with other people" (Akagi 2008, 23). This was someone desperate to be "nearly normal" (Berlant 2011). But Akagi went further. Not only did Katō lack a basic life, he had a life that lacked worth altogether. As a part of the precariat, he was a disposable human being. A "supernumerary" whose life, writes Robert Castel (2003) about the rising ranks of such laborers worldwide, is "superfluous":

> But the "supernumeraries" are not even exploited for, in order to be so, it is necessary to possess some skills that may be converted into social value. They are superfluous. . . . If they are no longer in the strict sense of the word "actors," because they make nothing that is socially useful, how can they exist socially? This is in the sense where to exist socially means that one actually holds a place in society. For, at the same time, they are ever present—and this is the whole problem, for they are in abundance. (Castel 2003, xxii)

Had he simply killed himself, as so many postings after the incident said he should have, Katō would not have been grieved or even missed. Only by killing someone else, as Akagi pointed out, could his life register in the national imaginary at all. To call attention to the ungrievability of his own life then, Akagi killed others who would be much more grieved than himself.

Recognition and Withdrawal: The Precarity and Precariousness of Youth

Writing about coming of age in Japan's "new management style" of flexibilization (ryūdōka), Amamiya Karin (2007), born in 1965, describes belonging to the "lost generation." When she entered the labor force in 1993 as a furītā, she found her job numbing for multiple reasons. She could be fired anytime, the pay was minimal, no one addressed her by name, and the work could be done by anyone. As part of the new "disposable labor power" (Amamiya 2007), she felt superfluous: unvalued in the work she did and voided of worth or recognition as a human being. Certainly, the job status of a furītā—or irregular worker (*hiseikikoyō*) is precarious. Pay is low and benefits are nonexistent. But Amamiya, who, with her goth style, dynamic public presence, and writing talents, has now emerged as something of the spokesperson for the irregularly employed and lost generation, is careful to define the risk of precarity in terms that are not just material. Employing the word *ikizurasa* (hardship of life), she defines it thus: "ikizurasa (hardship of life) is connected to poverty and labor issues. But, first, it's a problem of ningenkankei (human relationships). And that's where I start—with an emotional sense of hardship" (Amamiya and Kayano 2008, 9). Honing in on human relationships—the stuff of sociality—Amamiya describes the psychic turmoil of being a Japanese worker who lacks affiliation (*shozoku*). This is what companies once provided and still do for a few *seishain* (regular workers): a steady salary, protection if there is a crisis, and, every bit as important, an identity. Irregular workers, by contrast, are on their own, struggling to make a living, and bereft of a place that feels homey and secure (*ibasho*). More than anything, according to Amamiya, it is (dis)belonging—no recognition or acceptance by others (*shōnin*)—that troubles the young precariat. Calling this the biggest issue facing young Japanese today, Amamiya portrays the "hardship of life" as an insecurity that is not only material but also ontological. It carries with it a sense of existential emptiness and social negation. And, while anyone can be prey, those most at risk are the working poor at the bottom of Japan's increasingly bipolarized society (*kakusa shakai*): the flexible workers that the government embraces as its new "Japanese-style" labor force. It is these workers who are being treated like "foreigners": a treatment that feels particularly brutal in a country that is so unwelcoming to those who enter from outside and can lead, as Amamiya has observed, to a paranoid nationalism among the precariat targeted at foreign migrants.

At the heart of Amamiya's activism is the call to recognize, give voice to, and assist those having "difficulty in life" (*ikizurasa*).[19] At once pointed and plastic, the concept of ikizurasa resembles Judith Butler's usage of precariousness. That is, precariousness is both generalizable to life itself—"lives are by definition precarious" (Butler 2009, 25)—and differentially distributed in a population: "This differential distribution of precarity is at once a material and a perceptual issue, since those whose lives are not "regarded" as potentially grievable, and hence valuable, are made to bear the burden of starvation, underemployment, legal disenfranchisement, and differential exposure to violence and death" (25). Butler reserves the word *precarity* for that class most relegated or abandoned to precariousness by the state; for Amamiya, this is an economic class—those irregularly employed and insecurely waged as the precariat. By contrast, precariousness (Amamiya's ikizurasa) is the more generalizable condition of life itself: the susceptibility to harm, disease, and death that everyone is vulnerable to as a living being. For Butler the two concepts intersect. And while doubting that precariousness can be recognized per se ("we ought not to think that the recognition of precariousness masters or captures or even fully cognizes what it recognizes" [13]), she argues for a politics of social life premised on acknowledging precariousness as a shared human condition and on working for the grievability (and thus livability) of all lives, including those the state relegates to precarity: "precarity cuts across identity categories as well as multicultural maps, thus forming the basis for an alliance focused on opposition to state violence and its capacity to produce, exploit, and distribute precarity for the purposes of profit and territorial defense" (32).

Like Butler, Amamiya engages in a politics of social life. Preferring the word *activism* to *politics* (discounting, when I asked her in interview, if her work was a "politics of survival"), she advocates for both survival and life—for surviving hardship and living securely. Grafted onto the contingency of the precariat in particular, she is also interested in the broader (or more basic) condition of life ("hardship") that extends beyond those irregularly employed and deeper into existence than the dimensions of wages or labor alone. (Precariousness, for example, is the condition of risk that all Japanese are vulnerable to as a result of 3/11: to the dangers of radiation, contaminated food, a future earthquake, the national cost of recovery and rebuilding. But precarity is the differential distribution of danger by which certain segments of the population are at greater economic, job-related risk; for example, 90 percent of those who were working at nuclear plants even before 3/11 were part of the precariat as contract workers; today the number is about the same.) In her voluminous publications and public-speaking engagements,[20] Amamiya often speaks about the numbers of people she has known over the years who have committed suicide. Most, but not all, have been furīta who died from wounds as psychic and social as material and economic. Recognizing the complicity between precarity and precariousness, Amamiya is sensitive to how lonely life on the edge can be. Being materially, socially, existentially isolated is what she considers the scourge of twenty-first-century living in Japan, and the corrective is being stitched to a "place" (ibasho) of connectedness where one gains social recognition, human belonging, and material subsistence (or support when times are hard).

In her activism with haken laborers, for example, Amamiya works to overturn recent deregulation that—increasing the hours and kinds of labor companies can designate as haken without the security of contract or livable wages—makes work of this kind particularly risky and dangerous.[21] While pressing on issues of remuneration, hours, and job security, Amamiya is equally attentive to what she considers to be every bit as important: human or social recognition. Noting that companies categorize the salaries they pay haken workers as a property (*bukken*) versus personnel expense, she sees in this a sign of how disposable workers get treated as alienable matter (Amamiya and Kayano 2008, 55). Failing to be even recognizable as human—by one's employer, by society—is a "hardship of life" all its own and a problem difficult to address. This is existential vulnerability or ontological precariousness: a situation where even sensing oneself is up for grabs. And if feeling socially dead already, the option of suicide may not be much of a jump.

Asked, in a dialogue with the cultural critic Kayano Toshihito, to elaborate on this psychosocial dynamic of "recognition" (shōnin), Amamiya answered as follows.

Because we rely on others for self-confirmation, this becomes tricky when there is a strain or void in human relationships. I was raised in the boomer-junior generation [of aspirationally driven young people][22] and was particularly susceptible to needing confirmation from others. We all thought we were striving to enter the best schools "for us," but wasn't this something else: from being over-dependent on praise, and acceptance, from others? When we didn't reach these goals—or get recognition from others—it felt like an annihilation of the spirit [seishintekina ikizurasa]. And now we're in an age when this existential angst is spreading; affecting those with precarious jobs but also hindering those—like NEET and *hikiko-mori*—who don't have the spirit to find work in the first place. . . . Furītā are in a particularly hard position. If you're a student and working part-time [arubaito], then one is affiliated with the university. But most furītā don't have that, which, again, is one of the attractions of patriotism for furītā. Everyone needs a place, identity, affiliation: we need an ibasho that finds us necessary. This is what belonging to an ibasho means—unconditional acceptance. It's like the relationship between parent and child; a parent doesn't love the child because she's smarter than everyone else, right? Unconditional love means being loved no matter what. But it also means being made to feel special. (paraphrased from Amamiya and Kayano 2008, 38–39, 86–87)

What Amamiya describes here sounds to me like *amae*—the psychosocial dynamic of dependency that, embedded in the family and workplace, goaded the "Japanese style" productivity model of postwar Japan (see chapter 2 for more on amae). Amae affectively conspired in the aspirational normativity to be "number one," which rebounded in warm feelings of recognition and affiliation. We need an ibasho that finds us necessary, a feeling of being made to feel special. As Amamiya notes, but not enough to outweigh her longing for it, this is a mechanism that isn't precisely unconditional. Rather, it bears its own precariousness; acceptance is premised on productive performance. When one fails—or skids off track—belonging and recognition (even a parent's "unconditional love") may well be withheld.

This is what so many in the "lost generation" are stung by as well: the desire to be not only secure in everyday life but included as one of the "winners." This is a pining for what should have, what could have been, theirs as upwardly mobile youths who are hit instead by the stigma and rejection of (seeming) failure, of being a loser. Now susceptible to a precarity and underclassness that affected others far earlier (those who failed or dropped out of the academic credentializing society during Japan, Inc., for example), this generation still holds onto the desire to "feel special"—a desire fueling what studies show are the newly popular ambitions of young people today in fantasy futures such as becoming rock stars, idols, manga artists, or professional athletes (Yamada 2003; *Asahi Shimbun* 2007). (Still, teenage girls harbor more "ordinary" ambitions as well. A recent study showed that 85 percent desire to become a full-time housewife for the associations this carries with a "secure lifestyle," despite the fact that this is an increasingly unlikely option [*Hakuhōdō seikatsu sōgō* 2005]. A more practical, and almost as popular, ambition of Japanese girls, however, is to work in the nightlife scene [as *kyabajo*] in cabaret clubs that have risen dramatically in the last decade.)

Though she doesn't quite put it in these terms, Amamiya points to a "normativity hangover" (Berlant 2011)—the desire to find acceptance, recognition, and identification with something recognizable itself. But how likely is it that what is desired in the way of recognition will come from the social institutions, with their socio-affective relations, that operated in previous times? It would seem time, particularly as the government is doing so itself with its "new era" flexible labor force, to come up with a different rubric for measuring value, guaranteeing security, and assembling human relationships. Perhaps there should be a move away from a standard of work and productivity measured by capitalist value. This is what the Italian autonomist school (*operaismo*) advocates, as Amamiya knows from her connection with them (from whom she's adopted the term *precariat*, learned about activism around precarity, and been inspired by the EuroMayDays to help organize indie May Days in Japan). The feminist political scientist Kathi Weeks (2011) pursues this line as well in her postwork "utopian demand" for citizens to have a basic income driven not by productive output of workers but by the need for common reproduction — what creates the social life for an economy increasingly dependent on immaterial and affective labor.

Here, though, I want to stay with precariousness, and particularly the (precariat) affect Amamiya refers to as "annihilation of the spirit" (*seishintekina ikizurasa*) that festers around aspirational goals (and its supplychain of well-being) so sutured to a social and work affiliation of a very particular kind. It is not simply that post-bubble Japan no longer has the economic vitality to supply jobs and middle-class security to as many citizens as it used to, but it is also that the old nervous system is still, to some degree, intact, grinding down and spitting out "disposable humanity" in what is now a scarcity of social belonging. As Amamiya points out, what could be considered a holdover of the competitive society (*kyōsō shakai*) has only heightened in the competitiveness young people face in social media online and peer relations at school. While always precarious in terms of peer popularity and the threat of exclusion, the market in youth sociality shows signs of ratcheting up. Refugeeism from the social is becoming more ordinary every day. With the annihilation of the spirit, Japan is turning into a lonely country.

Nakamura Kyōko and Harada Yōhei, the two principal investigators of a study of teenage girls sponsored by the advertising company *Hakuhōdō seikatsu sōgō* (2005), discovered a form of competitive sociality fed by the intensity with which youths today are continually plugged into cell phones (and other digital devices). Virtually all of the girls in the study owned their own cell phones, and many of these girls were continually using their phones. But while this meant they were never—literally, digitally—alone, it also forced them to be proficient in what the two researchers labeled "instant communicative ability." Those who curried a high volume of phone transactions gained popularity, while those who couldn't feared getting cut from the social scene altogether. Like the market economy, energy was speeded up, and many of the girls said they felt jumpy: their sense of connectedness was contingent, frail, multiplied, and dispersed. In what others have noted about relationality in this digital era of information capitalism, interpersonal connections are at once spread across a broader network and devolve upon superficial, if constant, contact. As a young woman in her twenties told me, her friends only share what is *tanoshii* (enjoyable) in their lives—favorite foods, television shows, celebrity gossip. But the sorrows and hardships they keep to themselves to not burden friends and to stay popular in an age when knowing how to read, and stay in sync, with the mood of the moment—what is called *kūki o yomu* ("reading the scene" or KY—as in someone who can't)—is everything. In the era of the cell phone and Internet, *ijime* (bullying) is said to be on the rise among school students as KY gets played digitally, becoming a game of sociality whose stakes (winner versus loser) are as treacherous as effervescent (Amamiya and Kayano 2008).

Suicide rates are now so high that the government, and communities, are taking measures to intervene. Withdrawal is noteworthy as well: another form of refugeeism that has become only too "ordinary" these days in Japan and is symptomatic of the times. This social precariousness is linked to, but hardly coterminous with, that of the precarity of work, labor, and the economy today. Withdrawal is more common among those youths with families willing and able to support them: the middle class, in other words. Here too, there is a susceptibility to disconnection from others— the kind of psychic malaise or alienation of the social spirit Amamiya links to recognition. Withdrawal also takes multiple forms. Withdrawing from the active pursuit of job, school, or training are NEET who numbered 2.5 million as of 2007. This may, but not necessarily, lead to becoming a hikikomori (the socially withdrawn) who retreat to a delimited space (such as a room in their parent's house) from which they literally don't emerge. In addition to these two types, there is something more generic: what the feminist sociologist Miyamoto Michiko described to me as a "de-social" tendency among Japanese youths today to retreat from participation in society altogether. Whereas Miyamoto is not unsympathetic to youths and the challenges facing them because of the socioeconomic conditions of the times, she also wishes they had harder drive and more spunk. "How is Japan going to survive the next stage without youths pushing it to a more sustainable future?," she wondered.

Others, however, see even in the tendency of youths to withdraw a form of protest (or survival strategy) against society, the scarcity of options open to those coming of age, and the unwillingness of its authorities (state, social, familial) to protect its youths from the precarity and precariousness they are susceptible to. The cultural critic Honda Tōru (2007) takes this position. Writing specifically about the school system where the "competitive society" mentality is incubating an ever more virulent form of bullying, he tells young people to, first and foremost, protect themselves. If school is a hostile environment where their lives are literally at risk, young people really have only two options. They can stay in a place that is killing them, or they can choose to stay alive. The latter means leaving school and socially withdrawing. The title of Honda's (2007) book sums up his message: *Jisatsu suru nara, hikikomore* (If You're Going To Commit Suicide, Withdraw).

Refugeed at Home, a Warzone Outside

But to withdraw is to enter what kind of space precisely?

> I went to the store in my PJS, which I haven't been out of for months. Riding on my bike. To a store to buy two keys for my door at home so no one can get in . . . On the way home, an old man asked me to tell him where the hospital was . . . Yeah, well, I'm in my PJS so everyone thinks I'm a patient . . . I returned home. The TV was on and, like always, there was static, the sound of a sandstorm. With the sandstorm in the background, I locked the door. Now no one can enter my room. No one can shine a light on me. No one but me can give directions. . . . So started my life of only me in only my room. (Chihara 2007, 16)

In his memoir of his fourteenth year, the year he locks his door and becomes a full-blown hikikomori, the comedian Chihara Junior (2007) recounts the ordinariness and pain of his exile within one room.[23] Different from the time he was little—ill at ease in the houses of others, predisposed to drawing with bright colors and outside the lines — Chihara had been shunned by friends, by the neighborhood mothers (who didn't let their children play with him), and by teachers alike. As the years pass, he skips school more often and finds himself alone all the time. His parents, while decent, are clueless and his mother has taken to crying a lot. His father, self-employed in a small business he runs at home, putters in his workshop at night. Obviously stewing over their son, the two sometimes fight. The holes Chihara keeps punching in the walls lend brittleness to the home, which sometimes pains him. All his parents want, when he allows himself to hear them, is that he continue with school. But when he returns one day to give it a try (after, that is, he has stopped at a hair salon to dye his hair blond), a teacher stabs his head with a pencil. The event triggers a memory of another time, another teacher, who takes away a paper cutter he's brought to school for opening his mail. He's accused then of plotting to attack another student. In fact, though, the teacher attacks Chihara instead.

Throughout the memoir, Chihara recites a plaintive chant.

What will I do?
What will I become?
Who am I? (23)

And interspliced with this, he speaks (in his head) to his parents: "Please, wait just a little bit longer. It's only that I'm a little bit different kind of human being with a different way of thinking. Right now I'm searching for the path that is just for me. I'm different from the person I saw on television yesterday [a news show about hikikomori]. So, you don't have anything to worry about" (62–63). Meanwhile, he preoccupies himself with mundane acts: smoking cigarettes, watching TV, looking outside his window at the factory across the street, reading a book about Hitler, going out to the 7-11 in the middle of the night to get manga and food (because he refuses to eat the meals his mother leaves outside his room, knowing she laces them with antidepressants), pacing the floor, replaying scenes from his childhood in his head, staring at the television static at the end of the night that — increasingly as the year goes on — crawl with "bugs" that enter him and that he also "plays" with in what seem to be encroaching hallucinations.

Withdrawal, as evident from Chihara's tale of it, is pretty bleak. No wonder that this is a state (being *komotteru* from society; a hikikomori) whose associations, in the public imaginary, are exile, retreat, shut-in, cut-off. To withdraw from what can be a hostile world outside may keep one alive, as Honda Toru puts it, but it also feels deathlike—removal, isolation from other humans altogether. These are the accounts that trickle out on and by hikikomori. "Homeless inside of home," as the title one author gave to his period spent as a hikikomori (Tsukino 2004). An existence of the living dead in the account given by Murakami Ryū (2003) in his novel of a hikikomori, Kyōseichū. An everydayness of panic and jumpiness, where hostilities of the peopled world get (re)imagined and replayed—ad nauseum—according to its portrayal in NHK ni yōkoso, a book, manga, and anime that was serialized and broadcast on television whose author, a self-identified hikikomori, wrote it as a way to make a living by never leaving home.

Hikikomori are refugees from one kind of ordinary. But refugeeization for them would seem the inverse of that of net café dwellers who, free floating at work and living on the streets, only touch down—when they do—in overnight cubicles. Hikikomori, by contrast, are so housebound they rarely leave a cloistered existence of four walls for the outside at all. In terms of precariousness, however, these two contingencies share a lot in common: an inability to independently survive and marginalization from the stickiness of social, human connection. In a sense, they represent two ends of the same spectrum.

As a social phenomenon, social withdrawal became well known to the public just a few years before Mizushima's documentary on net café refugees in 2007. The pattern had started as early as the 1980s however as an outgrowth of another youth phenomenon that surfaced at that time—refusing to go to school ("school-refusal" or futōko) due to bullying or competitiveness around entrance exams. It was the much-publicized incident of "the busjacker" in 2000 that put hikikomori on the public radar. This was a seventeen-year-old boy who held up a bus for hours—during which time the news services broadcast the entire ordeal—before killing a hostage then himself. As he was profiled in the news, the boy suffered from psychological and social withdrawal and had been institutionalized (but out on furlough for one night) when he committed the crime. The incident spurred public interest in withdrawal. The NHK broadcast a special on hikikomori in 2003, the same year that the Ministry of Health, Labor, and Welfare (Kōseirōdōshō) officially labeled this condition and put out guidelines identifying hikikomori as "a person who, for a variety of causes, doesn't participate socially and doesn't spend time working or going to school outside of home." Though hikikomori are hard to access or count (in a country where mental illness still carries a stigma), Kōseirōdōshō put the figure at one million. According to another survey, the average age of a hikikomori is between twenty-six and twenty-seven, 76.4 percent are male, and 33.4 percent start out as kids who refuse to go to school (Kaneko 2006).

A number of theories circulate on the genesis of hikikomori. Some link it to dependency, claiming that those who suffer withdrawal either *amaeru* too much or are insufficiently allowed to do so in their affective attachments to their mothers and significant others. Related to this, others see in hikikomori a rejection of the dictum to be independent (*jiritsu*)—becoming stronger in today's atmosphere of jiko sekinin (individual responsibility)—or of the older (but still entrenched) aspirational normativity to succeed at school, marriage, and job. Another thesis is that *tōjisha* are overly sensitive to *sekentei* (how they are seen by others or recognition) due, in part, to the recessionary times, the freezing of job opportunities, and the marginality of irregular workers.[24] Unable, almost literally, to communicate (though many "chat" online and play video games), hikikomori are also seen as a symptom and result of wider sociological trends of the moment—the breakdown of communication and collapse of the family and human relations more generally (Kaneko 2006). But others, like the psychiatrist Serizawa Shunsuke (Nihon Kodomo Sōsharu Wāku Kyōkai 2005, 6), prefer to consider hikikomori as ontological rather than social misfits. Rather than not fitting into society, which is the common assumption, Serizawa argues that it is as likely that hikikomori can't find themselves (*jibunrashisa*) or a comfortable place (ibasho) in society as it exists. This leads to a condition he calls *sonzaironteki hikikomori* (ontological withdrawal) (6). The corrective, as he sees it, is not to return hikikomori to society in its present form—what a number of social and governmental initiatives aim, in various degrees and with different formats, to do—but rather to change society so that it is more open and accommodating to alternative modes of being and belonging.

What happens at the end of Chihara Junior's memoir of withdrawal is something a bit different. He takes flight. Abandoning not only the world he fled but the one he escaped into, Chihara shifts his "horizons of expectation" (Koselleck 1985) to something different, not yet known. One day Chihara's mother leaves a note outside his room telling him they must talk that night. When they do so, she says she can't take it any more—

the humiliation from the neighbors knowing of his "abnormal" existence within his room. The father has taken a new job in Osaka, and Chihara will go to live with him or he can try school again. Confused, not wanting to hurt his parents any more, not sure what path is right, the boy agrees to reenter school. Now it's upper school and he wears a new uniform: one of two—representing the two options for high school to attend—that have been hanging in his room, dancing in his imagination, for months. It's the day of the entrance ceremony (to upper school). His mother bangs loudly on his door.

> I've become a high schooler. But I am still searching [for my path] inside my room. Nothing has changed with me. I've chosen what kind of battle I am going to do; I've chosen what uniform [of what school] I am going to wear. That's my weapon. But is that all I'm searching for? If I don't find it soon. . . . Me, a high school student. I've come to be able to sigh a bit easier inside this room. Inside this low ceilinged room, I've become to feel narrow too. . . . If I don't leave this room soon. . . . (Chihara 2007, 154)

He puts on the uniform, pedals his bike to school, attends the ceremony. A teacher smirks at him and, though Chihara knows all the kids, only one, his one friend, greets him: "Long time, no see. I thought you weren't coming back to school." The words pierce his body and, sitting now in a new classroom, with a new uniform on, he realizes nothing has changed. Getting up, he's told by a teacher, "If you leave now, you can never come back." Chihara walks out of the room. Pedaling home, he stops at the bridge, and throws his uniform into the river below.

The same day, when he returns home, his brother calls. Four years older, he left home to work in Osaka about the time Chihara withdrew into his room, and though their relations were good growing up, he's never called his brother since. Told to meet him in Osaka the next day, Chihara is anxious. But he complies as nerve wracking as it is for him to make the trip. They meet up and his brother takes him to a training school for would-be comedians, introducing him to the teacher and announcing that Chihara will be joining the group. Those on the docket go up to the mike and tell stories meant to make others laugh. A delicate talk, some people smile (166). But Chihara can't manage even a smile and is amazed that the people in the room can engage in such an exercise. At the end, he realizes that it's the first time that he has gazed so earnestly upon people other than himself (168). His brother asks him what he thinks, and Chihara says he'd like to return. The comedy school is a world of smiles, and for the first time in his life, Chihara sees that a world like this is possible. His brother signs him up to take his turn the next day.

Traumatized at the thought of having to speak, let alone produce a story that would elicit smiles from people he doesn't even know, Chihara works all night long. He is a hikikomori, after all; communication is alien to him. But the next day he returns to Osaka. His brother meets him at the train station and they go to the school. When it's his turn, Chihara reads the story he's crafted. About the teacher who attacked him for bringing a cutter to school. The audience smiles; this is the first time people have smiled at something he has said. His brother hugs him: "A smiling world. A world my brother found . . . I've found the world I was looking for. Where people recognize me, where I can feel, where I can be myself" (170–71).

Chihara goes home. His room now feels small. He goes down to the kitchen to talk to his parents telling them how he can't return to school, can't ever wear that uniform again. His mother cries and his dad explains how, in a *gakureki shakai* (academic credentialing society), he'll be penalized without (at least) a high school degree. But going back to school means reentering a war zone, Chihara replies: hitting, being hit, breaking walls, spiraling out of control. Where he's headed academic credentials won't matter anyway. Because he's decided to make people laugh, to become a comedian. They listen. Then his dad says "*ganbatte*" (good luck), and his mom nods: "I throw the locks to my door away. It's been a year since I enclosed myself in this room. Tonight is the last time to see the fuzz zone out on the TV and I say good-bye to the *mushi* (bugs)" (188). When he leaves home the next day to start life in Osaka, his parents wish him well. It's his fifteenth birthday.

FOUR. HOME AND HOPE

Who are we? Where do we come from? Where are we going?
What are we waiting for? What awaits us? — Bloch 1986, 3

What will become of me? Who will I become? Where will I go?
What will happen to me? — Chihara 2007, 23

In *The Poetics of Space* Gaston Bachelard argues that where we live is at once shelter and dreamworld. How we take root day in and day out is our "corner of the world" (Bachelard 1964, 4): what anchors us and feeds the imagination. That it "shelters daydreaming" (6) is the chief benefit of the house, in Bachelard's estimation. For the home protects its inhabitants like a cradle or shell, but — with its nooks and crannies, secrets and dramas, memories stored and adventures concocted — this is a space lived as both virtual and real. Great dreamers, he writes, are intimate with the world; "they learned this intimacy, however, meditating on the house" (66).

In what he calls "topoanalysis," the systematic study of the sites of our intimate lives, Bachelard designates the house as a tool for analyzing the soul. Houses house the home — those we first lived in, ever lived in, and conjure up living in. This makes it a space that is part memory, part daydream, part physical domicile. Here we engage in what is most basic to human survival—eating and sleeping, having sex and making babies, warding off enemies and ensuring life. But this too is where we sprout dreams of elsewhere or of dwellings that open to an "everywhere" outside (51). All of this also makes the home a psychic state: one of deep, if complex, attachments that can be disappointing or cruel (Berlant 2011) and filled with the bitterness of what has been lost or never was. For Bachelard, the house must be understood not simply in the descriptive terms of its objective physicality but also in the psychological and phenomenological register of the intimacies it arouses in dwellers. To capture its poetic depths, the nest it provides for dreaming (what he calls the "oneiric house"), Bachelard turns to poetry.

In this chapter I too undertake a topoanalysis of sorts that looks at the home poetically, if not through poetry per se, and with considerations of time and space in mind.[1] Agreeing with Bachelard, that where and how we dwell not only shelters the body but also nestles the soul, I consider what has happened to the home in twenty-first-century Japan at a time when so many people complain of feeling homeless. The rate of the literally homeless has risen sharply under these conditions of economic decline. But my interest here is more in an existential or social sense of home and homelessness: what so many Japanese narrated to me as a breakdown of everyday security, the loss of whereabouts (ibasho), the "refugeeization" of groundedness itself.

Even if life has gotten harder for many Japanese, what does it mean to claim that the country has somehow lost its capacity to register as "home" for ordinary citizens, what I discussed in chapter 3, and that, instead of finding shelter for their dream making, many now feel exiled but not to anywhere else as much as to nowhere at all? There is certainly a sense of implosion today: of a place that has stagnated and retreated as much in space as in time. A friend commented upon her return from a quick shopping trip to China in summer 2008 that while not a fan of the Chinese, she saw in them something the Japanese had (already) lost: "You know, in terms of workmanship and quality of goods, China is nothing like Japan. Everything is done there just for business. But the energy and optimism of its people! Well, we had that too, you know. In the '70s and '80s when Japan was the cutting-edge of the world. We all worked hard, had great ideas, and were globally dynamic. But now we've slowed down, gotten tired, retreated into our island country (*shimaguni*). The Chinese are marching forward and the Japanese? We've kind of died."

The word *hope* (*kibō*) is much used today, sometimes in an attempt to drum it up but more often in a story about stagnated imaginaries—horizons of expectation that are ebbing or shutdown. This is the portrait Murakami Ryū (2002) gives in his book *Kibō no kuni no ekusodasu* (The exodus of a country with hope), which centers upon a country where people, too stuck in the immediacy of consumerist cocoons, can't see a collective or temporality beyond. Describing the bubble years of narcissistic materialism, Murakami longs for what the Japanese once had: when, in the lean years following the war, life was tough but dreams of a not-yet Japan drove people to work hard for the prospect of new possibilities. If nothing else, they had, in Bachelard's term, an "oneiric house," a dream of a house yet to come. But if the prosperity of Japan's postwar boom numbed the imagination by sating desire rather than feeding the soul, why didn't hope return again in the post-bubble period of economic decline and materially hard(er) times? It is this concept of hope—both as it is employed in the public sphere by figures such as Murakami (who still writes about hope in Japan today) and as it has been theorized as a political strategy by the German philosopher Ernst Bloch among others—that I place in conversation with that of home in this chapter.

Homes and hopes, how do these two arouse the imagination and implant strategies for life on the ground during this (second) "lost decade" in Japan?[2] For Ernst Bloch, hope arranges temporality and is always in, but beyond, present time. It is what, as a strategy or method, allows humans to get beyond an existential paradox; we live in a present that can only be contemplated after it has passed: "that I walk, speak, is not there. Only directly afterward can I hold it out in front of me. While we live, we do not see ourselves in it; we flow onward" (Bloch 1986, 17). The nowness of the moment isn't conducive to self-contemplation. For while we can act in the instant, it takes a delay to grasp the what and who that has (just) happened. Living in the now of the present catches us in our blind spot: a temporality where knowledge, of ourselves, of life, is clouded and dark (Miyazaki 2004). But this is relieved by what Bloch called the "not-yet-conscious," a consciousness that is formed in anticipation of the future. This contrasts, as Bloch intended it, with the "no-longer-conscious" of a repressed past at the heart of the Freudian notion of the unconscious. Found primarily in daydreams, the "not-yet" are presentiments of what we might, or would like to, become. Driven by hope, the "not-yet conscious" scratches at the inadequacies, frustrations, and hardships of present life. Thus, unlike dreams driven by desires smoldering from the past, daydreams, infused by futurist hope, can be productive. Existing more in the semiconscious than unconscious, they point to real possibilities that demand action in and for the future.

> The "Not-yet-Conscious." That is: a relatively still Unconscious disposed towards its other side, forwards rather than backwards. Towards the side of something new that is dawning up, that has never been conscious before, not, for example, something forgotten, something remarkable that has been, something that has sunk into the subconscious in repressed or archaic fashion. . . . The anticipatory thus operates in the field of hope. . . . The imagination and the thoughts of future intention described in this way are utopian, this again not in a narrow sense of the word which only defines what is bad (emotively reckless picturing, playful form of an abstract kind), but rather in fact in the newly tenable sense of the forward dream, of anticipation in general. (Bloch 1986, 11–12)

According to Bloch, daydreams are not in and of themselves productive. In order to be an impetus for action and for a person to move out of the present and beyond oneself, daydreams need to be shaped into images. This is the utopic potential of literature and art: to imagine a future that challenges, but also rearranges, the present sociopolitical reality. How we inhabit the world in the circumference of home forms part of this "anticipatory illumination" (*Vor-Schein*): envisioning a home that, while tapping into our experience of actual homes, also transcends reality and illuminates new possibilities. A home that "we have all sensed but have never experienced or known." Such a time (beyond the present) and space (at once safe and moving forward), Bloch treated as utopic (Zipes in Bloch 1986, xxxiii) — a solid daydream, a homeland yet to come — "the All in the identifying sense is the Absolute of that which people basically want. Thus this identity lies in the dark ground of all waking dreams, hopes, utopias themselves and is also the gold ground on to which the concrete utopias are applied. Every solid daydream intends this double ground as homeland; it is still unfound, the experienced Not-Yet-Experience in every experience that has previously become" (Bloch 1986, 316). Through the anticipatory illumination of a not-yet future and a home that is still becoming is laid an "architecture of hope" with its possibilities of radical change.

So, to put together the two notions of home I've introduced so far, that of Bachelard and Bloch, we get an image of a home that, nesting the imagination of a world and time beyond, prods the daydreamer to remake the here and now, to remake a hopeful home, a home that (day)dreams of the future.

Retreating Inward, Shrinking Japan

In 2008 I asked several Japanese people whether intimate lives had become as flexible as their economy these days. *Ryūdōka* (flexibilization) is the buzzword for Japan's de-structuration. While it usually refers to the deterritorialization of economic affiliations (jobs less sutured in place and over time to one workplace), does it also extend to the everydayness of human relationships, I wondered. Does it extend to how people are crafting and inhabiting the intimacies of their lived everyday? Most of those I approached though, from activists and students to scholars, workers, and housewives, were stumped when I asked if there was (or was emerging) a flexibilization of daily sociality. More to the point was that things had broken down, they told me. Far fewer people are marrying or having kids; more young adults are living with parents and never leaving home; old people are dying lonely; and the caregiving once provided by social institutions (family, neighborhood, work) is precipitously at risk. Even those with partners, families, or networks of friends and work colleagues (*nakama*), lamented the loss of something social—the "collapse" of the Japanese family (*kazoku no hōkai*), the dilution of human relationships (*ningenkankei*), the shrinkage of groupism in a culture now marked by solitude and loneliness (*kodoku*).

When answering about the state of a "flexibly social Japan," the sociologist Miyamoto Michiko voiced anxiety about the preservation of sociality altogether. Speaking of young people (a category increasingly hard to pin down, or move beyond oneself), she worried about their tendency to psychically and socially withdraw. Referring to the phenomena much in the news of youths who literally take themselves out of school, work, or human circulation—not in education, employment, or training (NEET), *futōkō* (school refusers), and *hikikomori* (the socially withdrawn)— Miyamoto was also making a broader statement about the "de-sociality" of the younger generation. As someone who works on and with youths and is sympathetic to the conditions they face today of dwindling opportunity and irregular work, Miyamoto's observation here was not spoken out of contempt. In an interview with Miyamoto in June 2008 she shared the following with me: "I don't think Japanese youths are as much antisocial as nonsocial [hishakōteki]. That is, they don't protest against society as simply don't participate in it to such a degree that they are not actually social. They're not active, is what I'm saying. And they're not very lively. Actually, they're not lively at all [zentaitekini genki ga nai]. Someone like Amamiya [Karin] is active; she's an activist. But this is the minority. Youths are generally withdrawn [hikikomotteru]; they're in a state that is close to that of a hikikomori [hikikomori ni chikai]." Citing a survey conducted with youths ages eighteen to thirty-four in Tokyo, she noted that, besides the twenty-five thousand who identified as full-blown hikikomori, 70 percent said they had the "sentiment" of being a hikikomori. For youths coming of age in twenty-first-century Japan, social withdrawal has become something of a structure of feeling or common affect, according to Miyamoto: the affective commonality of feeling estranged, disconnected, all alone. How can there be a future for the country when its young people aren't "there," Miyamoto queried in the middle of our interview.

But where precisely are they, I thought to myself, for it's not the case that many are leaving the country, seeking their fortunes or fantasies someplace else. The numbers of Japanese students studying abroad are way down these days, kept away by the fear of losing the few opportunities and the credentials needed for jobs at home. Japanese undergraduate enrollment in U.S. universities, for example, has fallen 52 percent since 2000 (and only one Japanese entered Harvard's freshman class fall 2009) in contrast to the rise of students in the same period from China (164 percent), India (190 percent), and South Korea (with two and a half times as many students now in the United States than Japan) (Harden 2010).[3] So, if it's not the case that youths are clamoring to leave, as they are in so many countries hit by global recession or the capitalist dreams of elsewhere, what is keeping them in Japan and where are they (imaginatively, intimately) withdrawing to?

Coupled with a sense of social retraction comes the ebbing of futurist hope in youths, about youths, and for the nation. Proclaiming Japan to be hopeless has become something of a national pastime, with a reference point clearly set in the past. Japan has broken down, dissolved, been irretrievably lost. Genda Yūji, a labor historian at the Institute of Social Science at University of Tokyo, traces the onset of this malaise to the collapse of Japan's economy and its stature as a global power: "Japan in the 1990s had lost confidence in itself and had no clear sense of where it was heading. As the economy continued to stagnate, the Japanese media referred to the 1990s as the 'lost decade.' What had been lost, however, was not simply economic income and wealth. Most Japanese had been deprived of any faith in the future. As Japan's economy toppled from the pedestal it had formerly occupied, its decline in international esteem only intensified the loss of confidence that Japanese felt" (2005, x). The Japanese are losing a sense of the future, as Genda sees it: a loss as great, if not greater, than anything material. For, rather than life getting better, the modernist calculus of steady progress over time, people are inclined to think things will only get worse: a prospect that makes futurity hard to invest in. If conceptualizing a time beyond the present is essential to the capacity to imagine, and to know and understand the self (Bloch 1986), what happens when life gets stuck in the immediacy of now, the blind spot Bloch pointed obstructing self-consciousness? This is not a situation unique to Japan, of course. The assumption that hard work will lead to a progressively better future is in crisis all over the world today.

As Jean and John Comaroff put it, lacking the means or opportunity to advance despite the ambition to do so is the hallmark of capitalism in its neoliberal, global manifestation: "This, after all, is an age in which the extravagant promises of millennial capitalism run up against an increasingly nihilistic, thoroughly postmodern pessimism; in which the will to consume outstrips the opportunity to earn; in which, relatively speaking, there is a much higher velocity of exchange than there is of production. As the connections between means and ends become more opaque, more distended, more mysterious, the occult becomes an ever more appropriate, semantically saturated metaphor for our times" (Comaroff and Comaroff 2001, 27). Anxiety about the stability and future of one's job even for those fortunate enough to have one is breeding a new toxicity in the workplace, as Noelle Molé (2012) writes about "mobbing" in neoliberal Italy. As in Japan, the increased flexibilization of employment renders work and the workplace precarious for employees: a precarity that extends far beyond the job itself and into a "'precarious-ization' of peoples' lives and of Italian society" more generally (Molé 2012, 25). Time gets troubled across the board; the present gripped by insecurity, the future incites feelings less of possibility than fear—of global warming, nuclear warfare, contagion and terrorism of promiscuous sorts. The uncertainty and risks associated with the future shapes what Marc Abélès (2010) argues to be a "politics of survival" where people across the world today are more concerned about their own ability to get through the day than what he calls the "convivance" of living harmoniously with others.[4] Speaking of the United States, Lawrence Grossberg writes that "from lotteries to reality television, we now expect that success comes in leaps and bounds, the result of matters outside of our control, having little relation to the ethical norms of society" (2005, 181). And as Charlie Piot (2010) describes of Togo in western Africa, it is a nation where everyone is playing the visa lottery to leave for the United States. This is not because the Togolese have lost their attachment to home but because they realize how unsustainable life there has become. Finding that even villagers are willing to abandon traditional customs to try out something new in their politics of survival, Piot sees the Togolese as acting on desires for a future that they feel if don't yet precisely know: what he calls "nostalgia for the future" (the title of his book on post–Cold War Togo).

But if anxiety over a present—of jobs, opportunities, ecological or nuclear risks—is a worldwide phenomenon, how precisely this affects one's notion of the future and attachments to home varies considerably. As I write this following the Arab Spring, there are new reports of self-immolations in northern Africa where college-educated precariat are killing themselves in Morocco to protest the paucity of prospects they face in a nation-state whose government has failed to securitize the lives and futures of young citizens like themselves. The Japanese precariat complain of the same, of course. Yet, while resonant with all the above cases, the situation in Japan is also different—a difference that has much to do with the genesis and degeneration of the family-corporate system in postwar, now post-postwar, Japan. This is where ambitions were housed, at an intimate level of the daily lunchboxes, outings to the hostess club, everyday regimes of hard work and competitive output.[5] A suffusing into the social life of just about everything that blurred the boundary between living and labor—a spread of work into the everyday that Berardi and others attribute more to the capitalist era of immaterial and cognitive labor (the capitalization of Facebook, the Internet, and texting) but that certainly predated it in the case of Japan, Inc. It is the contortions and liquidation of the relationship between human time and capitalist value (Berardi 2009,

22) at the level of the (re)productive family home that distinguishes precarity in post-postwar Japan. It is something that affects the dreams of an "elsewhere" (Bachelard 1964), and of a time daydreamt about tomorrow (Bloch 1986).

One sees signs of a turning inward in Japan. There are less "exit strategies" (Piot 2010) to places or futures beyond one's present home or homeland or the kind and degree of protests one has seen in North Africa or the Occupy movement in Europe and the United States.[6] More a sticking to home and the present. A friend in his late thirties, speaking of the Chinese influx (of money, business, development) into Africa in recent years, commented that Japanese were nothing like that today. "We're tired. We've become small." National, imperial ambitions have been reduced. For her part, Miyamoto sees a trend in Japanese youths toward de-sociality that she likens to hikikomori, retreating into a space and time encompassed by a single room. Aspirational normativity—this time at the level of the subject. In both cases mobility is greatly scaled down; there is a tendency to stay close to home even if "home" isn't what it used to be (in implanting ambitions of outward expansion and growth). In fact, this is exactly where the hikikomori live as delinked and incommunicative with those inside as outside home, becoming "homeless inside home" (Tsukino 2004) but kept biologically alive by parents nonetheless. Home reduced to bare life (Agamben 1998); a dis-belonging that starts at home; a home that goes nowhere. This thwarting of expectation—of national and social prospects that once were—produces a sense of "non-time," of a "time that does not unfold in connection with any aim or expectation that marks the end of the possible" (Bourdieu 2000 cited in Lucht 2012, 73). Such an attachment to "compromised conditions of possibility" is also what Lauren Berlant calls "cruel optimism" (2011, 24).

But the Japanese had what it is that the young precariat of Morocco or the Togolese applying for the lottery to enter the United States say they want—secure jobs, material prosperity, global belonging. And they had this dreamland of modernity at home: a Japan that even built its own Disneyland during the bubble economy so that this much-loved icon of American culture could be visited by the Japanese without going abroad— what Iwabuchi (2002) considers to be a "recentering" of U.S.-dominant global culture.[7] But the bubble burst in 1991 triggering decline. And from the poster child for a high-speed, high-growth capitalist economy, Japan has become the warning signal for economic collapse, ghastly financial failure, and market crash. This turnabout in fortunes shapes the contours of not only precarity but also the temporality with which both home and hope get rendered in post-postwar Japan.

As the Japanese know only too well, decline is the story about their country circulating the globe, and particularly the United States. This has been much reported on in the *New York Times*, for example. (Though a counterexample appeared on January 8, 2010, arguing that "the myth of Japanese failure" was being hyped in both Japan and the United States, and that it exaggerated the socioeconomic demise of Japan for presumably ideological reasons [Fingleton 2012]. In either case both views remain attached to a worldview of economic and national growth as the measure of value whose consequence for time and the inhabiting of world and home are the issues I'm exploring here.) For example, in a series of articles on the economic stagnation in Japan and the social effects this has had on the population that ran in October 2010, the *New York Times* reported on the demise of what was once a robust superpower—an economy so impressive it inspired the appellation Japan as number one (the title of a book by the Harvard sociologist Ezra Vogel in 1979 with the subtitle *Lessons for America*). The series noted that, despite predictions made by U.S. economists in 1991 that Japan would overtake the United States as the world's largest economy by 2010, its economy actually stayed the same over the two decades (gross national product of $5.7 trillion). Meanwhile, the U.S. economy doubled during the same period (to $14.7 trillion), and China overtook Japan as the world's second largest economy in 2010.

> And the future looks even bleaker, as Japan faces the world's largest government debt—around 200 percent of gross domestic product—a shrinking population and rising rates of poverty and suicide. . . . But perhaps the most noticeable impact here has been Japan's crisis of confidence. Just two decades ago, this was a vibrant nation filled with energy and ambition, proud to the point of arrogance and eager to create a new economic order in Asia based on the yen. Today, those high-flying ambitions have been shelved, replaced by weariness and fear of the future, and an almost stifling air of resignation. Japan seems to have fearfully pulled into a shell, meekly content to accept its slow fade from the global stage. (Fackler 2010, 14)

Strikingly, the *New York Times* used a photo of a thumb-sized home—capsule hotels akin to net cafés that working poor often sleep in these days—to frame yet another story it ran on Japan's economic decline. On the front page, under the headline "For Some in Japan, Home Is a Tiny Plastic Bunk," the photo is of a forty-year-old Japanese man crouched inside what looks like a doghouse in a row stacked double high. Appearing on New Year's Day 2010, the article starts off analogizing the man's home to death, a dreary commentary on another decade of plunging fortunes in Japan: "For Atsushi Nakanishi, jobless since Christmas, home is a cubicle barely bigger than a coffin—one of dozens of berths stacked two units high in one of central Tokyo's decrepit 'capsule' hotels" (Tabuchi 2010, 1).

Even at the height of it miraculous economy, the Japanese were belittled for their congested living conditions; "rabbit hutches" the U.S. press called the cramped urban homes of this nation of rising middle classers (with the industriousness of "worker bees"). But a rabbit hutch secured by a lifelong job is nothing like a capsule hotel for those in the ranks of the contingently employed and unemployed. As the article describes, Nakanishi leads a precarious life. But, having had enough jobs over the years to both save for and imagine something better, he still studies law in his free time and nurtures the dream of becoming a lawyer someday. But this is not the case with the next capsule dweller described. Once a tuna fisherman whose last job on a landfill ended a month ago, the forty-six-year-old man says he only has enough money for two more days at the capsule hotel. Not knowing where he will go then, Iwaya Naoto admits to being "on the verge of joining the hopeless" (Tabuchi 2010, 3).

Hopelessness comes from feeling stuck, the article suggests, from finding oneself in a world whose horizons have shrunk and timeline has stopped. A doghouse for a home, temp work for a job, economic stagnation for a nation in decline, and depopulation for an "incredible shrinking country" (as reported another article in the *New York Times* about Japan's low birth rate and fast aging demographics. Describing this as a dystopic scenario from science fiction,[8] it concludes that "for all our problems, twenty-first-century Americans should be thankful that we aren't headed toward the same sunset as Japan" [Douthat 2012: 7]). But not everyone is doomed to such paralysis. According to Yamada Masahiro (2003), in his book *Kibō kakusa shakai* (A Differential Hope Society), only those who can't imagine that life will ever improve give up on hope today. Adhering himself to the aspirational norms of the era of Japan, Inc., he equates those hopeless today with the "losers" in a society where fewer and fewer people can hang onto the Japanese dream of regular job, steady income, and a home with a wife and kids. As national fortunes decline and the population gets riddled by newly aggravated class divisions—the bipolarization of a divided society (*kakusa shakai*)—only certain people "win" stakes in a (capitalist) future. Hope is thus differentially distributed. By a calculus of temporality and well-being where futurity is mapped by the possibility of a certain kind of life and home, winners have hope. But no one else does, according to Yamada.

According to a survey he cites in *Kibō kakusa shakai*, only 15 percent of twenty-five- to thirty-five-year-olds think their own futures will get better over time. In another study half of fifth graders and over 70 percent of middle schoolers believe that Japan will never become more prosperous than it is now. Starker yet are the comments Yamada presents from the hundreds of *furītā* (irregular workers) he interviewed. When asked his plans for old age, a thirty-year-old *furītā* couldn't imagine five years into the future, let alone surviving beyond that. Unable to eat or live decently now and finding his life "useless," another, in his early thirties, assumed he'd be dead by the age of sixty. Save finding a husband who could support her (a highly unlikely prospect), a woman in her late thirties had no vision of the future, or herself in it, at all (Yamada 2003).

Flat Futures, Abandoning Hope

But how does one generate hopefulness about oneself in the first place and is it only from the shelter of a certain kind of my-home-ism, and from the ability to predict a progressively better future based on the (present-day) regularity and security of income and job? Though prosperity and being able to count on and enhance one's prospects over time is a sign of being a "winner" these days, that alone doesn't necessarily generate hope, Yamada Masahiro admits. Some young people don't aspire to anything beyond precarious employment when they can live off their parents' wealth and remain at home: a pattern Yamada (1999) has labeled "parasite single."[9] Such "parasitic" youths may well be enjoying a comfortable life: eating at boutique cafés, buying brand-name goods, traveling abroad (as more young women, than men, tend to do). But, according to Yamada, they've also become complacent and psychically or morally lazy: more spenders in the present than investors in the future—as Jeremy Rifkin has said of neoliberalism's effect on American workers (cited in Grossberg 2005, 178). This, as Yamada sees it, is the flat state of the futurity of (too many) Japanese youths and, by consequence, Japan itself.

When I spoke with young people, however, their take on this was quite different from that represented by Yamada. As many told me, it is not that they are unwilling or unable to work hard—at school, at work, at raising children. But, unlike their parents' generation when acquiring the credentials at school or years in the workplace would guarantee a particular lifestyle and place in society, the socioeconomic environment today is far different. A twenty-two-year-old university student who worked several part-time jobs but was pessimistic about her chances for regular employment in the *shūkatsu* season coming up (when young people undergo a rigorous "market" regime of finding jobs) described life for young Japanese today as a "crapshoot." In her case she went to university because her parents could afford it and it was enjoyable to her (*tanoshii*) in and of itself. But using this, or anything, to plan for tomorrow was an exercise in futility. Many of her friends didn't bother and had become *furītā* right off the bat rather than go through the hurdles and rigors of long years in school that may not pay off in regular employment anyway. Others she knew lacked whatever it was (energy, will, self-confidence—she wasn't sure) to even leave home and look for work in the first place, succumbing to withdrawal of various sorts (full-blown hikikomori, NEET, or those who just bummed around living off their parents when allowed to). Japanese of her generation are nihilistic, she admitted: "Nothing really matters and we don't take anything, including ourselves, too seriously." "Hope?" she repeated back when I asked her about this. "No, I wouldn't say I'm hopeful about either my own future or that of Japan. All I can say is that I'm *genki* [healthy] at the moment."

But outright happy is how another Japanese youth in his twenties assesses the affective state of his generation living in an endlessly flat present with little thought or hope for the future. In his book *Zetsubō no kuni no kōfuku na wakamonotachi* (Happy Youth in a Country of Despair), Furuichi Noritoshi (2011), a graduate student in sociology at Tokyo University, acknowledges all the signs of a shrinking Japan (economic decline, precaritization of jobs, low birth rate, and fast aging demographics) that make others despair. Nonetheless, he claims that the members of his generation are overwhelmingly happy, citing findings that 65.9 percent of males in their twenties and 75.2 percent of females report being satisfied with their current lifestyles (rates that he says not only progressively decline the older one gets but also exceed that of twenty year olds during the hardworking [*mōretsu*] baby boomer generation of the 1970s and 1980s).

> After the war there were many places literally of burnt fields, and we can say that the previous generation gave their lives to rebuilding [the country]. Thanks to them and to their era we are lucky; the wealth of Japan today is indebted to this history. But as much "one-hundred million en" talk there is [of everyone, or "one hundred million" Japanese, being part of the middle class during the postwar era], I would not want to become part of the boomer generation. Then there was radiation sickness, pollution was bad, foreign chocolates were not easily accessible, and of course, no cell phones. I prefer the prosperity of today, no matter what happens to the promise of economic growth from here on out. (Furuichi 2011, 234–35)

The baby boomer generation always worked and saved for the future. But this flattening of the present—deferral always for tomorrow—is not something Furuichi is willing to concede. Instead he embraces a mind-set of living in and for today: youths who turn their energies toward "action" in the present (as for social and political engagement, he says his generation is more likely to build a school in Cambodia than vote in elections) and to the pleasures and relationships of enjoyment. There are really only two things that youths like him need: enough money to live a moderately comfortable lifestyle (with cell phones and fashion from UniQlo)[10] and recognition (*shōnin*) via contact and acceptance from others that is easily available from social media online. Poverty is part of Japan's trajectory, Furuichi admits. But, for youths like him in their twenties, who have parents they can live with and off of because of the wealth they saved as part of the boomer generation, poverty is "Japan's future." Twenty, thirty years in the future, but this is not a future he cares to think about or plan for today.

Hope is not part of his lexicon. Acknowledging a radical shift in Japan's industrial status from global superpower to what he says will be the progressive turn to "farmer and factory work" (*nōminkō*) by young workers (he predicts this as the future trend of Japan, that half of all youths will eventually be precarious farm and factory workers [2011, 257]), Furuichi nonetheless claims that he, like others in his generation, can be happy.

"Youth poverty" (the phenomenon of net café refugees and youths becoming the new face of Japan's poverty, as discussed in chapter 3) only refers to material wealth, he points out. If one can be content with friendship instead and with not becoming rich, the potential for happiness is quite high despite being a part of the precariat. But the increased disparity in what is becoming an entrenched two-class society (with female and young workers disproportionately on the bottom) is a fact of life; so is what he predicts may be the collapse of Japan's democratic system (258–60). Still, Furuichi refuses to scramble after the aspirational norms—and the lifework this would entail—of a (would-be) winner: "If the standard for becoming an adult is becoming a 'seishain' [regular worker] or 'sengyōshufu' [housewife] . . . then more and more young people will not be able to become adults. They'll stay disconnected from age altogether, or simply stay [forever] a youth" (261–62). Such an identity, his identity, he calls: "the era of becoming one hundred million youths" (ichioku sō wakamono jidai)—a term that plays off that of the "one hundred million in the middle class" of postwar Japan.

This new generation—of the perpetually presentist, precariously employed, forever "youthful" youth—would seem an unlikely vanguard for leading the kind of political transformation of the social that people like Franco "Bifo" Berardi (2009) see as the potential of the precariat (a "class in the making," as Guy Standing calls it [2011]). Still, is there not a critique here of the relationship between human time and capitalist value that bears on the kind of dreams expected of life (once connected to, and now rejected by, my-home-ism)? There is a reclaiming of time, not the speeded up, manically hard-working student, mother, or sararīman (salaryman) forever deferring pleasure to the future but a slowed down sense of temporality; living in the moment, staying—forever—a youth. All the same, that this temporality may also accompany (or do nothing to prevent) a breakdown of democracy is something Furuichi seemingly accepts.

Hopology: Homes for Oneiric Selves and Shelter from Bullying

For Genda Yūji, a labor economist and public intellectual, hope is critical to the human condition as is linking this to the future—to future possibilities, horizons of becoming for the individual. Blochian in his approach to hope, he also takes a Bachelardian view of the home (and parents in the home) as sheltering the dreams and future selves children have the potential to become: an oneiric self. Ever since the bubble burst in 1991, sending the country into economic decline, structural readjustment, and an era of precarious un- and underemployment, particularly for young workers, Genda has been alarmed at what he sees as an abandonment and despair over the future. According to his own research on the subject—and strikingly at odds with the view taken by (the younger) Furuichi—one-third of all Japanese feel their hopes (in life) are unattainable or have no hope at all about the future. Inspired to both study hope and do something active about it, Genda started a hope studies (*kibōgaku*) project (called "Hopology" or social science of hope in English): an interdisciplinary research group within the faculty at the Institute of Social Science (*Shakaikenkyūjo*) at Tokyo University.

This group conducts research projects, many collaborative, all on hope in diverse settings and sites. It also hosts workshops and conferences, out of which a series of publications (including four edited volumes) have appeared. The objective is at once scholarly and political in the sense of not only studying hope but trying to actively produce it, as Genda told me. To this end, Genda is a committed public speaker who speaks to high school students, teachers, and lay audiences of multiple kinds. I have heard him twice in these settings: once at a small bookstore in Ebisu, Tokyo, and the other time at a motivational lecture for schoolteachers at Meiji University, where Genda instructed his audience on how to cultivate more hopefulness and optimism in their students. Throughout he emphasizes the importance of formulating active hopes—hopes that generate action. This is a concept that emerges from his own research, and that of other members of kibōgaku, on the practical efficacy of a hopeful imagination. In one study he conducted in 2005 with two groups of workers, one in their twenties and one in their fifties, for example, Genda discovered that most workers found their jobs meaningful (*ikigai*) while in the midst of actually working, and this was particularly true for those who had had specific hopes about work when they were young (2006, 65–66).

In a research study he did of lower- and middle-school children around the same time in Tokyo, Genda discovered that those who expressed more hope were more likely (than those who did not) to have parents who imagined (in them and for them) an anticipatory future: a future them. As he puts it, these are children raised with expectations and goals by parents, not necessarily normative, who help implant a potential in children beyond the immediacy of the present. When youths lack this—parents who cultivate a child's oneiric self—they are less likely to develop not only ambition but a sense of self-worth and recognition (something that seems akin to ibasho, a space and place where one feels at home). For Genda, it is as much the cognitive as emotional work performed by hope that is critical here. Content is less important than the fact itself of having plans, goals, some cartography of the possible: a self becoming a future. Unlike Yamada whose calibration of hope is tied to the normativity of the past (jumping through the hoops of a competitive society), Genda believes that any goal or interest suffices—wanting to travel around the world, open a café, work with the poor—as long as it grabs the imagination and inspires purposeful activity. Even when goals aren't met, they constitute an intimate space of sorts: an intimacy that, germinating within the here and now, gestures to a there and then beyond (Genda 2006).

Despite its importance to the human condition, generating a hopeful imagination (about the future, one's future self) proves a challenge as Genda admits. He finds many Japanese youths today complaining of feeling lost, invisible, and unmoored to anything solid or meaningful at all (ibasho). But, according to eight undergraduate women at a prestigious private university in Tokyo, whom I interviewed about hope and home in the summer of 2008, it isn't just a matter of imagining their future potential—a map mapping them onto a future germinated, in part, by someone else (i.e., a parent).[11] In an era when Japanese parents are said to be easing up on the rigid demands to study and excel, these women had all been raised to be high achievers. Still, half of them said that their parents urged them to be and do whatever they wanted (within limits, presumably). What they associated more with the ability to feel hopeful, now that they were young adults, was having a refuge to shelter them in bitter times growing up. None of these women, a fairly elite demographic, seemed to be at risk of the economic precarity facing so many Japanese, young and old, these days. But life could be traumatic nonetheless and, at these times, the "warmth" of family and home was what nourished their soul and, in some cases, quite literally saved them (for a future). The "education of the heart" (kokoro no kyōiku), one woman called it.

All the examples these women gave of ikizurasa (hardship in life) involved bullying (ijime) by one's peers—a phenomenon that, notoriously brutal in Japan, has reportedly worsened in the digital age of chat rooms and cell phones. One woman recounted how, when returning to Japan in the fourth grade after living abroad for three years, she was picked on mercilessly for being behind in *kanji* (Chinese character) acquisition. Then personal belongings—a pencil case, lunch bag, rucksack—went missing, being swiped, she assumed, by classmates. Though school time was torturous, she didn't tell her parents. But upon figuring it out, they told her she didn't have to go to school. Relieved, she started squirreling up at home whenever the ijime got bad. She'd then return to school for a few days before retreating again. When the teacher called the house complaining of the girl's absences, the parents asked if the school could protect their daughter from harassment. When told they could not, the parents asserted their prerogative in the matter. This, as the woman related it, exemplified the state and space of feeling safe, having a good home (ibasho): "When a child is bullied, you really need help from your parents. You feel really lonely and it's hard to face on one's own."

I've spoken to many young people over the years who have been bullied at school (and sometimes at work). Hardly all receive or seek out their parents' help, however. In fact, fewer do than not is my impression. Indeed, the parent who refuses to pamper their bullied child (*ijimerarekko*), thereby forcing them to become tough as nails, is something of a Japanese ideal. This is the story Naitō Daisuke who, after a childhood of bullying, remade himself to become both the World Boxing Council (WBC) flyweight champion and the Oriental and Pacific Boxing Federation (OPBF) flyweight champion. Made into a best-selling biography and popular TV movie (*Ijimerarekko no champion belt* [Bullied Child's Champion Belt]) that I just happened to watch the night I did the above interviews, the story is as much about the mother as it is the child. A single mom who works in a ramen restaurant, she refuses to coddle her son even when he comes home bloodied and bruised. Kicking him out of the house upon graduating from high school so he'll head to Tokyo to find work, she still won't praise him when he wins the championship. Tough love prods the boy to not only stay in the world but to kick ass—Japan as number one.

The personal stories I heard that broke this model haunt me still: young Japanese who are bullied at school and withdraw into self-destructive behavior find exit strategies with the imaginative help of their parents. Hope as anticipatory illumination, moving forward, an oneiric home. One young woman, gravely sick from anorexia after staying away from school for a full year due to bullying, was sent to a clinic in the United States at the age of sixteen. This represented a radical step and a leap of faith for her parents who, with a modest income and small-town views, had been advised by a doctor that this might be the only way to save their child. At the time (the late 1990s) little was known about anorexia in Japan and not much existed in the way of treatment. Still, neither parent had ever left Japan themselves and only had enough money to send the girl there on her own. Barely speaking English, she left and stayed away for a year. Today, the young woman is flourishing; she works at a nongovernmental organization (NGO) and has studied at graduate school in the United States. She is alive today because of the intervention her parents undertook, she told me.

Another woman who refused to go to school after a teacher harshly disciplined (and, in her language, "bullied") her in the seventh grade, started staying out all night, drinking heavily, and doing drugs. Angry and wild, she was spinning out of control. Then, again upon the advice of a psychiatrist, the parents sent her abroad: to Canada, then California, for homestays (where she attended school) that lasted three years. Having been told that leaving Japan might be their daughter's only hope for survival, the parents relented—albeit with much misgiving. Today, the woman—now in her late twenties, working at a full-time job, and married—attributes the fact that she is alive today to the strategy her parents adopted to send her away as a young teenager.

So, to nest hopes for the future, home (also) provides a safe haven—or strategic exit—from the harshness of the present. Exit as survival (and social critique) was also the theme of Murakami Ryū's *Kibō no kuni no ekusodasu*, where a group of kids leave middle school, and the normative middle-class path they have been on, to take up an alternative lifestyle (in a reimagined society replete with a new currency) in Hokkaido. But withdrawal presents another option. The cultural critic Honda Tōru (2007) advocates just such a path. Better to be alive and withdrawn than dead is his message about the riskiness of Japanese schools in an era when bullying, and competitiveness, has ratcheted to a new intensity. Withdrawal, for Honda, constitutes not merely a lifestyle choice but a political critique: a critique of a socioeconomic order that, based on a narrow conception of life, pressurizes and excludes (too) many of its citizens.

A self-avowed *otaku* ("geek" or fan of techno culture), Honda is also the author of *Denpa otoko* (Radio-wave Man) (2005), a manifesto proclaiming a radically different kind of intimate sociality from what he considers to be at the root, and reproductive, of Japanese capitalism—the heteronormative romance, family, and home. Here he takes on the fad phenomenon *Densha otoko* (Train Man): the hugely popular story about a twenty-three-year-old otaku who, thanks to the advice of a network of "friends" he keeps consulting on a chat website, manages to date a woman whom he meets when stopping a drunk from harassing her on the train. But, despite all its hoopla, Honda considers the story a cop-out. Spun into a novel, manga, television series, and movie and based apparently on a true story, *Densha otoko* ends with the protagonist transformed from a bumbling mophead myopically engrossed in his action figures to a cleanly groomed romantic lead, enjoying a full-blown relationship with an older woman. As Honda sees it, the message here is that developmentally stunted otaku must grow up and participate in the "love capitalism" (*renai shihonshugi*) of adult sociality: primping oneself to be attractive, going on dates to boutique restaurants, and committing to a long-term relationship with a gendered, human other.[12]

But otaku have other options. They can enjoy intimacy with a 2-D fetish (*nijigen fechi*) or imaginary girlfriend (*nōnai kanojo*) as found with an anime or manga character, a ball-jointed doll, or an interactive figure in a video game, for example. Such fantasy romance involves a "purity" unattainable with a flesh and blood partner, Honda claims. In tapping into a presocial sexuality, 2-D love also represents what he considers to be one of the only counterhegemonic masculinities available to young men today (Slater and Galbraith 2011). Others agree. In 2008 otaku organized a petition for legal recognition of 2-D marriage that garnered 2,443 signatures—not a significant number but the story itself became newsworthy in Japan. And, as I was told by a young reporter working for *Asahi Shimbun* in the summer of 2010, *himote* (not being attractive or popular) became something of a new fad. A Valentine's Day celebration was held that year at Loft+One, a live house in Shinjuku, where participants were given paper bags at the door (so they could celebrate the day with others while not being seen themselves). While it came nowhere close to the popularity of *Densha otoko*, Honda's book sold a respectable 33,000 copies. And, outside of stores selling *Densha otoko*, Honda's fans planted signs saying "Real Otaku Don't Desire 3-D Women."

Mothers at Home, Maid Cafés @Home

On a hot summer night, in one of those intimately delectable spaces Tokyo is famous for, I was savoring peanut tofu with a close friend. Someone with whom I have a special relationship—we met at a local *matsuri* (festival) when I was doing fieldwork on Pokemon in 1999 and have shared endless outings, adventures, and conversations ever since—Sachiko had arranged for me to live in her neighborhood that summer where we often met for beer, or food, late at night. As always, we chatted. This time the subject turned to the spate of violence labeled "*shōnen hanzai*" (youth crime) by the press. Often this involves families, youths, and household belongings turned into murder weapons: a girl stabs her father with a kitchen knife, a boy murders both parents with an axe from the shed, a boy kills his mother with the baseball bat he'd just practiced with for his school team. Intimacy and death; killing (in) the family. Wondering out loud what, in current conditions, was stoking such rage, Yoshiko became excited: "It's the homelife. Actually, it's the mothers—they're not feeding their children anymore. And when they do, the food is often just store bought and everyone eats on their own, at their convenience. What has happened to the family meal around the family table [*shokutaku*]? It's gone. This is the problem today in Japan."

Sachiko is not a mother. Single and in her fifties, she runs a local cooking school and lives by herself. And in the home of her parents where her mother, a successful businesswoman, rules the roost, her parents lived separately for decades: never talking, let alone eating together.[13] And yet this woman, who often eats alone, believes in the family meal and that, just as importantly, it be prepared by the mother in a tactile gesture that feeds something beyond the bellies at home. At the counter of *Shokuraku kūkan*—which translates as "space of relaxed eating"—we selected our sake cups from a basket and chatted with neighborhood friends. Meanwhile we watched the master prepare our food with elaborate care, rendering exquisite concoctions into pieces of art. The scene was soothing; our tastebuds piqued. As I sat there, sensually attended to, I wondered if this place, a space of comfort and food, was not felt (by us all) as a replacement somehow for the home. Food attentively crafted by someone who labors over it—a surrogate (m)other—feeding one's hunger for human touch.

Just days before I had been to another intimate space. This one, in Akihabara (the electronics and otaku center), calls itself @home and is a maid café. Food is served here as well but the signature is different. Rather than exquisite preparation, it is the service that counts; waitresses in maid uniforms address customers as "master" and kneel down to pour cream and add sugar to coffee cups. Dishes of food—like omelette rice and cheese toast[14]—also come decorated with a cute little bunny (*usagichan*) drawn in red ketchup on the top. The food is not exactly what customers come for, but it is a medium—as in Shokuraku Kūkan and the family meal—for producing an affect and a relationship through feeding someone else. According to Patrick Galbraith, author of *The Otaku Encyclopedia* and an anthropologist who has studied maid cafés, @home is "homey." Patrick was my guide the day I visited @home and though I noticed a lot of customers there alone (but also some in groups, women and men, and even one family, a middle-aged couple with their two young adult sons), he assured me that fans—who come back time and time again for forty minute sets[15]—feel a deep, intimate attachment. Many are furītā, he said, and they sometimes will spend all their meager earnings on maid cafés, needing to borrow train fare from him at night to go home.

The attraction is often to a particular maid who—because of a certain cut to her hairstyle, style of apron, or ribbons on her socks—creates an image akin to or precisely mimicking that of a specific character in a manga or anime. Customers will rarely exchange more than a few words or perhaps a game or two of patty-cake with a favorite maid, but those who are hooked call this attraction *moe*. Literally meaning "to bud" but also a pun on the homonym to burn, moe refers both to the character and the affect it elicits in someone—what Galbraith calls a "fantasy love or desire" (2009, 155) that is less physical or sexual than other media-bred fantasies such as lolicon (Lolita-complex). Associated with childlike purity, moe characters are youngish, often schoolgirls, and are sometimes rendered as "little sisters"—a new (home) trend in the maid café scene (*imōto café*).

The day after dining with Sachiko and recalling her words about mothers who (don't) feed their kids, I was riding a subway in Tokyo. Looking up, I saw advertisements for Japan's National Rice Association plastered inside the train. Inciting commuters to buy and consume Japanese rice, the message was illustrated with a cartoon woman leaning over to feed her child a bowl of rice. A bowl of rice that was also her head: a woman whose very body had sprouted what is considered to be the heart of the Japanese diet. Domestic rice as the mother's head feeding Japan. A flash from the past, I thought, recalling the *Anpanman* show my kids loved in the 1980s with characters made from food.[16] Anpanman, the hero, had a head filled with bean paste that he would willingly sacrifice to hungry kids, flying headless back to Jam Ojisan (Uncle Jam) to have a new head whipped up by Uncle Chef. Just what Japan needs today—the message seemed to say. An Anpanman for contemporary times. Heroes feeding the nation Japanese rice;

mothers sacrificing their heads to the family. Nostalgia for the past: for a social factory of my-home-ism feeding the national economy and also for (what my-home-ism often lacked the time for) the "education of the heart"—what the university students called the affective labor of sheltering the soul. In the restructuring of labor, the family becomes privatized and the intimacy of (a caregiving) home gets outsourced: the maid café and Shokuraku kūkan.

In interviewing the Marxist sociologist Adachi Mariko in July 2008, she spoke about caregiving as the critical issue facing Japan today. The modern nuclear family doesn't fit new capitalism at all, she agreed, even though many young people still harbor desires for its anachronistic gender roles: to be a stay-at-home housewife (*sengyō shufu*) and breadwinner male (*daikokubashira*). In such a gendered division of labor, caregiving is subsumed within the heteronormative family and home: not precisely part of the market economy but supported by the man's "family wage," when that still existed. But the era of the family-corporate system has ended. And what is needed now are new ways and resources for caregiving: a "sacrifice" that can't be reduced to, or only calculated as, market exchange. This also means a re- or post-gendering of young people vis-à-vis their intimate and economic investments; just as both women and men need to work (for a wage) these days, so do both genders need to caregive and raise children. But Adachi expresses concern about how this is turning out in practice. Already there is a tendency for strong women to be portrayed as cute— as if this makes their toughness more palatable to men. And while a new softer, "herbivorous" man (*sōshoku danshi*) is emerging as well—the antithesis of the hard-driving sararīman who, so wedded to job, contributes little to work at home—their image is mixed in the popular imaginary. They're portrayed as being sensitive to feelings, relationships, lifestyle, aesthetics. But, women don't necessarily want to get married to them. When, in the summer of 2011, I asked two different classrooms of Japanese undergraduate women what they thought of sōshoku danshi, they all laughed at the thought of marrying or partnering with one.

The market in commodified care, where childcare, elderly care, and intimacy of a wide variety is available for a price, is booming as well. This is the future of global affective labor, Adachi pointed out: not only sex work but care work as seen in the recent migrations of Filipina and Indonesian caregivers into Japan. (Who, despite the desperate need for them, have encountered stringent regulations. They're not allowed to enter "Japanese" homes, for example, and must pass a rigorous exam in Japanese within three years of entering the country. Wages for care work remain low as well. All in all, conditions are less than inviting to would-be foreign caregivers.) On the other hand, resources are being poured into research and development for care robotics: cultivating a labor force of technologized caregivers that, if less fleshy, are at least made in Japan. Another sign, it would seem, of the trend to look inward rather than to see or expand beyond familiar and familial Japanese horizons. What is of particular urgency, Adachi stressed at the end of the interview, is for the young generation to figure out a new way to raise children (*ikuji*). If young people can do this, they (and Japan, by implication) will have "hope."

The "Nuisance" of Care: Robots and Dogs

Late in a day darkened by rain, I discuss similar issues—family, caregiving, home—with three women in their early sixties. They all work part time at a supermarket, and we're meeting at the Denny's next door for supper. Two are married and one separated twenty years ago from her husband who, a gambler and philanderer, never agreed to a formal divorce. All three have children who are now grown. The stories they tell me of married life would not seem to be an endorsement of the institution. And yet, when asked what they think of the recent trend toward late marrying (*bankon*) or not marrying at all (*hikon*), they all find it regrettable: "I feel it's regrettable if someone doesn't eventually marry. I also think the trend today reflects on us; they don't have good memories of their own childhood and that's the reason young people don't want to marry themselves. Young people say marriage is *mendōkusai* [a nuisance]; they'd rather protect their money and time for themselves—for their own personal use." What they all agree is worrisome about remaining a bachelor (*dokushin*) is not having someone to "take care of you" in times of need: in old age, sickness, if one loses a job or falls into debt or trouble of whatever kind. People who don't have a pension (*nenkin*) are particularly straddled, and homelessness has been on the rise since Koizumi initiated economic restructuring in 2001. Escalating as well are families who no longer take care of their own members. But then, as another observes about the *danchi* (apartment building) she lives in, gathering spaces have disappeared, including play parks where mothers used to hang out and talk with one another and play with their kids. "Life seems more isolated and lonely today."

But the calculus of care is tricky. One tells me later in private how lonely and depressed she became despite having a family she tended to in all the ways expected of a "good housewife, wise mother." Her husband is a sarariman who travels a lot and drinks heavily outside home even when in town. And, after her two sons left the nest, she felt abandoned. It is the dog she recently acquired that feels more like "family" to her than husband or kids. Because, as she put it, "if I don't feed it, the dog dies. It's utterly dependent on me." Hearing her speak, I'm reminded of the *tamagotchi*—the virtual pets that, a craze in 1996, came "alive" by hatching an egg on the electronic screen that grew to adulthood by feeding, playing, and tending to it like a "real" pet (including cleaning up its poop). The prosthetics of presence here is fed quite literally (if virtually) by caregiving: what the designer of the tamagotchi called *mendō*. This means all those (bodily, basic, banal) chores that go into tending a pet (or raising a child) that are also *mendōkusai* (bothersome)—the very word that my interviewees attributed to the reluctance young people harbor today toward getting married. The paradox of the vanishing social today: the kinds of human connections that bring warmth have also come to seem annoying.

If tending to the needs of an-other is burdensome, it also ties someone to another life—whether that of human, animal, or digital creature. Producing an uncanny presence that feels lifelike was precisely what Yakoi intended when designing tamagotchi: a "strange lifeform" (*henna ikimono*) that evokes an intimate attachment in humans. An intimacy premised on care and built into technology—what I have called elsewhere "techno-intimacy" (Allison 2006). As I discovered in doing fieldwork on tamagotchi, Pokemon and other techno-intimacies, this is a play that, while multifaceted and complex, turns on fostering sinews of attachment that burrow into the nervous system "as if" humanly interactive, even social. And kids who grow up practicing social intimacy with a tamagotchi or digital companion will become the users of care robotics as they grow old—which will be ever more likely alone.

Needless to say, such prosthetic sociality—electronic goods that attach to the body and keep users continually plugged into circuits for information, communication, and affect—is percolating in the sociological gap left by the weakening of human ties in the family, workplace, and community in Japan today. Speaking about her five-year-old son, who was an avid tamagotchi player at the time, a young mother sounded pleased: "His days are busy with school, commuting, and homework. And, he's a loner, so I'm glad he has a companion now." In his research on Japanese robotics, the anthropologist Katsuno Hirofumi (2011) has discovered similar optimism around the affective potential of interactive technology. *Kokoro* (heart) represents the new cutting edge in the industry's techno futures; Japanese engineers are designing robots to render the human touch and intersubjective sensitivity of person-to-person relationships. Japan's robotic industry is the most advanced worldwide in its research and development of humanoid robots. And the key word here is *heart*: "in order to make a human-shaped robot truly useful for humans, it is ideal to establish a 'heart-to-heart relationship' [*kokoro no fureai*], which enables both the human and the robot to understand each other like human beings. In this light, the robot needs its own heart" (Sugano Shigeki cited in Katsuno 2011, 95).

Building a "heart" for a robot entails "tinkering with humanity," as Katsuno puts it (2011, 1). But what precisely of or in humanity gets tinkered with here? According to Katsuno, Japanese robotics are less redesigning what it means to be human than recreating a sense of humanity known, but perceived to be lost, in Japanese society today. It is no coincidence, he writes, that the humanoid robot took off at the end of Japan's "lost decade" (end of the 1990s). It is to quell the heartlessness of the times with a technologically intimate replacement—the robot heart—that the development of personal robots with communication skills is being spurred in the new millennium. New waves of both pet and therapeutic robots sell as consumer goods on the marketplace as part of an *iyashi* (healing) boom that has accompanied the post-bubble recession. These include Sony's high-end AIBO, which is a robotic pet dog, and the seal robot Paro,[17] identified by the Guinness Book of World Records as the world's most therapeutic robot (Katsuno 2011, 105). And, for kids, iyashi play comes in the shape of "sof-tronics" (soft electronics) with pet robots and electronic pals designed to promote companionship and communication—the twin themes of the Tokyo Toy Fair when I attended it in March 2000 (Allison 2006, 188–91).

What my interviewee said about her dog is a response I heard often about the appeal of tamagotchi: "It needs me. Without me, it dies." Of course, in the case of tamagotchi, the handheld digital toys had a reset button. So, when caregiving (mendō) stopped being fun and the player no longer fed her virtual pet, thereby killing it, the cycle could be restarted at any time. Pressing the reset button, a new tamagotchi gets hatched and the connection—of tending, having, intimacy—triggered all over. A game of life and death and a toy that is (also) a relationship. As inflected in its name (an amalgamation of egg plus watch),[18] tamagotchi is something one both wears and grows—a wearable life-form, a portable home, a prosthetic sociality, a heart as a personal toy for those who have the means to buy it.

In February 2012, another news story broke in Japan of bodies found in the home they'd lived in, dead from presumed starvation. A couple in their sixties along with a son in his thirties, they lived in an apartment where the electricity and water had been turned off and the rent hadn't been paid for months. A few bottles of water inside were the only sign of sustenance. An elderly neighbor said the woman had knocked recently on her door asking for help of some money but she'd told her to go to the landlord or welfare agency instead. Apparently the family had never sought out welfare—a common trend, as it was reported on in the press, of hesitance in seeking out help even by those in dire need. In the wake of two other similar stories in recent months (two sisters in their forties in Sapporo and an elderly couple in Kushiro, Hokkaido), the incident has triggered warning bells all over again of the "heartlessness" of the times and a society that has lost its humanity. A situation of life and death, of mendō (care of daily living) coming undone.

Touching Dementia: Touch at Cat Cafés

After finishing our food and returning to Denny's drink bar for coffee, one of the women launches into a story about caregiving. Tending to her invalid mother as a new mother herself, she was housebound by the demands of mendō yet she turned this into play for her young kids—a play haunted by death. I'd asked the women what they consider to be the most important factors in making (and maintaining) good family relations, and Takahashi replies first: "responsibility (sekinin) and feelings (kimochi)." As I already know, Takahashi married late (in her mid-thirties) after working for years as a hospital accountant. Her husband was a yōshi: adopted into her family, he'd changed his family name and moved with her into the family home. Takahashi's mother lived with them from the beginning— part of the marital arrangement, I assumed. Elderly, ill, and suffering dementia (which progressively worsened), the mother could never leave the house and demanded constant, fastidious care. Takahashi was her sole care provider (and doesn't say whether she could have afforded help or whether or not such help was even available). Meanwhile she gave birth to three daughters in fairly quick succession, and while her husband was a good enough provider, he never helped out in either the raising of the children or the care of her mother.

My mother was *boketeru* [deranged, confused]. But still she somehow knew what I, her daughter, liked. She could sense what song or piece of fruit would please me just like I knew how to rub her back or make her treats. She was basically housebound, which meant that I was too. For six years we never took a trip with the kids or went on fun activities outside the house. But I made taking care of my mother into *asobi* [play]. These became the routines that stitched the family together [this in answer to my question about what everyday routines keep families together]. The children didn't complain; they also saw their mother taking care of her mother. This is *aijō* [love]; we didn't experience caregiving as burdensome or hard. . . . I had my kids help me out a lot. It was necessary for them to help me. I told them—if they didn't help me, I'd be lonely [*kodoku*]. *Tetsudai* [helping] was important to me. But it was also important for them in the end. They helped. And, always, they helped without me having to ask them to. I now think that it was lucky that I had to take care of my mother. It made my kids help me. Lately, it seems that the emphasis for kids is only on studying and on doing well in school. And Japanese are living more solitary existences, apart from others [*tanin*]. Communication is lacking these days.

When asked what kind of chores her children helped out with, Takahashi answered with an example more of compassion. Of how, when sometimes making a long phone call because that was all she could do to stay tied to the outside world, her children would sit calmly off to one side, never disturbing her, giving their mother this tiny sliver of space and time—a zone within home to shelter her own imagination of something and somewhere else. How different a family scene from that in Kore'eda Hirokazu's aching movie *Daremo shiranai* (Nobody Knows, 2004) where the mother leaves the home altogether in order to indulge her desires for living beyond family and kids. Having kept the children out of school in her endless moves from one apartment (and man) to another, she ensconces them in a new place where she's forbidden them to ever go outside (and therefore be discovered). A free spirit, she plays sweetly with them when around, then goes off for days supposedly for work. But eventually she never returns, and soon the money she sends dries up as well. Meanwhile the four children she's left behind, the eldest only twelve, stay stuck in a home that is literally starving them. Based on a true story, one child dies but three survive in what Korēda captures as a poetry of at once death and survival: a topoanalysis of home that is almost (but not really) optimistic. Life, of a sort, continues by the children taking care of each other in the absence of a mother that they—as well as the audience—come to understand will never return.

In the case of Takahashi, when her mother eventually died, the loss pained her deeply. Even though this meant being liberated from tending to her, the two had shared a special attachment despite, and because, of the years and bodily surfaces tracked in the intimacies of care. When I asked if the mother had recognized her at the end, Takahashi said no; the mother had not cognitively known any of them for years before dying. But a sense between them always remained. A mother who held her daughter in sense if not recognition.

Caregiving, according to Arthur Kleinman, exposes us in the "divided meaning" of being human. It "burdens our resources" and can be deeply troubling and irksome (mendōkusai), but it also produces something deeply human in the one both giving and receiving care: "caregiving can enhance our compassion, solicit solidarity, and elicit a fuller, more human presence than we ever realized we possessed" (2010, 17). The human condition is one of incompleteness or precariousness, to use Judith Butler's term. Humans come into the world and certainly leave it at the end reliant upon others for survival: "precariousness implies living socially, that is, in the hands of the other. It implies exposure both to those we know and to those we do not know; a dependency on people we know, or barely know or know not at all" (Butler 2009, 14). If precariousness is the "social ontology" of humans, it is inscribed at the very level of body itself, according to Butler. Bodies that in their vulnerability to others leave us perpetually open: an exposure that makes us susceptible to touch of various kinds with and from others. Anything from pain, injury, maiming, death to love, affection, arousal, care: "We can think of demarcating the human body through identifying its boundary, or in what form it is bound, but that is to miss the crucial fact that the body is, in certain ways and even inevitably, unbound. . . . It is outside itself, in the world of others, in a space and time it does not control, and it not only exists in the vector of these relations, but at this very vector. In this sense, the body does not belong to the self" (Butler 2009, 52–53).

Touch figured prominently in the caregiving Takahashi gave to her mother and played at with her kids. Combing her mother's hair, cutting her nails, changing diapers, cleaning the orifices of a body whose mind had drifted elsewhere. This is a dimension of humanness dangerously missing in the lives of young Japanese today, psychiatrist Serizawa Shunsuke (who works with, and researches, hikikomori) points out. In an era of material accumulation and sterile decorporealization (*datsushintai*), young people who "float" the waves of "net society" have "informationalized bodies"— bodies that communicate through images and are mediated (as are the relationships with one another) through information. Eventually "bodies will be irrelevant altogether" (*Nihon kodomo sōsharu wāku kyōkai* 2006, 26), he predicts. But this is not merely a technological matter—the outcome of advanced digitality and roboticization of heart. Rather, "datafication" of the (inter)personal is closely related to the shutting down of family life in twenty-first-century Japan, according to Serizawa. Neither here nor elsewhere do Japanese youths find much in the way of "intimate spaces" where they can engage, or receive, human touch—something he believes that Japanese youths still desperately need (25). The young people he treats as hikikomori are emotionally stunted, hungry for a kind of love they rarely get from parents overly focused on achievement. Intent on programming their children into highly functioning competitors as winners on the socioeconomic marketplace, such aspirational adults treat their kids as investments. When parenting is so driven by an instrumental agenda to produce successful kids, intimacy can get little consideration or abandoned altogether when the child doesn't measure up. This is what Serizawa finds among the troubled youths he works with: kids in need of human touch.

One night, out drinking with three middle-aged Japanese friends, the subject of touch came up. As they saw it, everything has become overly mechanical, as in coldly abstract, in Japan today. Life moves too fast and attention on material things and making money eats people up. Two of the three are artists who do manual labor to make ends meet; the third is a woman who once supported their art before the recession set in. As they described it, social life was once more sensual. The conversation turned to their childhoods and what they remembered of eating together at the family table (shokutaku). "Our table was round," recalled one of the artists who, from a farming family in Niigata, returned every planting season to help his now elderly parents plant rice. "A square table has edges, but edges divide people. As a family, we weren't cut off from one another. We ate together and we listened to one another." Eating together, listening to one another, sharing food. The memory evoked a familiar, now nostalgic, sense of touch in them all.

Slowing things down, and reaching out to touch, and be touched, by another presence is the logic, in part, of the iyashi (healing) boom driving the market in prosthetic and robotic sociality. But one also sees this in new arenas of leisure that sell touch with pets on loan. These include rental dog services where customers pay to take dogs for hire on walks. Another variant are cat cafés—a newer trend in Tokyo that a twenty-two-year-old I know tells me about the same week of my Denny interviews. Busy with a part-time job and on-again-off-again school, Mariko doesn't have time for a flesh and blood pet (nor boyfriend, for that matter). But she does enjoy the Neko JaLaLa cat café on the blistering hot day we make the trek to Akihabara (the electronics and otaku headquarters in Tokyo) to check it out. We've heard that this place is a zone of stillness apart from the hustle and bustle of urban life. And, indeed, we barely find it down a little side street where it's located on the first floor of a nondescript white building.

Along with Mariko's friend, the three of us enter the café's premises, remove our shoes at the *genkan*, and go through the washing-hand ritual (soap, alcohol, and antiseptic liquid) that we're directed to at the washstand in the back of the shop. Ordering cold drinks, we sit down on cushions and start petting the cats wandering about. The premises are cozy and small. Soft chairs and low tables for drinks are spread throughout, and everything is stamped in the motif of cats: bookshelves with cat books, cat pictures on the wall, cat toys in baskets. Only ten customers are allowed in at a time (for which we pay 500 yen [US$6] for thirty minutes) to nurture the intimacy we're to have with the cats. During our visit we share the space with two couples, two single men in their twenties, and an older man alone. There are also three cat care providers. One stays in the front, one interacts with the customers, and a third serves the drinks and tends to the cats, brushing them with what looks like a toothbrush. Imagining this will be kinky, I'm pleasantly surprised at how gentle and low-key it all is; everyone does their own thing touching, and being touched, by the cats. The older man sits on a couch and gently bops a cat toy at a kitty; one couple eyes a lovely Cheshire, and when the woman reaches out to caress it, her partner starts giving her a back massage. Most are kitties: soft, fluffy, and cute; some are adult; one is monster-sized. A sign on the table reads "*otona mo wasurenai yōni*" (don't forget about the old ones too).

This is touch without the burden Takahashi faced in cleaning the wastes of her mother and maneuvering a body less cute than that of a kitty or tamagotchi. Touch is sanitized, aestheticized, channeled in Neko JaLaLa where—while sipping on tea and lounging on cushions—one can linger over the brushing of a cat's body while leaving the nuisance of care to the paid attendants. Affective or immaterial labor, such work is called. But, in this case, the affect sought is materialized through an inter-bodily (if trans-species) sensation of connectedness. "Good energy," Mariko proclaims after we leave the place, telling me how relaxed she now feels and purged of the "bad energy" she'd been dealing with lately at work. Complications in human relations have been making her tense. But with the cats it's just simple—a basic touch—slowing time down, staying in the immediacy of the moment, lingering over touch.

Homeless Middle-School Student: Hope for the Breakdown of Family

The same summer of 2008 filming began on the best-selling memoir of the winter before, *Hōmuresu chūgakusei* (Homeless Middle-School Student). This survival tale of a "normal" twelve-year-old who winds up homeless in a local park captured the precarity of the times in a blend of the graphic and ordinary—a story told about poverty that elicited both sympathy and laughter from audiences (Shimizu 2008, 129). At once personal and touching, *Hōmuresu chūgakusei* was also read as a fable for hope, highlighting the breakdown yet endurance of family and of the dreamwork as much as the reality of home. Written by comedian Tamura Hiroshi who performed it originally as a stand-up routine, it starts off when, coming home from school the first day of summer vacation after completing his first year of middle school, Tamura finds his apartment cordoned off and the furniture stacked outside. His two siblings (one in high school, the other studying for his entrance exams to university) are as surprised as he when they arrive home. But their dad doesn't show up until later when, sauntering up, he announces "it's regrettable our home is gone." He then intones "now scat [*kaisan*]!" before turning around and riding off on his bike. Their mother died two years ago and now their father has abandoned them.

Stunned but not wanting to burden his siblings, Tamura concocts a story of being sure he can stay with friends and heads to the local park (nicknamed *Makifunkōen* but also *Unko* [shit] for short) instead. Here, the twelve-year-old camps out: sleeping inside a fort-like slide, washing (his body and clothes) in rainwater, using leaves for toilet paper, and becoming a monster (*obake kami*) to the kids who throw stones at him. But, more than anything, he is hungry. Driving his energies and thoughts, hunger consumes him. The days and nights get reduced to an endless quest and desire for food. He buys an occasional *bentō* with change found by the vending machine but also resorts to eating cardboard softened by water and begging pigeon feed (stale bread) from an old man.[19] But the daydreams of the loving meals his mother once made him feed the boy's imagination. And, enwrapped in the nostalgic taste of Mom's food, Tamura survives his ordeal at "shit park."

In time (only a month, though it's made to feel as if much longer duration in the book) Tamura is discovered by a friend and brought home for dinner. The friend's family takes him in and, when learning of his siblings, arranges (along with another set of parents) to set them up in an inexpensive apartment. Home has been reconstituted thanks to the generosity of friends. But as they are not given much in the way of expenses, the three still struggle with money. Sharing a meager pot of rice for dinner, they play a game of masticating each bite of rice as long as they can—an image that, when she saw it on the made-for-television version, reminded a middle-aged friend of the lean years of hunger (and potatoes) following the war. Family, as Tamura recounts in his book, is what gives him the strength to keep going. But it is also the loss of his mother that almost kills him. When one of their benefactors dies, Tamura finally understands the finality of death. Losing the desire to live, he aches to see his mother again. A consummately generous caregiver, she had not only bathed and babied her youngest child, but constantly sacrificed herself for the entire family—making their favorite foods, apologizing to them for dying, deferring to her domineering husband. The sacrificial mom as soul of the home, and, with her death, the family dies too.

But not entirely as the plotline shows. The loss also crushed Tamura's father who tried to keep himself and his family going. But, after getting cancer himself and losing his job from restructuring, he started drinking and gave up. But "the family" survives. A kindly teacher rekindles Tamura's spirit and his siblings make sure he sticks with school. Later on, it is his sister's suggestion that he enter a performing arts academy upon graduating from high school and his brother who, sacrificing his own ambitions, works to pay for it. And Tamura succeeds in becoming a well-known comedian.[20] But his biggest break comes with *Hōmuresu chūgakusei* itself. Selling a million copies in the first two months (and two million by the next year), the book was a phenomenon. Made into both a television and cinematic movie, it was adopted as part of the school curriculum (in Japanese-language classes) and spurred tourism to the "shit park" where Tamura had been homeless. (The image of the slide he lived in at the park was plastered on the promo poster for the film as well as inside the cover of the book. A sign of that most familiar of play equipment now turned into a homeless shelter. But, given a bright blue color with clouds floating above it in the sky, the image also seemed designed to evoke humor.)

Part of a *geinin bon būmu* (boom of books by entertainers), the book resembled others in the genre, such as Riry Franky's *Tōkyō tawā* (Tokyo tower) also thematized around poverty, success, the loss of a mother, and broken families. Finding it an "interesting" story that did well when he first performed it as a comedy routine on television, Tamura's producer was the one who urged him to write a book: "Speaking about poverty just a little is good" (*binbō de chotto dake yokatta*) (Shimizu 2008, 22). The managing editor at the press (Wani Books) suggested that Tamura try to write it himself without a ghost writer, looking for.the "vitality" of an entertainer who could convey a story about poverty with "brightness" (29). And, indeed, this is how it was received. A review of *Hōmuresu chūgakusei* in *Oz Magazine* found the story tragic but funny too — "eating cardboard! Anyone will be surprised and then there are episodes that totally make you smile" (qtd. in Shimizu 2008, 31).[21] And, as Tamura himself has said, he sees in his own tale of survival one of "family love" (*kazokuai*): a belief in the strength of family that allowed him to endure hard times (*yahari dokoka de tsuyoku kazoku o shinjite ita tame*) (qtd. in Shimizu 2008, 67). Survival and success, born from the nest of a home that nurtured the boy's soul even when it failed to shelter and feed him or, at least, this was the story of *Hōmuresu chūgakusei*.

As Tamura told interviewers when the book was launched, he wrote the book to honor his dead mother and reconnect with his dad — from whom he and his siblings had heard nothing since being abandoned fourteen years earlier. Instead of the bitterness one might expect from someone essentially orphaned when still a young boy, Tamura expressed gratitude to both parents he had lost. Weathering the death of one parent and abandonment from the other made Tamura strong; he also learned how to survive hard times and be satisfied with life itself. This message of personal resilience was critical to the *Hōmuresu chūgakusei* boom. But so was that of family redemption, a theme that got played up by the discovery, quite literally, of Tamura's father, which fittingly took place on Japanese TV — as part of the show, FBI *chōnōryoku sōsa kan* (the twelfth episode), which tracks down lost family members and stages reunions that are broadcast live. In this one, Tamura's father appeared at the door of a run-down apartment: sixty-five, living alone, yellowed skin, and with only one tooth in his mouth. Immediately apologizing to his three children, he was forgiven in return by them. Coincidentally, this episode was staged right before the release of Tamura's book. And, as the news reportage kept track of the story, the family has continued to mend and the son has now invited his father to live with him, ironically (or not?) in the sumptuous mansion he bought with the money from *Hōmuresu chūgakusei.*

During the hoopla surrounding the book and its filming in the summer of 2008, I was in Tokyo. From talking to Japanese and reading postings about it on 2Channel (a Japanese Internet forum), I kept hearing how "extraordinary" but "ordinary" people found Tamura's story to be. That he had eaten cardboard and been told to "scat" by his father was shockingly "unimaginable." Yet Tamura also represented a "normal" Japanese boy who had fallen on, and risen above, hard times: someone people could identify with whose story also served as both a cautionary and inspiring tale. Struggling with a broken family, and broken spirits, herself, a twenty-two-year-old (the one I went to the cat café with) told me that she saw in Tamura a kindred "orphan" who had survived to become a huge success. At a moment when, following Koizumi's platform for neoliberal restructuring, the banner of "individual responsibility" (*jiko sekinin*) resounds throughout the country, *Hōmuresu chūgakusei* offers a myth of neoliberal individualism supplanting, but implanted within, the Japanese family. Isn't this the secret of the story's popularity? For the family does break down here and both parents, and the roles they have performed, are lost: the mother whose head feeds the family and the father whose lifetime job secures its livelihood. But the child lives on. And, as in any good myth, contradictions are resolved. The hunger and abandonment he incurred (by his father, the company that fired him, the nation-state that didn't step in to help either the father or children) are forgiven and Tamura succeeds, despite, or precisely because of, the collapse of family and a family form that no longer fits the socioeconomy of the times.

The story is almost too good to be true. And, indeed, according to a friend, the rumor on the streets is that Tamura manufactured it. Entertainer that he is, he spun a good comedy routine — poverty with humor — and then spun it some more into the megahit of homeless boy gets rich and saves dad. Certainly, Tamura has become a celebrity and fabulously wealthy to boot. His stardom is what many young people say they dream of today: of making it big in a designer profession such as rock music or the manga industry. Hopes built on such remote possibilities trade in ir-reality, says Yamada Masahiro, the author of *Kibō kakusa shakai* (2004). Since so few will realize these dreams, it would be far better, according to him, to stick with a more basic (and traditional) life plan: hard work and long-term commitment to school, marriage, and a job. But this, the postwar Japanese contract and dream, is what has become unrealistic in twenty-first-century Japan. By contrast, Tamura's tale serves up a fable for new-age hope by melding the old and the new: the old family that lives on — in the boy's memories, affects, desires — and the individual who succeeds in a path custom designed as his own. As a blogger on 2Chan-nel commented, how hilarious that the boy who once lived on cardboard in "shit park" has become a member of Japan's wealthy elite today. From being homeless, Tamura has emerged a "winner." A winner who can build his dream house and (re)make a familial home inside. An oneiric, mythic, flexible home where the child feeds and mothers the dad. The Japanese family reassembled, if not reproduced.

Tokyo Sonata: The "Cruel Optimism" of Home

Home, and what I call *hometime*, the temporality or spatiality given "home," pulses at the forefront of the public imagination today. Across multiple media — books, film, magazines, the Internet, video games, television, news coverage, and commentary — the precarity of the times gets played out in stories and storytelling about homelife. Homelessness falls at one end of the spectrum: of Japanese wandering the streets, crashing in net cafés, or creating shelter in local parks. *Hōmuresu chūgakusei* exempli-fies this along with such titles as *Ie no nai shōjotachi* (Young Girls Without Home) (Suzuki 2008) and *Kyō hōmuresu ni natta: 15nin no sararīman tenraku jinsei* (Today, I Became Homeless: The Lives of 15 Salarymen Who

Have Fallen Down) (Masuda 2008). But if displacement from home spells out one kind of existential precarity, another is found not outside but inside the space of home itself. This is the story told in a movie like *Tokyo Sonata* (2008) where the home, failing to shelter its inhabitants, breeds the social breakdown of the times. Directed by Kurosawa Kiyoshi, well known for his haunting horror films (*Cure, Charisma, Pulse, Akarui Mirai*) where the deadly and normal intimately collide, *Tokyo Sonata* is set in the quotidian landscape of an "ordinary" Japanese family. Throughout the film everyday routines get rehearsed, then disturbed in a pattern more disturbing as the film goes on.

The movie starts out with Megumi (the mother and housewife) cleaning the house. A wind distracts her from the outside and, opening the sliding door, she steps into it as if intoxicated or stunned. Meanwhile Ryuhei, her husband, is at the office, giving orders to an underling. Suddenly he is called into his boss's office and asked what particular skills or talent he can offer his company as it restructures. Ryuhei is confused, oblivious to the fact that the Chinese woman who just passed him in the hall represents the future of his corporation that is relocating some of its operations to China. Unable to respond, Ryuhei is fired. Packing up, he leaves the office. Once outside, he notices a number of other sararīman disposed from workplace like he has been, briefcases by their side, sitting on benches. He overhears one say he's been looking for work for three months. Another, a former classmate he runs into—dressed in a sharp suit whose cell phone is programmed to ring every few minutes simulating business calls—shows him the soup line. It is still light when Ryuhei makes his way home. When he tries to sneak in the side door, Megumi discovers him and wonders why he's acting so strange. Indeed, being home before dark signals something out of place.[22] But having been canned from work—the place more suitably his—is not a fact Ryuhei decides to share with his family. Henceforth, Ryuhei will enact a charade of leaving home every morning suited up, briefcase in hand, staying out for the occasional late night with colleagues from work.

The breakdown of everydayness would seem to start here: with the loss of a job that the head of the family so studiously masks. But, if this is the story, it is only part of it, for the interruption of tranquility at home—creepy and creeping as Kurosawa makes it—doesn't stem from economic rupture alone. Certainly, things unravel once Ryuhei loses what is not only a job but his footing in life: what, for this era of sararīman Japanese, was where one "belonged" and got socially nested. Having his customary way of life fall apart, Ryuhei is vulnerable to something besides mere depression: an ontological and temporal disconnect. Indeed, he seems less melancholic than ontologically at odds. Going off in "drag" in the morning, Ryuhei has no idea how to "be" anything but a sararīman. Rejecting the first job he is offered at the unemployment office because he finds anything but managerial work to be literally unimaginable, Ryuhei is genuinely confused. It's not merely that he finds custodial work in a big shopping mall (the job he eventually takes) demeaning, rather it's the sense that none of this registers—existentially, affectively, subjectively. Ryuhei can't see the world this way; he can't see himself—no future, no now, no self.

Ryuhei does cling to something, of course. The ghost of his past (which includes continuing to assert his authority at home). But this semblance disassembles; spotting him one day at the soup line, Megumi realizes he's lost his job. Even worse, for Ryuhei at least, is being seen by his wife at the mall dressed in the orange uniform of a custodial worker. Caught without his props—the suit and briefcase he dons when leaving the mall—Ryuhei is devastated and, stepping in front of a truck that night, almost dies. Being stripped of, in essence, himself is the existential predicament of this ghostly sararīman. But, if life now gets emptied, there was already an emptiness to how life got enacted and inhabited by the Sasaki family. As the movie shows, homelife—particularly around the family table eating the meals Megumi still endlessly prepares—is something of an empty prop as well. Even the morning after Ryuhei has lain all night in the street after being hit by the truck, he comes home to eat breakfast with his wife and son. They, too, as it turns out have had their own traumatic adventures away from home; Kenji was in detention, caught for shoplifting, and Megumi had been abducted by someone who broke into the house. Yet all three sit down to eat breakfast. No one speaks and no one knows, or asks, why the others look a mess. This is an ordinary family where no one communicates, as Kurosawa has said of the Sasakis he created in *Tokyo Sonata*. Or to put this differently, this is a movie about what is ordinary in the (de)sociality—disconnectedness, incommunicativeness—of Japan's *muen shakai* (relationless society). Families where no one speaks; communities where a longtime resident can starve to death without seeking or receiving help from a neighbor next door.

As depicted by Kurosawa, the breakdown of what is everyday in the Sasaki home—the mechanical routines of everyone assuming their place and assembling together for family meals—is not necessarily something to mourn. Indeed, neither son in the Sasaki household is headed on a path that will reproduce that of their father's. The older son, a college student, finds school so meaningless he enlists in the American army—an absurd twist added by Kurosawa. The younger son, ready to graduate from elementary school, is drawn to music rather than school; he wants to study piano and, despite his father's dictatorial opposition, takes it up secretly on his own. While both sons seek an alternative to the life options they're presented with, Megumi is more stuck in the home that is now imploding with no exit to the outside. The one dream we see her indulge—a fancy new car that entrances her at a showroom—is only realized when an unemployed man breaks into their house and forces her to drive the BMW he's stolen. Needless to say, this flight turns out badly and, like her husband, Megumi falls into despair.

While far short of a happy ending, things do end on what the director intended to be a "hopeful" note. Ryuhei is shown energetically scrubbing a toilet, resigned to his new job. The older son, home on a furlough, seems to have mellowed out. And the younger son has been allowed to audition for a music academy. In the final scene, the boy mesmerizes the entire room with the brilliance of his rendition of *Moonlight Sonata*. His parents recognize his genius and are affected by the beauty of his performance—a poetry that opens up new possibilities for not only their son but, as we are to imagine, the family as well. In a home that doesn't fall apart and moves beyond a present that "is not enough" (Munoz 2009), there is a glimmer of a (not-yet-known) futurity and the willingness to start letting go of the past. Still, as with *Hōmuresu chūgakusei*, salvation is pinned to the exceptional luck and abilities of a child: as comedian turned pop celebrity in the case of Tamura and as budding pianist with the promise of stardom for Kenji.[23] Hopeful daydreams of a home at once extraordinary and mundane.

Radical Hope: Queer(ing) Home

Hope is a wish for something to come true by action. —Genda 2006, 295

In the face of radical change, there is also the potential for radical hope. As Jonathan Lear defines the latter, this is the "possibility for the creation of a new field of possibilities" (2006, 51). Being able to see beyond a present, brokered on the past, into the future calls on the imagination. Needed are new poets who can take up the past "and—rather than use it for nostalgia or ersatz mimesis—project it into vibrant new ways" for living and being (Lear 2006, 51). Such a poet, according to Lear, was the last great chief of the Crow Nation who became a spokesperson for both the death and rebirth of his culture. Overseeing the Crow's transition from nomadic buffalo hunting to resettlement on a reservation, Plenty Coups certainly viewed these events as traumatic: "when the buffalo went away the hearts of my people fell to the ground, and they could not lift them up again. After this nothing happened" (qtd. in Lear 2006, 2). With the disappearance of their way of life, existence and time seemed to stop. This condition Lear calls "ontological vulnerability": existential precarity when the rules and regularities of a shared lifestyle no longer compute. Because even food preparation was part of a cultural flow geared toward buffalo hunts, terminating the latter made everydayness itself incomprehensible. Once their grammar of how to be and act in the world was taken away, the Crow Nation suffered a kind of existential death in addition to all their other losses.

Plenty Coups grew up in the traditions of his culture. But at age nine he had a dream that foresaw the disappearance of buffalo. The elders took this dream seriously and, by interpreting it as a sign of impending crisis and a call for radical change, they embarked upon a course of practical action—willingly giving up hunting and negotiating to hold onto (a modicum of) their land. To survive this transformation, the Crow recalibrated the terms by which they lived life and viewed themselves. It was a course of action germinated by Plenty Coups's dream and fueled by what Lear calls radical hope: "Through the interpretation of the dream the tribe surmised that the traditional ways of life—and thus the traditional ways of being a Crow—were coming to an end. And yet they gathered confidence that they would survive. In this way, the Crow hoped for the emergence of a Crow subjectivity that did not yet exist" (2006, 104). Hope is at once a poetry and a methodology for life in ontologically vulnerable times. Taking a leap of the imagination into a space, future, even a subjectivity that does not yet exist is what enables new possibilities—and also a practical means for survival. According to Lear, this is what Plenty Coups, acting as a radically hopeful poet, did for the Crow: "Here by 'poet' I mean the broadest sense of a creative maker of meaningful space. The possibility for such a poet is precisely the possibility for the creation of a new field of possibilities" (51). Being able to envision a "then and there" alternative to what is missing or flawed in the "here and now" is also how José Munoz in his book *Cruising Utopia: The Then and There of Queer Futurity* (2009) defines hope (which he equates with utopia). But his interest stems not from the collapse of a traditional culture (as in Lear's case) but from the exclusions such cultures enact on certain individuals and lifestyles. In a dominant culture ordered by reproductive futurism, for example, those who don't biologically reproduce are "people without a future" (2009:98). Denied futurity, "the present is not enough. It is impoverished and toxic for queers and other people who do not feel the privilege of majoritarian belonging, normative tastes, and 'rational' expectations" (2009, 27). Rather than trying to make a place for oneself (as a gay family, for example) within this dominant order—or fleeing it altogether (the position taken by antirelational queers)[24]—Munoz advocates for what he sees as a more hopeful path: envisioning and working for a different kind of collective belonging. This entails remaking subjectivity and the world at the same time, which takes hope a step beyond the practical (if poetic) trajectory laid out by Lear: "This 'we' does not speak to a merely identitarian logic but instead to a logic of futurity. The 'we' speaks to a 'we' that is 'not yet conscious,' the future society that is being invoked and addressed at the same time. The 'we' is not content to describe who the collective is but more nearly describes what the collective and the larger social order could be, what it should be" (Munoz 2009, 20).

Borrowing from Bloch, Munoz views hope as not only poetic but also political. This involves, in part, a rejuggling of time: incorporating "traces" of the past and figments of a not-yet future to retemporalize a present in which one is stuck—"'queerness' time is a stepping out of the linearity of straight time" (25). But reimagining the world also means changing it. If being queer "casts one as hopeless," then seeking hope means being willing to not only not settle for but to actively disrupt the present. To Munoz, demanding a world and a future of new possibilities involves a "collective futurity, a notion of futurity that functions as a historical materialist critique" (26).

Hometime Beyond Family: A Poetics of the Socially Withdrawn

That there is something menacing or missing in the present is a sentiment one hears often in Japan these days. Home (or homelessness) and hope (but, more commonly, hopelessness) are two of the most common tropes for expressing this. An ontological vulnerability that is connected to time. If time is preeminently social—how we measure labor power but also those rituals, both quotidian and sacred, marking membership in groups—what does it say about hometime that this has become the crucible for so much anxiety at the onset of the twenty-first century in Japan?

As I have argued in this chapter, it is the breakdown or liquidization of the relationship between human time and capitalist value at the level of the (re)productive family home that marks the form of precarity and unease experienced in post-postwar Japan. For many, the present seems fraught, particularly when the reference point is a past remembered, or reinvented, as idyllically stable: a time when jobs and marriage were secure and a future—of more of the same—could be counted on. But belonging, even then, came at a price: an extraction of a particular kind of—constant, competitive, intense—labor. A sacrifice, some say, of everything else, even (or particularly) the soul: the time to touch a mother with Alzheimer's or to shelter a child getting bullied at school or to simply enjoy the rhythm of slow eating with friends. As this kind of temporality and sociality was already getting squeezed by the market mentality of the family-corporate system of Japan, Inc., some find it better to remake the kind of human connection people long for when they buy a care robot or visit a cat café with a home different from the past. A form other than reproductive futurism, with a different construction of hope.

Such an example was given me by Suzuki Takayuki.[25] Aged thirty-three when I interviewed him in Niigata City in 2008, Suzuki had grown up in Sado Island where, underindustrialized, the only secure employment came from going to Tokyo and acquiring the academic credentials to get a job elsewhere or return as a public official (kōmuin). His parents pressured him to excel at school. But, regrettably for him, he was a lousy student. Looking at childhood photos of himself now, he sees that all the strain he was under gave him bald spots by the age of five from pulling his hair out at the back of his head. His mother hounded him, and his grades always disappointed her. "There was no home (ibasho) for me at home," he told me. School offered little relief. Short for his age, a poor student, and not very good at sports, Suzuki was bullied right from the start. Without a single friend, everyday life tasted harsh (tsurai). He thought about suicide all the time and released the pain inside by cutting, making small slices in the skin on his hands and up and down his arms. Suzuki also escaped into books (history and literature), took up shoplifting, and—when the *fami kon* (video games) came out in Japan—played games on the TV. He watched a lot of movies on video as well. Not surprisingly, he has grown up to be a filmmaker as an adult and peppers his conversation with references to the movies he's watched now for decades.

In a world premised on value of only certain sorts—academic for kids, economic for adults—Suzuki saw himself as did others as a boy: worthless. Only by fleeing reality did the child survive. By middle school, his parents started ignoring him, shifting their aspirations to his younger brother and getting absorbed by their desire to accumulate ever more wealth. With the bubble economy still strong and stocks going up, life became ever more prosperous at home. But, with all the pressure placed on him, his younger brother cracked. Sent to a psychiatric hospital at the age of sixteen, he had a long recovery (and still carries the designation of handicapped today; Suzuki takes care of him now in Niigata where the two share a home). At the time of our interview, the "indiscriminate attack" by a twenty-five-year-old temporary (*haken*) worker in Akihabara, killing seven people, had occurred the month before and Suzuki told me he could see himself in Katō Tomohiro, the perpetrator. Like Katō, his situation at home, and in life, had been existentially bereft. And, like in Katō's situation, communication floundered between parent and child. His parents didn't "get him." And, as Suzuki tells it, he grew up not talking, quite literally, with his parents nor basically anyone at all.

Rather than giving up on life, or taking that of others, Suzuki started reeducating himself. This led him to reassess the worldview and view of self he had been raised with. During a period of being NEET upon graduating from college, Suzuki voraciously read. Learning about child abuse from books like Claudia Blackson's *Mother and Child*, he started questioning his childhood. Denied love and recognition for his failure to measure up to the norm, he had been discarded as human waste because he was not much good at academics. Drained of confidence and spirit, he now needed to establish self-worth and a place for himself on different grounds. With this intention, he moved to Niigata where he joined a self-help group, started studying social work, and pursued filmmaking. Committed to helping youths like he had been himself, Suzuki now works with NEET and hikikomori throughout the city. As he put it, one of the most pressing problems facing troubled youths today is the inability to find a place within society (*yakuwariga mitsukerarenai*). Unstitched from the milieu around them or a life plan that is moving forward, these youths lack hope. But, as Suzuki admitted, generating hope is difficult. One strategy he has come up with on his own involves making films where each youth is assigned a part: camera operator, screen writer, sound producer. In this, everyone assumes a role (*yakuwari*) and, just as importantly, learns how to "work together, communicate, and see something through" as part of a group.

Speaking as someone who couldn't find an ibasho at home or anywhere else as a kid, Suzuki noted how high the numbers of hikikomori, NEET, and otherwise withdrawn, disabled, or anxious youths are in Japan today. Even for those graduating from the highest ranked universities, there is less and less guarantee of a stable job or a secure role in society these days (he cited a figure of 20 percent unemployment for those graduating from Tokyo University). For just about anyone these days, the future ahead and the present society can feel shut off despite having what it once took to become a winner, as I've already discussed. As Suzuki sees it, in order to "belong" today, the stakes for existence and connectedness (*tsunagari*) must be recast to open up new realms of possibility. This was Ryuhei's dilemma in *Tokyo Sonata*, of course, and also the glimmer of hope Kurosawa Kiyoshi implanted at the movie's end. And in this we can see Munoz's call for a "collective futurity" that, making a place for those excluded in the here and now, also operates as a materialist critique of a heteronormative order that reproduces itself on the basis of only one kind of child.

When I see Suzuki again, in the summer of 2010, he tells me about the film he has made with a crew of three self-identified hikikomori. A local friend wrote the screenplay, and the actors, all acquaintances, performed without charge. Made on a shoestring budget—for only 30,000 yen (about US$320)—the film was his brainchild: a strategy for involving hikikomori in a creative, productive endeavor that would help ease them back into a world of labor and social life. The plotline, somewhat fanciful, revolves around a bombastic protagonist in search of dreams, but the "motive" of the story, as he puts is, is rekindling the family. The film is titled *Ma-kun ni wa yume ga nai* (Mr. Ma Doesn't Have Dreams) and, written up in the *Nīgata Nippō* newspaper, the subject of a special news report on the local television channel, it has earned kudos for socially engaged filmmaking. It would seem to be an expression of life—a poetry of and for survival, a methodology for social belonging in ontologically vulnerable times. Production of the film has been sponsored by Suzuki's new nonprofit organization: a support network for youth that is codenamed a *bansōsha* (the partner who runs alongside a bicyclist giving support). Given that hiki-komori, by definition, don't communicate, Suzuki's strategy of arousing them into human activity and collective talk through the mechanics of co-producing a film is quite extraordinary.

Suzuki seems wearied during my visit to Niigata this time. Something weighs on him; he's had a health scare, and a doctor told him to curb his drinking. Life is strained, he admits. But when he speaks of *Ma-kun ni wa yume ga nai*, Suzuki smiles broadly. The project was a success. His crew stuck it out to the end, and the film is now earning some recognition. The night it was finally finished, Suzuki invited all three of his work crew over to his house for food and drinks. The mere memory of it makes Suzuki laugh. Awkward, ill at ease, ignorant of even the most basic social etiquette, these were hikikomori partying. Sharing food made not by a mother but by a former misfit just like themselves. They all got drunk and stayed the night, Suzuki tells me. And this, in itself, is something. A con-tinuing "to do something as long as they refuse to do nothing" (Povinelli 2011:191).

A queer home that sheltered a family—of strange sorts—for an evening.

FIVE. THE SOCIAL BODY— IN LIFE AND DEATH

On June 30, 2010, the byline of *Asahi Shimbun* reads: "Lowest Wages, Can't Buy Stability." In a series on the upcoming elections in the House of Councillors on July 11, *Asahi Shimbun* reports on the scene. In this article the subject is precarious workers, now seen as a useful lens for assessing the political mood of the country.

It is nine months before Japan's triple crisis of earthquake, tsunami, and nuclear reactor meltdown on March 11, 2011. And it is nine and a half months after Prime Minister Hatoyama Yukio's landslide victory. Riding into office on a reformist agenda, his party, the Democratic Party of Japan (DPJ), ousted leadership from the conservative party, the Liberal Democratic Party (LDP), that had held it for half a century. June 2010 comes midway between these two seismic events, midway between an event auguring hope (for political change and social reform) and an event unleashing devastation and death (the fourth largest earthquake in recorded history).

By early summer though, the midpoint is tipping already. By now, the optimism garnered by Hatoyama's victory is gone as is the prime minister himself. Brought down by tax evasion, political scandal in his party, overspending, and, in the end, reneging on his campaign promise to press the United States to move its military base on Futenma, Okinawa, off the island, Hatoyama has been forced to resign earlier in the month. The fourth prime minister in four years, his departure signals further erosion of public trust in Japan's national leadership, given that no one can muster whatever it takes to last long. He is replaced by his finance minister.

Kan Naoto will be in office at the time of the earthquake the following March. But, amid charges that the government is ineffective in handling the disaster, Kan too will lose popular support. Five months later he resigns in what will get read as now ordinary even amid the newest crisis: turnstile prime ministership and a government that more and more Japanese say they distrust. Precariousness emerging on multiple fronts: political, economic, and—just around the corner—the natural, national, and nuclear disaster of the Great East Japan Earthquake.

The article features two workers from Miyazaki Prefecture,[1] where wages are the lowest in the country. The first is a thirty-year-old man who, at the same job in a convenience store for thirteen years, earns 630 yen (US$6.70) an hour. Even working six days a week, his monthly pay (130,000 yen, US$1,381) puts him (far) below the poverty level. By living at home with his folks, the man avoids destitution. But, taxes and health insurance take half his salary. And, while there is a woman he would like to marry, her parents won't allow it. The future makes him anxious. Sleepless at night, the man says all he wants is to earn enough to live independently (*dokuritsu shite kuraseru*). But at the wage he currently makes, and has been stuck at for thirteen years, he can't "buy stability" (as in afford a stable life).

The second case is of a worker in the same *konbini* (convenience store): a single mom with three kids. Given a small child allowance from the government and help from her parents in covering her children's school expenses, the woman survives despite her low wages. But her parents are in the livestock business and were hit hard by the outbreak of foot-and-mouth disease earlier in the year. In her forties, she doesn't want to ask for help anymore and reckons that, with a wage of just 800 yen an hour (US$8.50), she could manage. Though she works full time, the woman doesn't earn enough to provide even a "basic life" for herself and her kids under present conditions. She, too, can't afford what it takes to live safely.

Lessening the ranks of such "working poor" (*hataraku hinkonsō*) is one of the agendas of the ruling party, the article reports. For example, the government made raising the minimum wage for those at the bottom of national statistics (to 800 yen an hour and eventually 1,000 yen, $10.70) a priority in its most recent growth strategy announced in June. And all the political parties are similarly oriented in this campaign season: working toward "upping" not national growth but everyone's standard of living (*Asahi Shimbun*, June 30, 2010, 14). Precarity, as the article would suggest, has entered public discourse, and, as its corollary, securing daily life for even those on the bottom registers as a political issue in the upcoming elections.

I am reading this newspaper article on the *shinkansen*, the network of high-speed railway lines ("bullet trains") that, designed and first constructed in the period of reconstruction following the war, became a sign of Japan's miraculous recovery and, with its rapid economic growth, emergence as a global industrial power. By 2010 the moment feels radically different. As reported in the news, Japan is struggling with a long-lasting recession, political instability, an aging and declining population, and, among the people, rising levels of homelessness, poverty, suicide, and existential despair. This is what I have come here to study. The contemporary moment and how people are dealing with the insecurity of the times in navigating, quite literally, the ecology of life and death. It is June 2010 and I have six weeks this time for fieldwork: my third summer on the project. Based mainly in Tokyo, I am pursuing social sensibilities, and fractures, of survival: how relations with others—of care, belonging, recognition—are showing strain but also, in a few instances, getting reimagined and restitched in innovative new ways. Social precarity is what I'm now calling this.

This is why today I am on the shinkansen, returning from Osaka where I have gone to check out a social welfare program devised to serve people needing help with the basics of life. It is through another newspaper article that I've learned about what the reporter dubbed a "welfare bank" (*fukushi ginkō*): a system that stores and lends "welfare" in a country where citizens are increasingly living and dying alone but also expected to maintain an ethos of individual responsibility (*jiko sekinin*) in getting by. As I've heard often from Japanese—and will hear again in the wake of the 3/11 disaster—self-reliance is valued and dependence upon others abhorred. Not wanting to burden their children is the number one reason elderly give for choosing to live alone, often at great risk to themselves, the investigators of a study on Japan's *muen shakai* (relationless society) discovered (NHK *Muen shakai purojekuto* 2010). The welfare bank caters to just such a contingency: providing a resource for daily living that doesn't depend on money, the family, or the state.

Officially called Nippon Active Life Club (NALC), the program operates through a currency of caregiving calculated in time. Started in 1993 by Takahata Kei'ichi in Osaka, NALC now has 135 branch offices and over 30,000 members all over the country. It is run entirely on its own resources (raised from the annual fee of 3,000 yen [US$32]) that members pay and also from donations of cash that users, without stored time, may give as compensation).[2] The foundational principle is its chief mode of operation: the "time-savings system" (*jikan yotaku seido*) whereby one hour of labor earns one point that is recorded in a bankbook (*techō*). All labor is equal whether it is raking leaves, making a meal, or more so-called intellectual work, such as teaching a computer class or running seminars. Members are divided into two categories—users (*riyōsha*) and donors (*teikyōsha*)—though the assumption is that a donor is a future user (true so far for only about 10 percent of current users). In principle then, caregivers are proxies for their future selves; one gives care while still able and cashes in when needing care oneself. But recipients can also be family members (defined as spouses, parents, and disabled children) and, if a donor dies with unused points, family members can apply to activate them. More pertinent for the way the system has utility for families is its convertibility across not just time but space. If someone donates time in Osaka, for example, she can convert this into care for her aging mother in Tokyo. In this case the caregiver in Tokyo stands in for the absent or distant family member—a process by which the family's potential for care labor is stretched across both body (a stranger substituting for family member) and space. In fact though, while open to families, the currency of care here operates more on the assumption of the family's absence or erosion as primary caregiving unit in Japan. And, organized like a bank, NALC donors and users are transacting the labor of care primarily as individuals.

Sitting in a barely air-conditioned room in their offices in Tenmanbashi,

Osaka, Takahata, still *kaichō* (chair) of NALC at age eighty, told me that what inspired him to start this program was a lecture at the Miami School of Law in the early 1990s given by Edgar Cahn. When I look Cahn up later on Google, I discover that he is an innovative figure in the field of social welfare and social justice in the United States. A lawyer who, along with his wife, founded the Antioch School of Law, he is the president and founder of TimeBanks USA with its concept of "Time Dollars," a local, tax-exempt currency designed to reward and recognize the work of the disenfranchised in their struggles to hang onto and rebuild their communities. Cahn has been successful in getting the government and major philanthropic organizations to fund Time Dollar initiatives in multiple arenas ranging from juvenile justice to immigrant worker rights and elderly care. And in 1995, two years after Takahata started his own version of Time-Banks in Japan, Cahn initiated another radical welfare project called Co-Production, where recipients of service are enlisted as co-producers of social change. In my interview with Takahata, his account of what in Cahn's work led him to start up NALC is a bit perplexing. "Time is money," he tells me in English, though this adage of American capitalism touted by Ben Franklin would seem the very inverse of NALC's system of brokering time in an equivalence of not money but care. Yet, like capitalism, value is produced through labor performed by individuals and measured in discrete units of time. And by treating it as a currency like money, NALC converts care into an impersonal medium that can be brokered between strangers rather than relying on one's personal ties of family (and thus abstracts and homogenizes into exchange the use value of care) (Marx 1978, 304–5). As Takahata elaborates, what drives the need for care in a program like NALC is scarcity. There is a "care deficit" gripping Japan today that starts, though hardly ends, with the elderly.[3]

The example Takahata gives is of elderly dying alone. And, given that this is Japan, there is a word for the phenomenon—*kodokushi*, which literally translates as lonely (*kodoku*) death (*shi*). Loneliness (kodoku) is a pain all its own these days: what one hears from young people to old about existences spent too much alone, isolated from others, and disconnected from the social fixtures that (once) anchored identity and human relationships such as the workplace. NHK (the national broadcasting network) televised a special in 2009 on *muen shakai* where, among all the other stories, it highlighted the escalating rate of elderly who die alone (the figure given was 32,000 deaths in 2009: a figure that kept appearing on the screen in large numbers). As Takahata describes the phenomenon to me, kodoku-shi is increasing nationwide with more and more discoveries of putrefied bodies of elderly who have died solitary deaths days, even weeks, before. One just happened next door in New Town.

As Takahata shows me, this is the lead story in the monthly newspaper NALC puts out: "*Hayaku ugokidashita mimawaritai kodokushi dasanai machi zukuri e*" (Neighborhood Watch is On the Move — Building a Town Without "Lonely Death") (NALC, July 10, 2010, 1). Life is risky, and not just for the elderly, Takahata points out. Many people have needs in managing everyday life and insufficient resources (human or financial) to tend to them, such as being an invalid who needs to get to the doctor or a single mom whose kids need to be picked up at daycare before she can get away from her job. Sitting next to Takahata is Nishimura, the person who co-ordinates all the work transactions for NALC in Osaka. This is a job she works at five days a week from 10 AM to 4 PM on an entirely volunteer basis (which, she admits, is "quite a job!"). It is Nishimura who enumerates the diversity of care needs and services that NALC trades in: everything from teaching children to swim, fixing wheelchairs, and building a kids' adventure park in a forest close to Osaka to tending to the elderly by making them tea, drying their hair, and accompanying them to the public bath. As she cheerfully observes, what gets exchanged is driven by not only need for a specific service but also the desire for something pleasant (*tanoshii*): the pleasantry of having human companionship. The two merge here. For, as described in the pamphlet I'm given, NALC runs on the logic of love and mutual contact ("*aijō to fureai no ronri*"): drawing on, and filling the gap in, human relationships. As NALC implicitly acknowledges, there is a care deficit and a deficit in sociality in Japan today.

Lonely elderly are dying alone.

I START THIS chapter with these two stories — one about low wages and campaign promises to raise peoples' living standards and the other about a volunteer "welfare" organization that calls itself "a storehouse for the future" (*mirai no kura*) — to draw attention to what I see as a new focus of personal and collective interest in Japan today around the issue of life. Needless to say, these are troubling times all across the world, and there is nothing unique about the sense of desperation or call to survival that so many Japanese experience these days. In political and social theory as well, there is a convergence of interest over issues pertaining to bare life

(Agamben 1998), humanitarianism (Fassin 2008, Redfield 2013), biopower (Foucault 1998, 2008; Rose 2001), suffering and pain (Das 1997, Asad 2011), belonging and abandonment (Berlant 2011, Povinelli 2011, Butler 2009), survival and care (Muehlebach 2012, Jackson 2011, Lucht 2012, Han 2012, Garcia 2010), and the politics of affect and love (Hardt 2011, Hardt and Negri 2004). In theoretical discourse, practical life, and social activism, people all over the world are confronting a reality of growing scarcity, daily insecurity, and the risks enjoined by everything from natural disasters and military warfare to runaway speculation, bank pullouts, and the shortage of jobs.

Drawing on this work of others, what I examine in the context of twenty-first-century Japan is how the insecuritization of the moment is gnawing at the soul, triggering the pain of unease (*fuan*) and dissatisfaction (*fuman*) with the precarity of existence. People are suffering. And, becoming fed up with suffering alone (which is part of the pain), some are activating around collectivized forms of survival and care. This is a biopolitics of life (and death): an investment, not only in the (re)production of life (what oriented labor, productivity, and economic growth under the postwar era of Japan, Inc.) but in the protection of everyday existence (where "life," in these post-bubble times, is beginning to shift its calibration, from lives of hard work and consumerist rewards to lives valued more by well-being and being well cared for). In times marked by the uncertainty of the moment, the unpredictability of the future, and the stretching—but thwarting—of horizons of expectation, the political imaginary shows signs of an epistemic shift. Away from a politics of living together—of prioritizing the "convivance" of a collective, social whole beyond individual interests[4]—to a politics of survival: what Abélès sees as the biopolitical dimension of global neoliberalism today (2010, 15–16). Where is the possibility of hope in such a landscape when a better tomorrow seems far less certain than it was only yesterday?

It is the biopolitics of life in this period following the collapse of Japan, Inc., that I am interested in here. This means the question is one of not only "life" but of life in what sense, for whom, according to what standard, and with what consequences for those who both make it and don't. Do calls to raise the standard of living include foreign migrants, for example; what assistance is available for those in need and how—and for whom—does this get defined, ascertained, and dispensed; what is the relationship (of any of the above) to the state, capital, and collectivities? In an era where energies and anxieties congeal around survival, there are signs of both a collapsed futurity and a desertion of sociality into loneliness: "a profound dynamic of decollectivization, reindividualization, and insecuritization" (Castel 2003, 43). Yet despite, and alongside, this uncertainty is something else. My suspicion—perhaps desire—is that germinating in Japan today are seeds of what the Italian autonomist Franco "Bifo" Berardi (2009) has called the "soul at work" (what I turn to, as a continuation of this chapter, in the next chapter). When humans lose the ability, or opportunity, to be human—living under conditions too ragged to nourish enjoyment or compassion toward (or from) other humans—the soul slips into depression. But when circumstances are such to engender a collective depression—when, as Berardi says of late-stage capitalism, energy is frenetically fixated on the extraction and abstraction of labor into a thingification that can never satisfy and when, under restructuring and deregulation, even jobs and everyday security (and connections with other humans) get threatened for ever more of the population—the deadening of life that occurs may also be, or inspire, a call for social revolution or, at least, a call, a demand, for a reconfiguration of the social, "a social otherwise" (Povinelli 2011, 16). It could be an unwillingness to die, a demand to live (better), an insistence that society must change: "the soul on strike" (Berardi 2009, x). The soul working out its pain to build new "social zones of human resistance" (220) and "extra-economic networks of survival" (219) where the soul can be soulful again.

Is there any evidence that the soul is on strike in Japan today?

Suicide

On a warm night in June 2008, I went with my research assistant to a live house in what is known as the seedy sex district (Kabuki-chō) in Shinjuku, Tokyo. In the basement of a seven-floor building, we find Loft+One: a place well known for its subcultural rock scene in the 1980s and, these days, for an array of edgy events from sm demonstrations to discussions of socialist literature. In what is a series of talking events ("talks live house"), tonight's theme is the prevention of the latest suicide trend: hydrogen sulfide suicide (*ryūka suiso jisatsu*). Apparently so common at the time to be a daily occurrence, news of it spread through a net posting of instructions on how to assemble the ingredients from two household detergents that are available anywhere. Besides being easy and cheap to concoct, ryūka suiso jisatsu is known to be a relatively quick and painless way to die. A downside however is its toxicity; anyone who walks into a room after it has been used is at risk of death themselves. As my research assistant points out, suicide goes through trends just like everything else in Japan. Last year it was charcoal. And still popular is the fad of going online to meet partners with whom to die together—a suicide dateline (*deai*) or what Ozawa-de-Silva calls "shared death" (2010). Here, as I soon learn, the aim is quite different: to share stories of near-death experiences as a means of assisting each other in not dying but trying to stay alive.

Tonight's event is called "STOP ryūka suiso jisatsu!" and, after paying 1,500 yen (US$16) plus 500 yen (US$5.30) for two drinks, about seventy of us gather inside. Sipping our beers, we sit on chairs that have been set up in the middle of what is a dark but cozy space lined by sofas, a bar, and manga library. Right on time, the moderator, a young man in his mid-thirties, walks onto the stage and introduces two of the performers with whom he starts bantering. These are Tsukino Kōji, a man in his mid-forties who usually performs in pajamas but tonight is wearing jeans and a shirt, and Kacco, a male in his mid-thirties wearing a red gingham dress. After describing the format for the evening, the moderator invites the rest of the participants onto the stage. Things start off by him asking each of the five guests, all *tōjisha* (those with the experience of, in this case, attempting suicide) essentially the same four questions: Under what circumstances did you feel like dying, have you ever felt like killing someone, what helped you get through these hard times, and what message do you have for people who are *tsurai* (having hardship)? The circumstances of each is different. Kacco, for example, describes how, because he always wanted to be a girl, school was difficult, making him want to kill everyone. In middle school he got pierced and had a "yankee" period (becoming part of a *bōsōzoku*, motorcycle gang, when a teenager). For five years he was also a *hikikomori* (socially withdrawn into his room, never leaving for job or anything else) and his message to the audience is, "it's okay to run away. Get out [of whatever, wherever] in order to survive."

Aiko, a soft-looking woman in her early twenties, recounts a history of domestic violence and years spent dreading school because she had a hard time interacting with people and couldn't, almost literally, speak. Eventually the men in her household left or died and life is better today. Her message is: "You can always fix things [*yarinaosu*], so don't give up!" Shirai, a forty-six-year-old man, tells of living at home until the age of thirty-three with a father who got drunk every night. Fixated on sex but unable to connect with women (and still a virgin), he was enraged every time he saw couples on the train. Still working on his addictions to alcohol and sex, his message is to "disconnect from bad living environments and learn to care for yourself, and others." Amamiya Karin, the social activist and author in her mid-thirties who is dressed in goth, describes how she was bullied (*ijime*) as a middle-school student, which continued through high school when she started cutting herself. Desperately lonely (*kodoku*) and deeply depressed, she was too distracted to perform well on entrance exams, so she became a *furītā* (irregular worker) instead of going to university. This was the worst period of her life; treated as "disposable labor," she was repeatedly fired and never secure when it came to a job, money, or life itself. At age twenty-one she eventually discovered that she wasn't alone in her *ikizurasa* (pain or hardship in life), which is the single most important thing that ever happened to her. Her message to the audience: "You are not alone. You are not a freak. You're okay, and we're here with you."

Tsukino Kōji, a performer, author of three books, host of an all-night radio show for hikikomori in Niigata, and founder of Kowaremono ("broken people," a performance group where each member self-identifies as having a handicap), relates a long life of being tōjisha: struggling in school, dropping out, becoming an alcoholic, cutting himself, living as a hikikomori at home, overdosing and almost dying (multiple times). After joining a support group during one detox stay at the hospital, he stuck with it and is still sober twenty years later. Tsukino, like all the guests except for Amamiya, also delivers a performance (while Aiko sings and Shirai reads poetry, Kacco and Tsukino perform spoken word). And it is here, in detailing the dynamics of a difficult relationship with a father who has just passed away—a highly successful *sararīman* who, pushing his son to achieve, continually berated him for failing to do so—that Tsukino's message to the audience is the strongest. Indeed, he bellows it out, shouting it over and over like a mantra: "*shinanai, korosanai, ikitai!* SHINANAI, KOROSANAI, IKITAI!" (I won't die, I won't kill, I want to live!). Then turning this to the audience: DON'T YOU DIE, DON'T YOU KILL, DESIRE TO LIVE! Cutting the air with soundwaves that strike—and keep striking—a nerve, the performance is stunning. Speaking at once to his father and to us—of wanting to die, to kill, but now to live—it is as if Tsukino is giving voice to his soul.

The soul on strike that strikes through affect. The whole night, at three hours plus, is deeply affecting. And it continues to be when, after the interviews and performances, there is a question and answer period. One woman, now aged twenty-five who worked one year at nineteen but has not been in education, employment, or training (NEET) ever since, asks how to go about finding a job. A number want to discuss the recent killings in Akihabara, where a twenty-five-year-old Japanese male, irregularly employed with strained family relations and no friends, drove a rented van into a crowded crossing and jumped out to stab more victims.[5] One asks why the perpetrator didn't target the business or government district (like Kamiyachō) instead of Akihabara, associated more with irregular workers and *otaku* (techno nerds) like himself. A couple questions are about familial relations: shouldn't parents praise children more and is it okay to still rely on parents (*amaeru*) even as adults? The final question is by a woman who, standing up at the back, identifies herself as a hikikomori who constantly feels like killing herself. Until tonight, she hadn't left home for a year and says the evening's event was helpful. But, breaking into tears, she wonders how she can keep going. How is she going to stay alive in the face of this throbbing urge to die? At this Amamiya thanks her for coming out tonight and praises the courage this took. Telling her how brave she is, Amamiya also reminds her that she no longer is alone. "You can email me anytime." Then she urges the woman to keep living. "Please, try to stay alive just a little longer. Stay alive. For us."

I am struck by the power of the event. Precarity from below; an effort to generate life for, and from, those who come here to share the condition of psychic teetering on the edge. Suicide is a national problem; the rate escalated in 1998 (to about 33,000 suicides a year where it has remained for over a decade) and the highest (and fastest growing) demographics are men in their forties and fifties and young people (for whom, those between the ages of fifteen and twenty-four, it's the leading cause of death). The precarity of the times is both reflected and implicated in this trend; 60 percent of those who commit suicide are jobless. When I return in 2010, I notice even more stories about suicide in the news, more subway stations with track protection (meant to prevent people from jumping), and reports about the new measures the government (alongside those by private businesses, local prefectures, NPOs, and individuals) are taking to stop suicide. A symptom of a depressed nation-state; a depression that people, and the state, are just beginning to talk about. How different things were in 1993 when, at age twenty-eight, Tsurumi Wataru published his manual of suicide techniques (*Kanzen jisatsu manyuaru* [The Complete Manual of Suicide]). Society didn't recognize suicide then at all, he tells me when I interview him in summer 2010.

> For example, at my own university, among the "new left" of which I was a part—those involved in the antinuclear arms and antiwar movements—we thought only about other problems far away. But no one was willing to address our own lives, our struggles [*ikiteru kibishisa*], what we were having trouble with [*nayanderu*]—such as having a hard time going to school or in our relations with other people [*ningenkankei*]. The small things in life that are hard [tsurai] for us. Of course, there are these major problems—of war, the economy—we need to face. But for people contemplating suicide, where does one turn? How does one put this? These are problems of the heart [*kokoro no mondai*]—going to school, being picked on—these too are matters of human rights just like those of being discriminated against as a minority or a woman. So, my intention with the book was to liberate this contingency in Japan. (Personal interview, July 2010)

The book catalogues multiple methods of suicide: drowning, freezing, carbon monoxide poisoning, car collision, hanging, wrist slashing. Each entry gives explicit directions for carrying it out alongside details assessing relative pain, efficiency, and speed of death. *Kanzen jisatsu manyuaru* sold over a million copies. It also generated controversy when copies of the book were found alongside the bodies of several suicide victims (including a number of middle-school students).[6] The controversy was painful, Tsurumi admits, for his aim had been not to promote suicide as much as to "calm people in giving them the knowledge that they have a choice." In his own case, Tsurumi had endured years of solitary suffering, crippled in his isolation from others and sense that he was pathologically unique. In writing the book he intended to give voice and legibility to an experience of "life pain" (*ikizurasa*) accorded little recognition in Japan at least at the time. It does this in the form of a methodology for death. A manual for killing oneself that could also serve as a tactic for life. A young man I know in the United States who spent his high school years severely depressed, basically alone, and immersed in Japanese anime and manga told me that reading Tsurumi's suicide manual in English provided him a source of great comfort. For, as desperate as he felt in his everyday skin, the knowledge of an exit strategy and of others sharing similar experiences—around which he sometimes bonded online with the only "friends" he had, some of whom eventually committed suicide—provided a link, of sorts, to life. This young man, now in his early twenties, is alive and thriving in a center of recovering addicts.

Communication, if not precisely community, of pain is what the "stop suicide" event generated as well. It promoted a stepping (if only a step) away from what Robert Desjarlais, in his ethnography of the homeless in Boston, describes as the "social and linguistic isolation" of, in this case, street dwellers: "Since dwelling on the street could mean months of living on the margins of language, communication, and sociability, some found it difficult to return to living 'inside.' A person's very nature changed, particularly one's capacity for communicating with others. The longer people lived on the streets, the less they lived as social beings" (Desjarlais 1997, 122). But, after living on the margins of sociability, how does one reconnect with anyone else? From her work as an attendant in a detox center for heroin addiction, the anthropologist Angela Garcia notes the constant "ache" of her patients and the "ache" elicited in her watching and attending to them: an orchestra of aching through the long nights she's on graveyard duty that, while experienced collectively, stops short of being shared. One can only move (so far or so fast) toward others when gripped by life pains of particular kinds. One undergoes detoxification "entirely alone," Garcia writes. And yet, "besides the evidence of dislocated humanness and detached sociality," there were also those moments, those gestures, those touches, of rupture and "shared singularity." Seeking an ethics of healing across incommensurability, these are the occasions when Garcia can "imagine the possibility of a new kind of care" (2010, 51). This description—of shared singularity around pain—fits the account of the young American man reading Tsurumi's suicide manual who then tried to give "care" to the new online friends he met struggling to live. It also captures the "stop suicide" event at Loft+One.

Immediately after the first manual was published, Tsurumi tells me he retreated from the public eye. But the next year he wrote a second edition (*Bokutachi no kanzen jisatsu manyuaru*, 1994) that he describes as more about "matters of the heart" and how to live without committing suicide. The book was also made into a film, *Jisatsu manyuaru*, in 2003. When I ask Tsurumi what he thinks about the "stop suicide" event I attended at Loft+One, he suggests that his book may have been the inspiration. There was nothing like this before his book came out and such events have steadily increased ever since. And after giving Amamiya a copy of *Kanzen jisatsu manyuaru*, Tsurumi has been invited to speak at a few "stop suicide" events himself. Reacting to the performance of Tsukino Kōji, which he has also seen, Tsurumi calls it powerful: "When someone with experience (tō-jisha) shares his heart's weakness and tears with the audience, this is far more effective than simply being lectured and told to hang in there [*gan-baru*] by officials." The event and performances are a theater of the soul, a theater for the soul to be healed, rejuvenated, collectively restitched. In this (and perhaps only this), Tsurumi sees a glimmer of hope for Japan's future.

ALLISON: What do you think Japan's future will be?

TSURUMI: I think the level of despair [*zetsubō*] about the future will increase. We're no longer a society that can rely on the corporation; the family is falling apart; individuals are more on their own, making connections through the Internet. . . . Somehow we'll have to figure out how to get along. We have no other choice.

ALLISON: Do you have any hope?

TSURUMI: Well, I had no hope [*kibō*] until I was in high school, and then I entered what was the worst period of my whole life. It felt like nothing would ever change or get better. But just in the last half year, things are opening up. Social movements are starting, people are beginning to talk more, there is something happening.

Throwing Up Frustration

Later in the same summer, on a day when the air is at its steamiest in Tokyo, I interview Yuasa Makoto—the codirector of the NPO Moyai, author of *Hanhinkon* (Reverse Poverty), co-founder (along with others, including Amamiya Karin) of the *Hanhinkon netto wāku* (Reverse Poverty Network), and one of the leading figures in activism for precarious workers, dispatch workers, the homeless, and working poor. As described in chapter 3, I have seen Yuasa often this summer of 2008—talking at anti-G-8 events in June, twice at Moyai, where I have gone to observe, and at a host of symposia and talks I've attended—one at the Buddhist temple on war and labor, another at a university on poverty and youth, and the last at a citizen's meeting just today giving the keynote on social difference (*kakusa*, the new word for class) and solidarity (*kakusa to rentai*). Politically savvy and razor-sharp smart, Yuasa dropped out of Tokyo University in 1995 where he was a graduate student in political theory to do local activism for Iranian migrants and homeless men around Shibuya, and he has expanded his activism ever since. He is thirty-nine when I meet him in 2008 and by 2009—after masterminding *Toshikoshi haken mura*,[7] where hundreds of homeless and temporary workers camped out in Hibiya Park at New Year's and, tended to by volunteer groups and engineered as a spectacular news event, the government was incited to come through in the end with more permanent assistance, housing, and jobs—he was given his own cabinet position by the Hatoyama administration.[8]

In our interview we talk about the state of life in Japan these days: what Yuasa has described elsewhere as the "refugeeization" (*nanminka*) of the country. A reference to the rise of net café refugees (see chapter 3), Yuasa considers this to be not only the "new face" of Japan's poor but a troubling sign of the country's inability to guarantee a "reasonable" life, as the constitution mandates, for (all) its citizens.[9] Like Tsurumi did with suicide, Yuasa's agenda is to give face and voice to a social problem too little recognized in the society at large. It is a travesty that Japan is the second poorest country in the Organisation for Economic Co-operation and Development (OECD), 14.5 percent children are now growing up poor, 70 percent of homeless have no jobs—and this in a country that, despite its troubles, still retains the third strongest economy in the world. As Yuasa keeps reiterating wherever he goes, these statistics, and the people behind them, are not the mere exception, "they are us." A Japan that, by abiding the bare lives of too many of its people, is no longer "home" to enough. Japan in exile from itself. Japan refugeed from its soul. This is Yuasa's work, and he is tireless in pursuing it: making poverty visible in Japan and trying to remake the country through structural reform, grassroots activism, and face-to-face volunteerism with people in need. His speaking engagements alone are extensive, he has now authored or coauthored racks of publications, he still co-runs both the national *Hanhinkon netto wāku* and Moyai (where I have seen him counsel drop-ins for hours on, among other things, how to apply for welfare using a manual on the subject he has written himself), and—when I attend another "stop suicide event" the summer of 2010—Yuasa, even as a cabinet member, is the first speaker (detailing statistics about poverty and resources on where people can go for support of various kinds).[10]

As he stresses to me the day I interview him, poverty is not merely an economic situation; for that, the word is *binbō* (poor). But *hinkon* means poverty in a deeper sense. Not just a lack of money, but the "emotional" (*seishintekina*) sense of deprivation that comes, for example, from not having a support system of family and friends and being stranded from human relationships (*ningenkankei*). Under "corporate society" (*kigyō shakai*), people were tied into a network of relationships—the company, the family, school—that anchored their place in society and provided welfare if also extracting duty, conformity, and hard work. But that family-corporate system has broken down (*kowareta*) under the deregulation and restructuring of neoliberalist reforms in the 1990s. Corporations no longer provide (much) lifelong employment, and the family has not "been adaptive to the times." And, given that Japan isn't, nor ever was, a welfare state (*fukushi kokka*), the collapse of what once served as people's "safety net" means the desertion of "human resources." A desert in humanity itself. The word he uses is *tame*, which he is careful to point out doesn't literally mean resources though this is how it's translated into English. Financially, tame is something one saves. Less a resource that is used (or used up) as much as a cushion, a reserve, a reservoir (*tameike*) for the future or hard times. "Tame is not a condition (*jōken*), but energy," Yuasa stresses. Potential is what he seems to mean. Potential for living and for staying alive, whether this is savings in the bank, academic credentials, or the social and personal tame of human resources. (A "sociology of potentiality in which potentiality is always embodied in specific social worlds" [Povinelli 2011, 14].) This is what he stresses the day I speak with him: the support of family and friends in times of need but also the self-confidence and psychic stamina to survive hard times. And, without this, broken potential. People living on the edge, lacking backup, energy zapped.

As a public speaker and writer, Yuasa fills his politics and activism with the fleshy details of real-life cases. He is brilliant in dissecting, in clean, comprehensible terms, the structural conditions of precarity—in policies, practices, and regulations involving everything from labor and welfare to taxes and housing. But Yuasa is also a storyteller whose stories, much like those I heard at the "stop suicide" event, graphically disturb (as I've earlier described, in chapter 3). Anatomizing the despair he knows deeply and close up, these are stories of a jobless man who has lost his family and now the means to stay at a net café; of a mentally handicapped woman who was denied welfare and lives on the streets; of a middle-aged man, the sole caretaker of his elderly mother, who killed himself and his mother when he couldn't take it anymore; of a worker, who after working for decades, died all alone in his apartment craving a rice ball he couldn't afford.

Yuasa adopts here an epistemology of affect: wanting his readers and audiences to know poverty by feeling the pain of those experiencing it. Putting a "finger in the wound" to make us at once more intimate and more complicit with the pain.[11] His is not a politics of hope, as Yuasa clarifies when I ask him about the word in our interview. We've been discussing the case of Katō Tomohiro: the perpetrator of the Akihabara rampage in June that left seven dead and triggered a slew of copycat attacks in Tokyo throughout the summer. Many Japanese, and particularly young people, share circumstances similar to Katō's, Yuasa stresses: contingently employed, detached from social networks, dismissed as human waste. And, like Katō, their sense of being in the world is not only existentially precarious but socially dead: a deathliness that can easily turn violent. But far more common, according to Yuasa, is turning this violence inward—as in suicide, cutting, or withdrawal. Still precarious sociality is a state that endangers not only the person himself but everyone. For it represents less a virus that is spreading than an implosion of the spirit (*seishintekina tame*) in the population at large. "Behind this incident," Yuasa says, "are the cases of many workers who give up hope for a better life, who don't fight for better conditions. These are workers who don't say 'no.' This can't be considered a good thing. Hurting others isn't good either, of course, but how many people and workers are living like this in Japan today? Hundreds of thousands." No, when I ask, Yuasa doesn't see much in the way of hope on the horizon. But what he does see is a scratching at the wound, the beginning of what he calls venting—*hakidashi*, a word that also means throwing up.

> I'm not sure if there is hope [*kibō*]. But in this last year, at the very least, more people have vented [*hakidasu*] their frustration toward the society outside [*soto*]. And from this venting alone, people have started healing. These hurts [*kizu*] that people feel inside and give to others, this is a social problem. Amamiya Karin is a good example of someone who, hurting inside, wounded herself [Amamiya often tells her personal story of years spent cutting her wrists when she was bullied at school and a furītā]. But she has stopped and has started speaking out. People like this with such experience are in-

creasing and, in that, I see the start of something that could become hope in Japan.

As I listen to Yuasa I am reminded of what the sociologist Miyamoto Michiko told me earlier in the summer when we were talking about the same subject—precarity, youth, and the state of life in Japan. Youths are "de-social" today. And not only do they not actively participate in society, more and more (60 percent was the figure of Tokyoites she'd cited from a survey the year before) report experiencing the sensation, if not actual state, of being hikikomori. Social withdrawal as ordinary affect (Stewart 2007). An affect that, if common, is shared alone.

That something is dead and needs to be brought back to life in those feeling the deadest, Miyamoto and Yuasa are in agreement. There is something corporeal, socially corporeal, in this call to both survival and politics. People need to live and to feel alive, and rekindling both means a new kind of future for Japan.

Sensing a New Everyday

My friend is having a house party. Four of us sit at her table and, over homemade dumplings and chilled sake, the conversation drifts to my research. What this is, Sachiko tells the others, is basically "life—you know, hikikomori, young people, homelessness, family." At this, she starts up on something that has been annoying her of late: the rise of Chinese in Japan. Not only are more and more coming as tourists (and just this summer, the restrictions against granting visa cards to Chinese have been liberalized to encourage even more), and the economy is depending more and more on Chinese investments (such as Laox, the biggest electronics store in Akihabara that a Chinese firm bought out three years ago), but—and this is the real crux—"the Chinese have something the Japanese have lost. They have *yaruki* [the will to do something]." Like many middle-aged Japanese raised in the baby boomer generation (*dankai*) following the war when, as Murakami Ryū has put it, no one had anything but hope (and, by implication, the drive to work hard), Sachiko tends to blame the younger generation for Japan's downturn these days. Despite all the political and economic reasons involved about which she is very knowledgeable, there is a spiritual void (as in void in character and fortitude) in the country that concerns her more than anything else. While this occurs in adults too, it is particularly worrisome in youths who show, as she sees it, a wimpiness of the will.

The term Sachiko uses is *resource* (*shigen*), as in the productive capacity of human labor to generate economic growth. The emphasis is strikingly different from the word *tame* employed by Yuasa to denote the capacity, including that of human relations, that one draws upon to survive and sustain life. Both terms, as heard in public discourse these days, reference loss. To Sachiko, Japan is losing its most precious resource, the drive of its people that has driven national growth. That, poor in natural resources, Japan must rely on the hard work of its population to fuel its economy is a truism I have heard ever since first coming to the country in the late 1970s. Rice agriculture, with its backbreaking labor and demand for group effort, stands as the iconic example with its history going back over two thousand years. But youths no longer feel driven as they once did, according to Sachiko, and for this she blames a laxness in the schools. Once it was the school system and its principles of academic credentializing (*gakureki shakai*) that undergirded Japan's enterprise society—the era of its high economic growth globally recognized as a "miracle economy" by "Japan as number one." What schools one attended as a child became the currency of one's social and economic capital as an adult. This is a system that some say is even more intense today given the scarcity of "seats at the table," as one interviewee described the difficulty in landing regular employment now. But, as Sachiko tells the story, something in the system has lost its edge, or at least the edge it once bred in those going through its hurdles. This started with changes implemented to make the curriculum looser, broadly referred to as "loose education" (*yutori kyōiku*) (for which Sachiko largely blames the leftist teacher's union). But even after this new structure was abandoned and the old one—the so-called competitive education (*kyōsō kyōiku*)—readopted, children are not being sufficiently channeled to compete and work hard. Few will sacrifice to be the best they can be, as Sachiko puts it: "Youth today, they're fine with however they turn out. Do you know that over 50 percent don't care how much money they earn? I mean, okay, they don't all have to strive to be number one. But everyone needs a goal that they're willing to give up everything for, whether that is looks, academics. How can you settle for just being anyone?"

At this point I turn to Tanaka, sitting next to me, whom Sachiko has introduced as a former high-ranking employee at a big IT firm who quit and now delves in chocolate making as a hobby. Is she an example, or counterexample, of the highly driven Japanese Sachiko prizes so highly? I ask about her job. It was prestigious, she admits, but the work was ceaseless: "As soon as one project ended, the next had already begun. I got home after midnight every night and the only time I saw my husband—who worked as hard as I did at his own job—was on Sunday." For twelve years she worked like this. Then her husband had a heart attack. Though she obviously thought about it—long and hard, she stresses—Tanaka decided to quit. For a while she tended to her husband. Then he improved and went back to work. She, however, stayed at home. The tempo and flavor of her life now vastly differs, working as she does part-time as a consultant from home. She is forty-two. Doesn't she miss her job, I ask her: "Not for one second. I worked there for twelve years but that was my entire life. After I quit, we got a cat, Mikan. The joy I experience with her is indescribable. I stay at home, playing with Mikan, listening to music, making chocolate. Every night I cook now for my husband; he's slowed down as well and returns home every night by seven so we eat together. This is a good life, a life I never had before. I regret that my husband got ill but, frankly, it was a good opportunity for us."

In telling her story, Tanaka lingers over the details of its present presence (Lefebvre 2004). It is deeply corporeal: the chocolate she kneads with her hands, the cat's fur brushed with fingers instead of a comb, the music that singes the air as she cooks. This is evidence of a life she (now) loves, a corporeality that has (re)animated her marriage and home and also her network of social relationships. It is from a blog she posted on chocolate that Sachiko made contact with her in the first place. Sharing recipes, they became friends three years ago: a friendship that Sachiko calls her newest in a social milieu where the making of (new) friends is notoriously tough. And, when we leave at the end of the night together, Tanaka tells me that this is the first house party she's been to in years. By her own account (but the term I give to it), she has radically undergone reterritorialization. The way she senses, and inhabits, the world. Someone who lived for work and worked in the immaterial labor of information technology, she was a member of what Berardi calls the cognitariat: workers in the cognitive industry of producing "semiocapital," whose very labor demands a "removal of their own social corporeality." Members of the cognitariat "can isolate themselves in a pressurized and hyperconnected capsule. They are physically removed from other human beings (whose existence becomes a factor of insecurity)" (Berardi 2009, 104). In the case of Tanaka, it would seem not merely the kind of abstract work she did but the abstraction of human she became as worker—one project endlessly looping into the next—that numbed her. A life that, when she looks back on it now, was no "life" at all.

According to Berardi, it is not just those doing cognitive labor, but all those bred by the competitiveness and abstractions of late-stage capitalism who are at risk for what he sees as the two psycho-pathologies of our times, panic and depression: "As an effect of capitalist development, industrial labor loses any relation to the concrete character of activity, becoming purely rented out time, objectified in products whose concrete and useful quality does not have any interest other than that of enabling the exchange and the accumulation of plus-value" (2009, 60). Wealth becomes the measure of value: a "projection of time aimed at gaining power through acquisition and consumption" (81). Over time, and in everyday life, there has also been what Berardi calls a "generalized loss of solidarity" (80). Fixated on performing, producing, and accumulating, people have little time for anything (or anyone) else. Things are sped up, but a sense of accomplishment eludes us. And, in the neoliberal turn with competition ratcheted even higher, more and more feel doomed to the rank of loser: "The social context is a competitive society where all energies are mobilized in order to prevail on the other. Survival is no longer based on reaching a position of sufficient preparation and abilities, but it is constantly questioned: if one does not win, one can be eliminated, in a few days, or a few months" (101). As elsewhere, the levels of stress have skyrocketed in Japan today where people panic over being able to manage or make it. Depression is on the rise as well. There is a smothering of a sense of possibility (*tame*) and futurity in lives spent teetering on the edge of failure and sometimes sociality as well. More than anything, in Berardi's view, depression excretes one's investment of energy. Once someone can no longer sustain the tension of competition—either because they haven't made it or are unwilling to compete any longer—energy in and for life retreats. Demotivation occurs, a "zero degree of the exchange relations between the conscious organism and the world" (102). Potential is broken, energy is zapped, as is the draining of those reserves (*tame*), including reserves in the self, that provide the wherewithal to keep going.

Might not "demotivation" be what Sachiko sees as an ebbing in the competitive edge of Japanese youths today? Is it a matter of youths competing less (well) or of a change in the conditions of competition in an era where even the "proper" academic credentials no longer guarantee a secure future or job and where doing anything else is considered a failure? The futility, and brutality, of the stakes these days has become a familiar theme in pop culture, particularly in that targeted at youth. In the blockbuster hit of 2000, for example, Japan's competitive society showcases as a dystopic inferno: one that, quite literally, is killing youth. *Battle Royale*, a sensationally violent film based on a novel by Takami Kōshun and directed by Fukasaku Kinji, inspired a manga, video game series, and sequel in 2003. The story takes place on a deserted island where, in an annual ritual mandated by the government, a class of ninth graders is forced into a three-day competition of survival; in its logic of kill or be killed, only one student will be left standing at the end. In this arena, ensured to reward savagery and self-interest, the players become killers, resorting to whatever polymorphously perverse violence they can come up with to keep living at the expense of someone else. Slicing, hacking, dismembering, pounding; death after death in this thrillingly horrific rat race of Japanese school kids competing to win "battle royale" (the prize being their own life).

To survive here means thinking of no one but oneself and treating friends as deadly enemies. In *Battle Royale* life becomes precarious as does humanity. The politics of survival played on the terrain of the (no-longer) human. As Talal Asad writes about suicide bombing, what makes it so horrific (and much more so to Westerners than the conventional warfare that kills vast numbers more) is the "unbearable intimacy" (2007, 66) with which bodies and warfare collide. When a man dressed in jeans explodes on an ordinary bus in the middle of the day, the bus ride turns into a warzone, his body into a weapon, and the passengers into military targets. No zone is excepted, and no one is safe from anyone else. Borrowing from Stanley Cavell, Asad argues that horror is the "loss of that ordinariness in which human identity resides" (71). In *Battle Royale* it is the state that turns the school into a competitive bloodbath that strips kids of that ordinariness in which human identity resides. The battle of competition (*kyōsō shakai*) that makes middle school a warzone and ordinary school kids killers or the killed.

What Kind of Life Is a Good Life?

In interviews I did with eight undergraduates at a high ranking Japanese university in the summer of 2010, I asked them what kind of life they considered to be a good life. They answered with life goals that struck me as surprisingly balanced and modest. Six had already passed through *shū-katsu*: the employment market of finding jobs that has so intensified and sped up that it now starts, and consumes the bulk of, one's junior year. All six had been successful in securing stable jobs that they would commence as *seishain* (regular, lifelong workers) upon graduation. Yet when asked what they envisioned as their ideal life and job course after starting to work, one answered simply "I want enough money to be able to live [*ikiru*]." Another said: "interesting (enough) work, a job that stays secure, marriage and family, time 'for myself' [*jibun*]." Virtually all eight said a version of the same thing; all but one (a woman) was sure they wanted kids, all stressed work environments that would be agreeable (a congenial atmosphere and not too cutthroat), and none mentioned being driven by a high salary or prestigious corporation. Saying they were willing to work hard during the week, most emphasized carving out time at night, and particularly the weekends, for friends, hobbies, and simply themselves. And here, quite pointedly, they (and particularly the males) differentiated themselves from their fathers. As one twenty-one-year-old put it: "I respect my dad and the career he has had. But work consumed him and we, his family, never saw him. And, because he works so hard and has so much pressure on him, he's always grumpy when he is around. This is not what I want to be, and it's not the life I want (for either myself or any kids I will have)" (personal interview June 18, 2010).

As a number point out to me, theirs is the generation of youth that came of age after the collapse of the bubble economy. For them, life expectations have been shaped by the experiences not of "Japan as number one" but of those who have struggled to find jobs or been laid off by restructuring. One mentioned his father's depression and the suicide of a family friend when speaking of the insecurity of business these days. The job market is jittery even for those with elite credentials like theirs. As they know, the bursting of the bubble triggered an economic recession that, after a "glacial hiring freeze" in the 1990s that spurred at least two waves of "lost generations" for those coming of working age, Japan has not emerged from yet. Adding to the anxiety of the job search is the short window young people face in securing the gold standard of regular employment following graduation. If this hasn't been attained within one or two years of being on the job market, the person may well get stuck in the type of irregular employment described in the news article at the start of this chapter. As with the two workers profiled there, jobs such as in convenience stores typically fail to provide a liveable wage. Without benefits, incremental wage increases, or even the assurance of a job the next day, workers can't build lives, or futures, that feel the least bit secure.[12] This specter of job precarity fills the airwaves today. On the very day I wrote this, in fact, there was another article in the newspaper, this one a letter decrying the vast differential in wages between those with regular jobs (seishain) and those working part-time, dispatch, or contract jobs like the author of the article himself. The writer, already sixty-three, says he is not worried about himself. But it is the young people who worry him. Those who, even if they work tirelessly, day after day, can't manage to live a "straight life" (matomo na seikatsu) and "are in constant fear [bikubiku shite] of being fired. . . . If you get treated, and knocked down, like this when young, a person has no dreams of life." And if youth have no life dreams, "Japan has no future" (Asahi Shinbun, July 14, 2010, "Opinion koe," 12).

Potential is another way of calculating labor and life. Eaten up by the mere scramble for jobs that fail to realize one's potential or inspire hope that the future (self) will be different, the precariat are often struck by panic and depression—affective responses that would seem all too appropriate (but are also dismissed, as we've seen, by those precariat who refuse the worldview of regular work altogether and reorient their horizons of expectation away from the past, as well as the future, to a present of, in the case of Furuichi Noritoshi [2011], everyday enjoyment).[13] What of those, however, like these university students who seem on the path of actually being able to secure regular employment—and all the social accouterments this will open up—proclaiming that "just living" defines their aspirations? Does this come from relief at getting a job, depressed drive and ambition, or the scaled-back, reoriented life goals of post-bubble Japan? As I pushed them to elaborate on what they regarded as a "livable life"— not only for themselves as future seishain but also for the irregular workers many said they encountered in part-time jobs—the students stressed life outside, as much as inside, work. For themselves, they saw (much) more to life than work and wealth. And, not wanting to get used (up) by jobs as had their dads, they hoped for an everyday existence with inbuilt reserves for pleasure and people. They wanted social corporeality, time for jazz, said one, time for family and wife, voiced another, time to give care to an aging grandmother and parents should they ever need it, ventured a third.

And what about those stuck in such low-paying jobs who have to work longer hours with less pay and stunted resources for family, caretaking, or jazz? All but one of them didn't read the lives and livelihoods of the working poor or precariat in such bleak terms. (As one put it, "the media plays up the darkness of our times.") Rather, those they worked alongside at konbini (convenience stores), donut shops, and bars struck them as resourceful in having found something (outside jobs) that made life worth living as well. I was told, for example, about a long-term worker at a konbini who had an amazing manga collection he loved and a forty-two-year-old single mom and high school dropout at the donut shop who was excitedly planning (with the help of her coworkers) to return to school.

Oddly, or not perhaps, only one of the eight students I interviewed saw in the current conditions of job precarity and divided society (*kakusa shakai*) an inequity and injustice that they themselves were motivated to do anything about. Not that they were heartless or cold. But compassion—in the sense Berlant (2004) uses it, of feeling moved by an-other in life straits different, and less fortunate, than one's own—was not part of their affective (or social) makeup. Such an attitude seemed to noticeably change in the aftermath of 3/11 when vast numbers of Japanese (and hordes of young people among them) responded to the crisis by volunteering in various shapes and forms, some quite sustained and profound. I speak about this in the last chapter. For now, though, I am writing of the pre-3/11 moment: a moment when the eight undergraduates I interviewed all, except one, discounted the activity of volunteerism as something they would ever do or that was even culturally salient. "We Japanese don't volunteer; it's not part of the tradition," one stated. The group concurred, and another exemplified this by saying that going up to a homeless person on the street and giving him money would feel as shameful to the recipient as to the giver. "It's not done here." Not by them, at least. Giving, connecting to someone outside their zone of social belonging—stretching their notion of "we"—seemed pretty unfathomable to these young people, at least at this moment (pre-3/11).

What I took from the students was a moral common sense (Kleinman 2010) of "self responsibility" (jiko sekinin) that has been much promoted by the government in its swing to neoliberalism under Koizumi. Meaning everyone needs to take care of, and make do for, themselves, the credo could also be read as a refusal to extend sympathy and support to anyone else. This certainly was the message given to three young Japanese who became the targets of national scorn after becoming hostages in Iraq. Having traveled there in connection to the war, the three—two aid workers, one photojournalist, and all of them furītā—were captured by insurgents in April 2004 who demanded that the Japanese government withdraw all 550 of its troops and funds allocated to the U.S. invasion to secure their release. Prime Minister Koizumi refused to negotiate with the insurgents, and an official spokesman denounced the hostages for irresponsibly "causing Japan so much trouble." Just as their beheading appeared imminent, a high-ranking official of the Foreign Ministry scolded the hostages at a press conference, claiming that because they had forsaken the "basic principle of self-responsibility" (*jiko sekinin gensoku*), the government similarly had the right to deny responsibility for them (Driscoll 2007, 181). While the three were eventually released, they returned to a barrage of public scorn at home. Signs saying "you got what you deserved" greeted them at the airport, and the government billed them for their airfare back to Japan. Harassed by hostility and hate mail once back home, the three experienced more trauma in the treatment given to them by fellow Japanese, according to the psychiatrist treating them, than the abduction they'd endured on foreign soil (Driscoll 2007).

Another sign, or symptom, of a care deficit troubling everyday life in precarious Japan: the tendency to feel oneself, and foist onto others, disbelonging (Hage 2003, Appadurai 2006).

Missing Elderly

Despite their ubiquity in a country that is demographically aging (*kōreika*), old people are disappearing in Japan. Or at least that was a lead story in August 2010: the case of the missing elderly. On August 4, the headline in *Asahi Shimbun* read: "Fourteen Elderly, [Status] Unknown," (*Kōreisha fumei 14nin ni*). By the next day, the number had risen to thirty-one nationwide. And by August 6, forty-nine centenarians couldn't be found: "whereabouts unknown" (*shozai wakaranu*), "existence unclear" (*kōreisha fumei*), elderly gone.

August is marked by searing heat and memorialization of the dead. This is the season for Obon, the Buddhist custom of returning to the family grave to honor and rejoin deceased spirits. This makes it (also) a time when Japanese go back to natal homes, often in the countryside, for a short respite from work and hectic lives to gather with families. As things slow down and bygone times get revisited, Obon stirs up an affective cocktail— of nostalgia, anxiety, warmth—around home: what Kore'eda Hirokazu (the director of *Daremo shiranai*, Nobody Knows) brilliantly captures in his film, *Aruitemo aruitemo* (Still Walking, 2008) about the strains of familial longing and (dis)belonging in Obon of post-postwar Japan. It was in this season, of dead spirits and heat, that police investigated the whereabouts of the missing centenarians. What started things off was a would-be birthday greeting. But when local officials visited his home in Adachi ward, Tokyo, on what should have been his 111th birthday, Katō Sogen turned out to be a mummy, dead for almost three decades. A 79-year-old daughter admitted she had kept his body since the late 1970s to pocket the man's monthly pension payments (for which a granddaughter was later charged). In a nation priding itself on having the best longevity in the world (86.4 years old for women; 79.59 years for men) and on keeping fastidious official records on all matters of life and death, the news disturbed people. Local governments responded immediately. Sending out teams of investigators to check on the whereabouts of their own centenarians, they discovered that many, in fact, were missing, unaccountable, or already dead. This was the case with what would have been the oldest resident in Tokyo; the woman (who should have been 113 years old) couldn't be located. The same was true of a woman who, recorded as 125, was listed at an address that, upon inspection, turned out to have been converted into a park in 1981.

In some instances, it was clear that deaths had been willfully concealed so family members could gather pension payments. But, more often, neglect seemed responsible. Neglect in the reporting of death by family members and in sloppy record keeping by the governmental offices assigned this task. And neglect in the treatment of the elderly themselves by a society, and families, who were paying too little attention to the lives, and deaths, of its old people. Often the police learned that families simply didn't know where their elderly had gone or even whether or not they were still alive. In the case of a resident in the Minato district of Tokyo whose records reported him to be 105, the family responded to the phone query, saying that "he left home several years ago. But where he went, we don't know. And whether or not he's alive today, we have no idea" (*Asahi Shimbun*, August 4, 2010, 1). After a month of investigations, the government announced the tally; more than 230,000 centenarians who had been listed as still alive on government records were actually missing and assumed to be dead. But there was one upside to the story. Regarding Japan's claim to the greatest longevity in the world, the government assured the country that this statistic, at least, was still intact.

The case of Japan's "disappearing old people" (*kieta otoshi yori*) rubbed a raw nerve. It was just another sign of Japan's "loss of relationality in family and community alike" (*kazoku ya chiiki to no tsunagari no sōshi-tsu*) (*Asahi Shimbun*, August 6, 2010, 1), as the commentaries decried. Evidence, as NHK took up the story, of Japan's muen shakai: the title of the special it ran in January 2010. Here, in gritty relief, scenes showed the desperate straits of isolated elderly trying to survive bare life alone as well as the cleaning service that comes in to mop up after they've died—throwing everything away, in most cases, because no one is willing to claim it. The remains of a person's life, and that life itself, treated as garbage. On the screen, the number 32,000 kept flashing to indicate how many elderly die alone every year in Japan. Friends sobbed when watching this, they told me. But losing track, or regard for, Japan's elderly isn't just a natural evolution, a new stage in the de-sociality of society. Rather it comes from the calculus given human worth—in what counts and who counts as having a grievable life (Butler 2009)—and the role played by social institutions (like family) in upholding this. For, as observed by Takahashi Hiroshi, a professor at International University of Health and Welfare in Tokyo, this newest phenomenon of the missing elderly demonstrates "a type of abandonment, through disinterest" (*New York Times*, August 15, 2010, 6).

But what does it mean that families become "disinterested" in their elderly? Is disinterest akin to disbelonging: a part that becomes extraneous (as waste) to the entity to which it once belonged? The quality of being needed is "the first and most common use of the word human," Tova Höjdestrand writes in her book on homelessness in postsocialist Russia (2009, 10). The homeless are "needed by nobody"—a Russian expression that signifies worthlessness, the condition of someone or something losing utility that equates with becoming waste and, in the case of a person, no longer human (2). In Russia homelessness is tied quite literally to residence; those without the compulsory registration papers at a permanent address (*pro-piska*) become officially designated as *bomzh*, "without a specific place of residence" (5). But housing, in both the official and conventional sense, is precarious and has been for decades; 2 percent of the population in 1999 lacked a propiska. Without proper papers or a residence, a person becomes excluded from the "moral community" (8). Stigmatized as "purportedly unreliable nonpersons" (9), the homeless get treated as social waste. Citing Zygmunt Baumann (2000), Töjdestrand argues that social waste is a result of modern social design: of creating human "leftovers" because "its resources — including housing — are always distributed to some particular model of society and its members" (3).

Human leftovers get created in Japan too, of course. They do so according to a social design premised on productivity: on tying belonging to the work and place one occupies and the family and roles one assumes in a competitive economy — the family-corporate system ("my-home-ism") much discussed in this book already. In this model of society the moral community is an amalgam of work and family where utility and waste tally according to the social design of each member of the family and corporation in their assigned place (father at work, mother at home, children at school), laboring to be — in Sachiko's articulation of this logic — the "best one can be." Designed according to a model of competitive capitalism, the family serves as social factory, functioning to prop up and (re)produce the labor and skills needed by waged labor in multiple ways: as a distributive mechanism (for extending the "family wage" of the breadwinner), as a privatized machine of social reproduction (that ensures longer working hours and more labor extracted from core, male, workers), and as a disciplinary apparatus (that schools, and extracts, high-fueled competitiveness from its members) (Weeks 2011). In Miranda Joseph's terms, the "community" of family serves as a supplement to capital: "a surplus that completes it, providing the coherence, the continuity, the stability that it cannot provide for itself, although it is already complete" (2002, 2). Supplementary (but instrumental) to capitalism, the family engineers competitive productivity in return — as the bargain is supposed to go — for security and prosperity of daily life.

But as the neoliberal marketplace shifts more to irregular labor and away from the lifelong jobs of the sararīman so tied to the male breadwinner and female caregiver familial model, the logic of the family is in crisis, particularly for those un- and underemployed. If the logic of familial and social value is economic productivity, then those who are un- and underproductive (or extraneous) risk being abandoned as waste, needed by nobody, abandonment "by disinterest," suffering the fate of the missing elderly. In the investigative study that NHK did for its TV special and follow-up volume of *Muen shakai*, it tracked a number of the cases of the 32,000 who die alone every year (*muenshi*). Typically, ties with families — by birth or marriage or both — have been stagnant for years. This was the case of Fujita-san who died relationless at age fifty-five in April 2009 in Fukuyama. Having been raised in a wealthy family that went bankrupt, he inherited nothing and, after his father got sick, the brothers dispersed. He subsequently married as a *yōshi*, thereby assuming his wife's family name, and was gainfully employed in construction and then as a taxi driver for years. But after divorcing, he didn't stay in touch. When later, in his fifties, he lost his job and became sick, Fujita was all alone—the state in which he died (NHK *Muen shakai purojekuto* 2010).

As in many of the cases of muenshi they investigated, the NHK research team discovered that, when the next of kin is contacted by the municipal office, they often refuse to claim the belongings or bodies of the deceased. To the researchers, this "refusal to claim" (*hikitori kyohi*)—belonging as much as belongings—symptomizes the deterioration of family and social connectedness (*tsunagari*) in Japan's relationless society today: "32,000 muenshi. But when we investigated, most of them had families who survived them. But why, despite being relatives and families with blood connections, did they refuse to claim them and let them die relationless? To us, family is the most minimal social unit. Something abnormal has happened [in Japan]" (NHK *Muen shakai purojekuto* 2010, 72). When they tracked down his next of kin, his ex-wife said that she hadn't heard from him for twenty years and his relatives told them that, since he'd changed his family name upon marriage and had never changed it back, Fujita was no longer part of the family registry (*koseki*) and couldn't be buried in the family plot (*haka*). To be alone in life continues then into death. For those "with no place (*ibasho*) in life, it's the same with no place to go (*yukiba*) when dead" (83). Some Buddhist temples accept such human leftovers; often located in the countryside, they are sent the unclaimed dead by municipal offices in the cities. This is true of Takaoka *daihōji*, located in Toyama Prefecture. As its head priest commented on the "*muenbotoke*" (relationless "Buddhas," as the dead are called) to the NHK research team: "This could happen to any of us. But is this ok? To let life have no value like this?" (84). At his temple, the unclaimed ashes go in a special container, what looks like a coin locker.

But there is another destination for the unclaimed dead, as the NHK team discovered in the case of Fujita. This is as corpses "gifted" to science in Japanese public hospitals or research institutions. Fujita wound up at Nīgata Hospital where the officiating doctor told the researchers that, due to a shortage in their supply of medical corpses, the hospital had started turning to municipal offices for unclaimed bodies—always, he reassured them, seeking permission first from any next of kin. Apparently Fujita's brother had signed off in his case (being given the legal right to dispose of a member that the family no longer claimed in any other sense). This became Fujita's endpoint: "*kentai* [gifted corpse] #94" at Nīgata Hospital. A gift, in death, to the state. In the registry, next to the reason for donation, is written "didn't have a survivor."

As "the function" of family changes in twenty-first-century Japan (NHK muen shakai purojekto 2010, 99), so does the capacity to give recognition and care—a duty once assumed by family but increasingly by no one or nothing definitively these days. Without a "blood relation to claim one's body upon death, there is no one to be recognized by as a general rule" (98). This leads to not only missing elderly and relationless dead but also abandoned souls—a pressing issue after 3/11 when thousands of bodies remained missing even months after the triple disaster. But the "refusal to claim" is not just the effect of soulless families abandoning their useless members—the lean and mean model of capitalist efficiency at home. Increasingly, Japanese themselves are choosing to limit (or eliminate) their dependency on others by living alone (currently one-third of the population) and embracing an ethos of self-responsibility (jiko sekinin). Self-reliance, self-independence, self-sustainability—selfness itself is the new credo of post-postwar times. And, along with this, is the desire (or injunction) to not bother anyone else, which seems to circumscribe moral community sometimes to an entity of one. This is what the NHK team uncovered when interviewing a number of the residents living alone (30 percent of the total) in a large *danchi* (housing complex) in Osaka. For 48 percent, their days were spent basically alone, sometimes uneasy (*fuan*)—such as when having no one to help them if they fell down going to the store. But whereas only 12.8 percent lacked kin altogether (and 70 percent had children), only 4 percent answered "yes" to the question of whether they planned to live with family in the future. For those who said "no," the overwhelming reason given was not wanting to bother anyone.

Care as a burden. Burdening others extends to the need for recognition and grief. But the desire—to be recognized by others (when alive) and grieved by loved ones (upon death)—remains all the same. This is the story of *Noriko no shokutaku* (*Noriko's Dinner Table*),[14] a parodic film about the dystopic landscape of relationless Japan where families, disjoined in real life, restage attachment in a fictive, commodified form. In one scene, halfway through the film, an elderly man appears to be dying. Flat in bed and body totally inert, he seems finally gone, which triggers wailings of grief from the distraught family members gathered around. Clutching the bed, shrieking their adieus, and gushing tears, the familial drama lasts a few minutes. Then the old man abruptly jumps up and laughs in glee. Satisfied by the performance, he happily pays the actors their fees before they rush off to perform somewhere else. As if investing in a proxy for the familial grief that won't come when he dies (all alone), the man has purchased the services of a rental family.

Playacting "family" repeats throughout *Noriko's Dinner Table*. Though done for comedic effect in *Noriko's Dinner Table*, renting family is an actual practice in Japan where a family of four, for example, will visit an elderly couple on a Sunday afternoon, sharing a meal, showing off well-behaved kids, and fussing over the old man's bonsai or woman's tea utensils as if the kin, and attachment, was authentic. The act here revolves around gestures of family living out, and standing in for, familial life itself.

A Room of Sickos

It is a different idiom, and age bracket, for human waste I encounter when interviewing members of the Kowaremono: a performance group that, started by Tsukino Kōji (the lead performer for the "stop suicide" event described earlier), literally means "broken people." Each member, ranging in age from their early twenties to their mid-forties, identifies as having one, or more, disabilities — eating disorders, alcoholism, sex addiction, cerebral palsy, panic or anxiety disorders, fear of others, social withdrawal. As tōjisha (someone with firsthand experience) of social, physical, and psychic brokenness, they speak, and perform, their stories on stage. The day I meet them in Nīgata in summer 2010 at the local community center, four are gathered: Kacco, Aiko, Tsukino (these three I had seen earlier at the "stop suicide" event), and Suzuki (not an official member but a social worker and filmmaker who has made a documentary of the Kowaremono; Suzuki appeared in chapter 4). Introducing themselves as all "sick" (*byōki*), they describe what they do on stage as a form of performance (called *saiten*) that doubles as public therapy: metaphorically vomiting (*hakidasu*) the pains they've incurred in life as a tactic for psychic and social survival. (Hakidasu is also the word Yuasa used in reference to disgorging the pain of life and the injustices of the working poor.) Tsukino discusses this from the perspective of being an alcoholic who sees Kowaremono like the support group he attributes to saving his life that he still meets with twenty years after becoming sober:

> TSUKINO: I'm an alcoholic and when I want to drink, I close up inside myself and this happens every single day. So, when I joined a no-drinking support group, well—when that feeling comes over me and I want to die—I share this with them. We laugh, they listen to me, I listen to them. I receive sympathy and can breathe out. This is very effective. I'm alive today because of this. They are my friends [*nakama*]. . . . Doing this on stage is fundamentally the same—it's like therapy. Many in the audience have mental problems. So, it's the same thing: talking, listening, laughing, irony.

> KACCO: Saiten is performing this on stage. Rather than keeping ikizurasa inside; it is a relief to be able to "vomit" it up in front of everyone. And when doing this in front of others who also have their own problems. . . .

> TSUKINO (*interjecting*): It's like being in a room of *chōbyōki* [where everyone is sick, a room of super sickos] [*everyone laughs*].

> KACCO: Well, everyone talks and receives support from one another.

While their injuries are different, Kowaremono share the condition of being "sick": a state that has disabled them, to various degrees, from securing the type of (regular) employment that would provide them an independent livelihood.[15] Of course, as they readily point out to me, they are hardly alone in that regard. Half of all young workers are irregularly employed: a condition they have heard amply about from neighbors and friends working the contract, dispatch, furītā jobs of the precariat, where workers are treated as "disposable humans."[16] This is one variant of waste—workers living on the edge of the labor market where wages are too low and jobs too unstable to guarantee "life security" (*seikatsu hoshō*). As we discuss that day, it is in the name of workers in this condition, the working poor, that Amamiya (a guest member of Kowaremono) has issued the rallying cry, "*ikisasero!*" (let us live). The title of one of her books, ikisasero has become a slogan for activists, community groups, and concerned citizens across the country for calling attention to the plight of the rising tide of Japanese struggling without the life security of regular employment today. As Kacco puts it, Japan remains a "work-like society" (*shigoto teki na shakai*) where work, and the kind of work one performs, remains the currency of value: how people get calibrated as having social worth, which, in turn, converts into the means and reserves to live a safe life (full of hope, futurity, jazz, or kids). Those demanding "to live" (ikisasero) are asking for something both material and ontological: an existence secured by jobs where pay, security, and workload are livable. For, as Kacco continues, echoing Berardi, the anxiety (*fuan*) of daily existence wears people out, producing a nation of wearied Japanese. This is the toll precarity has on peoples' souls—and mental health. As he puts it, ikizurasa is only going to worsen so we'll be seeing a lot more depressed Japanese—what he calls "plus-diseased."

But even apart from all those working outside the ranks of *seishain* (regularly employed) are those not in the workforce at all. The employment rate for handicapped is only 8 percent nationwide and is even lower in Nīgata, Tsukino mentions. And then there are the ranks of NEET and hikikomori: those (mainly if not exclusively) young people who, by the standards of education or job, aren't socially productive at all. Too often such people are hidden, if taken care of, by their families who see in this condition something terribly "strange" (hen): a disease of nonproductivity that marks someone as socially deformed, even dead. But what has incubated this condition if not the family in the first place, Kowaremono muse out loud: an institution that has so one-sidedly fixated on producing and reproducing wealth through work that it has depleted its ability to nurture its members in any other aspect of humanity. *Pus* (*umi*), with its imagery of waste oozing from a wound, is how Kacco portrays the social corporeality of the family and capitalist system he grew up in: "We're living on the debt [we incurred] from the previous generation today [*mae no jidai no tsuke*]. They worked so hard, too hard; this overwork produced pus. These are the times today—times of pus coming out [*umidashino jiki*]. Because this is all they did—worked, worked, worked; so this is what is left over now. Pus. This also means, in terms of social security, we're okay for now. This amount of debt [*tsuke*]—we have this as a remainder." While *pus* refers here to capital—money generated from the ceaseless labor of the hardworking generations of postwar Japanese—it also signals a disease, a wound, something putrifying in the very body that has produced such wealth in the first place. As Kacco uses the word, it becomes something like a floating signifier—referencing money, family, children—that, expected to yield a return, comes up short.

> I was raised in a *gakugyōshakai* [school and business society]. I had a training regime [*kunren*] that was intense; I was pushed to study, study, study. As long as I performed well in school, things were okay. But once I started to deviate just a little—they [parents, teachers] went to the extreme and started treating me incredibly coldly. When I started resisting, they didn't tell me to study. Instead they said—well, if you don't study, this is the kind of salary you'll be stuck with for the rest of your life. This is for your benefit—your life [*seikatsu*]. But is it? Is it the child that the parent is thinking of? Or is it the parent? They're thinking about how they're going to spend their last days when they're old and, for that, they need my salary. They're thinking how prices are going to go up. When parents talk about being anxious [fuan] about the future and wanting to be safe [*antei, anshin*], they're thinking about their own old age and how their oldest son [Kacco is an oldest son] should take responsibility [*sekinin*] for them. And now as the economy has fallen . . . we've all become strangers to one another. Society today is very cold.

According to the accounts that four members of Kowaremono relate to me that day, family caused more wounds than it provided nourishment. This is where they first became broken, or failed to get stitched together, when young. For all but one of them, their mistreatment festered around their failure to academically excel. Poor students, they were hounded to do better and harassed for being inadequate and undeserving of, as one put it, not only parental love but even human recognition. Aiko grew up being told she was *gomi* (garbage); Suzuki that he was a loser; Tsukino that he had failed; Kacco that he was sick. The "sickness" they claim as adults is a condition that, if not entirely caused by their familial situation, was certainly provoked and exacerbated by it. For each, childhood felt painful and the shards of memory they share with me in the Nīgata community center unsettle the air. Hurling his emotions, Kacco shouts at one point, "the family should be nuclear-bombed!" Given the symbolism of nuclear energy even in pre-3/11 Japan, the statement is incendiary and intentionally so. Angry and riled up, Kacco repeats it even louder for affect: "THE JAPANESE FAMILY SHOULD BE NUCLEAR-BOMBED!" The others now respond; clapping their hands and slapping the table, they heartily agree.

But in the laughter that erupts, uneasiness scrapes the edge and the hilarity quickly dies down. For, even in their own storytelling that evening, I have heard how these broken people also rely—in many ways and sometimes, over and over—on families to sustain them. Two of the four still live at home, and all admit they receive financial support. And in his book titled *Ie no naka no hōmuresu* (Homeless Inside of Home) (2004), Tsukino describes his years of alcoholism and the time, when totally down and out after quitting a job in Tokyo, he wired his family in Nīgata to return home on the shinkansen. Had he not had family to help him out, he would have been homeless or dead on the streets. Family saved his life, Tsukino admits, and they harbored his existence for the years he went in and out of the hospital, overdosed and attempted suicide, and became hikikomori.

So what kind of institution is the family in an era when its ties to corporate capitalism, and the nation-state, are collapsing in a residue of pus? Sutured to both welfare and wealth, the family meal and competitive output, it is ambiguously pitched. A resource—for the nation, industry, members themselves—it is also expected to be a cushion: safeguarding those who don't make it, age beyond the system, or need help (and just the basics) in daily existence. In Berardi's (2009) terminology, this is an institution that uses the soul to extract value for competitive capitalism, engineering the kind of drive, hard work, and productive performance that not everyone (as Kowaremono can testify) is equally able or willing to deliver. Not only does this create a tension, a pressure-point that rubs high-level performativity into (and out of) the heart of family life, but it depletes what "my-home" is (also) supposed to be: that something else, in excess, remaining over and beyond this extraction of competitive labor potential that informs the fantasy, at least, of what people are working for in the first place. When Kacco imagines that his parents were thinking of their own future by pushing him to work hard and get a good job, the kind of "secure life" they were envisioning surely involved not only material comfort or social status—the perks of having a well-placed son—but they likely harbored the hope too for some kind of corporeal relationality: visits from grandkids, family gatherings at Obon, perhaps even living together someday with their eldest son, particularly if and when they needed care. But what is the likelihood that Kacco, little nourished as he felt growing up, will nourish such dreams of his parents in old age? And what are we to make of the fact that such gestures of familism and care seem to be at such a deficit across the spectrum and landscape of Japan today?

When one of the "disappeared elderly" shows up as a bunch of broken bones being carted around in the rucksack of the son who was cashing his mother's pension checks, this would seem a sign of disappearance motivated more by (self-)interest than disinterest. The mother died in 2001 at the age of ninety-five. Needing her pension and not having the money for a funeral, the man held onto the body. Three years later, after it had mummified and he was moving residence, the now sixty-four-year-old and unemployed son washed the bones in his *furo* (bath) and put them in his rucksack where he had been carrying them ever since. Meanwhile, Mitsuishi received his mother's old age pension (including a supplementary bonus for centenarians the last three years) (*Asahi Shimbun*, August 21, 2010, 23; August 24, 2010, 22). Oddly, or not perhaps, this story reminds me of another that hit the news three years ago involving an adolescent who toted his mother's decapitated head around with him in a bag. In this case, it was a seventeen-year-old boy who killed his mother after she came to visit him in the apartment where he and a younger brother had been living to attend school. Apparently already troubled and prone to rage, the boy snapped during the night and targeted his mother. After killing her, he cut off her head and, putting it in a bag, carried it with him to an internet café. After chatting online for awhile he went off to a karaoke club and finally to the police station where—still carrying the head—he confessed to the crime.

A mother's head in a bag, a mother's bones in a rucksack; both stories, as reported in the news, are iconic of the "disappearance" of family ties in contemporary Japan. But what precisely is the icon here in the fragmented body and relationship carried, in withered form, by the child? And who or what exactly is responsible for the violence, for carving up a parent's body to render it as life support for oneself, and for removing a mother's head from a family that, in some sense, was de-animated already?[17] Is it the death of, or clinging onto (the trace, fantasy, fragment), a familial relationship that we should read from these stories?

In the case of Mitsuishi, the sixty-four-year-old, he had a motive, other than money, for holding onto his mother's bones. When apprehended by the police, he confessed to concealing his mother's death to cash in on her old age welfare pension. The day he saw her die (June 12, 2001) is clearly recorded in the diary he turned over to the police. But so is the attentiveness he showered upon his mother in the months and days at the end—as she became bedridden, needing to be fed, subsisting on yogurt, finally refusing food and medicine altogether. When the police asked him about the bones, Mitsuishi responded affectively about a mother he stayed close to through these bodily remains and about a relationship he lingered over past death. It was not the severing of a tie—as waste—but something quite different: "I put the bones in the rucksack because I wanted to be next to her until I die [*Hone o ryukkusakku ni irete motte ita. Shinumade issho ni itakatta*]. This way, I was doing a continual *kuyō* [memorial for the dead] (*Asahi Shimbun*, August 24, 2010, 22).

Dead spirits, familial intimacy, pension checks, is the logic—of (dis)-interest—so clear after all?

National Security: Securing the Nation or the People?

As Arthur Kleinman observes, the capacity to tend to those incapable of surviving on their own is essential to humanity.

> Only then . . . through the demanding practice of caregiving do we begin to realize the fullness of our humanity, as well as the limits of our capability to transcend the self and develop the interpersonal moral potential of what it means to be human. . . . It is not just that the reality of concentration camps, killing fields, and the "grey zone" of predatory local worlds tells us that caregiving is fragile and can be negated. In a quieter way, indifference to and, at worst, abandonment of the seriously impaired by family and professionals through denial and avoidance of human needs tells us much the same thing. Caregiving needs to be sustained in the face of such very real threats as poverty, war, stigma, and indifference. (2010, 18)

But who precisely is responsible for caregiving in an era when the family, (once) assigned this responsibility, is losing its capacity to carry it out? I agree with Kleinman that "caregiving needs to be sustained in the face of very real threats" such as economic recession, job irregularization, and indifference. But who or what is going to sustain this: care not just of and by the self ("self-sustainability") but of and for one another (what I have been calling soul)? A sense of insecurity, of not being materially or humanly sustained, unsettles the country as noted by the political scientist Miyamoto Tarō. In his book about the "security of life" (*seikatsu hoshō*)—a term that has become something of a catchword for the times—Miyamoto attributes the lack of it to not only the instability of jobs and depletion of human reserves (tame) but also to a growing suspicion that the market economy, into which the country has given such priority and resources, is coming up short. (This, too, will be one of the reactions to 3/11). Endless public surveys reveal high rates of dissatisfaction and uneasiness in Japan's turn to a "society of unequal distribution." Seeing in this an implicit critique of the status quo, Miyamoto was curious as to what kind of socioeconomic institutions Japanese do want. Posing this as a question in a nationwide survey conducted in 2009, he gave respondents three options: a society like America, a society like former Japan, or a society that prioritizes welfare such as northern European countries. The results were telling: 62 percent answered the latter, a welfare state. Further, in answer to how they would personally feel about expanding citizens' responsibility for social expenditures through taxes or national insurance payments, 54 percent responded that they would be in favor (Miyamoto 2008, 16–17).

It is more at a level of everyday survival that Japanese see, and feel, the issue of national security today, Miyamoto argues. As he points out, security is a concept with multiple rubrics and implications. When used by George W. Bush to launch war against Iraq or by Prime Minister Koizumi to initiate his economic restructuring initiatives, its meaning is intended as the maintenance of public peace and order. Here, security is framed as self-defense against an enemy, whether that is the Taliban or the failure of an economy to rebound (let alone grow). The question here becomes, whose security are we protecting in the name of national interests and against whom or what? But when *security* is used in what Miyamoto claims is the original sense of the word in Latin, the meaning is one more of safe living (*fuan ga nai*): protecting daily life for the people. At the base, living safely is a matter of human (whether personal or collective) survival where the issue becomes survival for whom, in what terms, and at what expense or assistance (by the state and non-state)?

Currently the state does little in the way of ensuring basic survivability for people. Japan ranks low among OECD countries in the percentage of the national budget it spends on social expenditures. In a ranking of thirty countries, Japan was 17th (in 2009) in terms of gross public social expenditures (at 15.9% of its GNP) (OECD Social Spending). But survival, in a very basic sense of guaranteeing life itself to people (Miyamoto's "life guarantee," seikatsu hoshō) is becoming more urgent, as are the demands that it claim more political attention and commitment on the part of the state. This is a global trend, Marc Abélès has noted, arguing that concern over survival marks a transformation in the nature of the political in the twenty-first century.

> The hypothesis that I propose . . . is that the emergence of a new transnational is above all the effect — and not the cause — of an unprecedented transformation in our relationship to the political realm. This relationship is now played out around a representation that puts the preoccupation with living and surviving — what I refer to as survival — at the heart of political action. Moving backward from a tradition that places harmoniously living together (convivance) as the highest aim of social beings, the political field finds itself overrun by a gnawing interrogation concerning the uncertainty and threats that the future possesses. (2010, 15)

In the case of Japan, a preoccupation with living and surviving has indeed moved into the heart of political action. Raising social expenditures to the end of securitizing everyday existence for citizens was a platform endorsed by virtually all the political parties in the campaign season leading up to parliamentary elections on July 11, 2010. It was also on a socially progressive platform — promising initiatives that ranged from job training to raising welfare — that Hatoyama Yukio was able to oust the long-standing LDP with his election to prime minister the year before. While his leadership was soon tarnished by scandal, Hatoyama's short-termed prime ministership signaled a shift in political sensibilities nonetheless. Away from the dominance accorded corporate interests, cronyism, and U.S.-Japan alliance, Hatoyama advocated for more investment, in both money and governmental attention, to issues involving the security of life for average Japanese citizens. As one of the actions taken during his brief stay in office, Hatoyama brought Yuasa Makoto into his cabinet as a consultant for his new committee on emergency relief.

In the usage intended this word by Miyamoto, *seikatsu hoshō* is an umbrella term that encompasses (but delinks) labor and life: the need for stable employment and, the related but separate, need for a secure existence.[18] In an era where employment has become far less stable or assured and even those with steady jobs are not necessarily guaranteed a living wage, work is no longer the mainstay of the social or political order as it was under Japan, Inc. People can no longer depend on a stable workplace — and the social relations formed in connection with such a workplace, including the kind of family it enjoined—to ensure seikatsu hoshō. In the face of encroaching precarity, greater expectations are being placed on not only the individual (under the urgency to be "self-sustaining" and individually responsible) but also the government to help people manage life. But life defined how, for whom, and with what measures—and at what expense—on the part of the government? Two of the biggest issues driving the political campaign for parliamentary elections in June 2010 both involved welfare and life. One was a 10 percent consumption tax proposed by Hatoyama (and taken up by his replacement, Prime Minister Kan Naoto) to pay for increased social expenditures—to cover job-related services such as job training for NEET but also heightened support in such areas as mental illness (measures to curb suicide and depression) and daily assistance for single mothers and the elderly.

The other issue, interestingly enough, involved investing in children— increased state support in the form of a "children's allowance" (kodomo teate)—to help families shoulder the expense of reproduction. Japan has long given financial assistance to parents of young children; I received "milk money" from my local prefecture when my first son was born in Tokyo in 1982, for example. But the proposal, this time, was to significantly raise and extend child payments: to give a monthly payment of 26,000 yen (US$276) for the upkeep of any child not yet graduated from middle school (approximately age fifteen). Before leaving office in June, Hatoyama had already instituted this reform, which was being implemented in a number of prefectures across the country. Covered widely in the news and taken up by each political party in their "manifestoes" (strikingly, the word political parties used to announce their campaign promises) leading up to elections the following month, the issue of child allowances generated heated debate. A huge expense for the prefectures—one of the biggest complaints against it—it also put on center stage not only the problem of Japan's low birthrate but also, as its corrective, state support of the child-reproducing family.

A re-embrace of the principle of reproductive futurism, now with the state allocating even more resources to it, the proposal was explained in public service ads, one of which I saw in Asahi Shimbun on June 10, 2011. Running two-thirds of a page and supported by the cabinet, the Ministry of Science and Education, and the Ministry of Health, Labor, and Welfare, the ad struck me immediately with the placid smile of a newborn linked to the words "our country" and "our future." A smiling bubble, like a toy, in the corner sums up the message: "all of us together, raising children, Japan" (*minna de sodateyō Nippon*). The image of the baby fills the center: yawning, eyes closed, held by a generic anyone. Faceless with checkered shirt, this person holding the baby is less gendered as mother than generalized as Japanese. It could be anyone. It could and should be YOU! Over this couplet—of baby in arms—stand the words "OUR FUTURE" (*mirai tachi*). And, written underneath: "This is a new life. Today we hear the voice of this newborn. This is a new future that starts in an instant. Congratulations. Believing in a future without limits, we move ahead together. Our country is a country that we raise together as a people. With this, and the many dreams we have, we will be first in the world. This is what we want: to be a country that can have pride like this. Japan has entered an era that emanates from all of us. Announcement: to our future" (*Asahi Shimbun*, June 14, 2010, 12).

If "placing one's future in the image of the child" is the cornerstone of a modernist state (Edelman 2004) and "no future" the anxiety of a nation troubled by decline (of babies, of economic growth), then one sees here the attempt to reclaim reproductive futurism: reclaiming the newborn as the potential for a nation whose competitive edge is and should be productivity. Becoming "first in the world" again; a "country that can have pride." But, if the nuclear family served as supplement to capital under the family-corporate system of Japan, Inc., families are now understood to need the help of others: the community of Japan. The rest of the ad contains three short sections laying out ways in which the state, the workplace, and the community can ease the burden of childcare for parents today. In the one on the state, a graph shows Japan near the bottom of the OECD countries in social expenditures devoted to child raising (0.44 percent of Japan's GDP which falls behind Germany, Italy, England, France, and Sweden—the top at 2.17 percent—but above Canada and the United States, which is at the bottom at 0.27 percent), but it lays out its new policy of child allowances (*kodomo teate*) intended to start remedying this. The section on the workplace outlines new policies related to working parents; a working parent of a child under three years old can opt to work only six hours a day, refuse overtime, and be given time off for a sick or injured child. The third section emphasizes the role community residents (*chiiki jūmin*) can take in assisting with childcare—picking up the children of working parents at daycare, for example. At the top of the page, the headline reads: "let's give assistance to child raising all across society" (*shakaizentai de "kosodate" o ōen shite ikō*).

In talking to Japanese, I often heard a similar sentiment: the importance of bearing and raising children to Japan's future but also the limits of a privatized family in shouldering the burden. When asking college students what image they held of Japan's future, one responded the following way: "The image I have of Japan's future [*nihon no shōraizō*] is dark. The birthrate is low and things are only going to get tighter. What can be done? The government needs to help people raise children naturally [*shizentekini*]." Such a view links child raising to not only the family as the social unit to "naturally" bring up children but also to the state that owes families assistance in doing so. In fact, the government has become aggressive in devising and implementing policies to support, and mandate "work and life balance" for working parents. Two recent initiatives, for example, were the Angel Plan in 1994 and the New Angel Plan in 1996 (Kimoto 2008, Roberts 2005).[19] But despite the flurry of attention around the low birthrate (*shōshika*) and the flurry of new faddism around marriage (one of the newest "trends" in the summer of 2009 was *konkatsu*, a commercial "marriage market" along the lines of the job market),[20] the assumption that children represent the life-force most valued—and in need of protection along with resources—is not universally shared.

One woman I interviewed dismissed the low birthrate as of any concern at all. Not seeing this in national(istic) terms—a refreshing change from how this issue is usually framed in Japan—she said that the world is overpopulated as is and not everyone should have children, which includes a lot of young Japanese. In her small shop stocked with the kinds of things she loves (baby clothes, old tea cups, good books) that serves coffee and cake and has an art gallery upstairs, Kawada gave me her worldview: people should live meaningful lives and be independently resourceful. In her case, she lived in the back of a small house she shares with one of two daughters and the parents of her husband who died relatively young eight years ago. In her mid-sixties, she said that her life—of caregiving, supporting local artists, and doing a bit of business—was good. Her shop embodied its name: *Yumeya* (Dream shop). A retreat within the everyday: just what the window with its antique baby shoes and poetry books always signaled to me—two doors down from a pachinko parlor.

In the same neighborhood, Eifukuchō, where I used to live and return to visit whenever I'm back in Tokyo, I had dinner with four middle-aged women who similarly discounted the gravity of Japan's low birthrate. When asked about it, they expressed worry instead about the loneliness and neglect they saw escalating to epidemic proportions in Japan. "The low birthrate? It doesn't worry me in the least," one said. What did was the rising rate of "lonely death" (elderly dying alone) and the incidence of neighbors she dealt with as a volunteer deprived of a pension, health insurance, family to care for them, or even—in a recent case of a man who died—sufficient food.

The evening we had this discussion coincidentally fell on what her neighborhood had just started up as a biweekly "night patrol": volunteers who patrol the neighborhood on the lookout for elderly residents in danger of dying alone. (The concept stumped me, I must admit. How does one look for what is hidden inside?) Deciding to join them, the five of us rushed out in a cab and met up minutes later with the small group just disembarking from a local shrine. Donned in bright yellow jackets, carrying foot-long red flashlights, and all but one over sixty, seven of us set out on our hour-long patrol. Meandering the backstreets and greeting neighbors, the leader told me their agenda was simple: make their presence known and keep an eye out for signs of anything amiss in the residents of the elderly they were watching. The seventy-year-old man added that "this is what the Japanese neighborhood (chiiki) used to be like. No one was alone and we all watched out for one another."

In a word—my word—these night patrols were intended to reterritorialize the neighborhood: give life to the community by preventing death suffered alone. It was national security at the level of the everyday, remaking solitary living and accompanying the lonely into death. A politics, or humanism, of survival—social corporeality reanimated.

SIX. CULTIVATING FIELDS
FROM THE EDGES

MY HOME
A place that we built by giving life to an empty house;
this is a home [*jikka*] where we receive energy and can comfortably give
and receive help from one another. Here we can meet others, eat
a meal with others, talk with others, and also laugh.
— Website for Niigata City *Chiiki no cha no ma*; *uchi no jikka*
(Regional Living Room; My Home)

In the promotional material for Nippon Active Life Club (NALC), the "welfare bank" program where one donates and deposits care time, it is called a "storehouse for the future" (*mirai no kura*). The word *kura* (storehouse) has a specific connotation in Japanese. Referencing the traditional warehouses of sake, silk, or rice merchants, it is a structure that both contains, and protects, something valuable. A resource that converts into wealth. In the case of the NALC, what is stored is caregiving, a service rather than a good, whose future is not for sale on the marketplace but is converted back into care itself. These would seem to be different economies, and currencies, of value. The one encodes capitalism: storing a material (rice, silk) that, exchanged for an abstract currency (money), is used to buy something else in the future—Marx's classic formula of commodity-money-commodity (C-M-C). In NALC, by contrast, what gets stored is the currency it pays out in — caregiving — and the only abstraction is the calculus for quantifying the labor involved: one point for one hour of (undifferentiated) care labor. If capitalism is a system of alienated labor where workers sell their labor, produce commodities whose use values are for others, and live in a social order where wealth is unequally distributed, NALC would seem to represent a post-capitalist system — with a circuit of exchange that could be represented as care-care-care (C-C-C). Use value and exchange value align here. Alienation and inequity are mitigated (if not eliminated altogether). And the system operates on a currency of welfare rather than wealth. Posed as a "storehouse for the future," NALC envisions life in a very different way from that of new birth — and raising children for and as a nation — trumpeted as Japan's future in the public service ad mentioned above.

Time, as explained to me by Takahata-san, the founder of NALC and still the head of its Osaka branch, is the heart of this "time savings system" (*jikan yotaku seido*). One donates time in the form of care as an investment in one's future. But this is not the only temporality at work here. Speaking for himself, Takahata recounted how, in a society where people retire in their sixties and are living twenty years longer, volunteering fills up one's time with an activity at once meaningful and productive.[1] Now aged eighty, Takahata related how busy he was. Rather than sitting home alone, cut off from the social world that, for four decades, he'd been tied to through work, Takahata felt both useful and alive — a far cry from the loneliness and isolation suffered by so many elderly (and other precariat) in Japan today. Staying active in the present then is another form of life insurance in what is labeled, after all, an "active life club." And this was what Takahata seemed more invested in himself. Having donated care at NALC for seventeen years now, he'd accrued a sizable "savings," but he imagined he could well die before spending any of it. The thought pleased him immensely.

Something to do, a place to be at, utility in life (when one has outlasted productivity on the job market) — this is what NALC gives Takahata as volunteer. The rhythms of an everyday life, of being "nearly normal" himself (Berlant 2011). As such, NALC's currency of care serves as an alternative economy in a society where, because productivity is the medium of social value, those beyond (or outside) regular employment get left, or dumped, out, being "needed by nobody." This is how the activist Amamiya Karin describes the exclusion she felt working as a *furīta*. In serial jobs where she could be fired anytime, wages were minimal, and anyone could do the tasks she was assigned, Amamiya became a disposable laborer (Amamiya and Kayano 2008). Yet even more pressing, alongside job insecurity and an unlivable wage, was the sense of disbelonging—of lacking recognition (*shōnin*) from others—that she found the hardest to bear. The experience of being cut off from society and existentially irrelevant filled Amamiya with a despair that drove her to cut herself, overdose, and attempt suicide (multiple times). In her mind the lack of shōnin is the biggest hurdle facing those in her generation (the "lost generation" or the precariat—of a certain age at least). It also foreshadows the fate of someone like Fujita who, in his case, was "disclaimed" by (even) family upon death in NHK's investigative study of Japan's *muen shakai* (relationless society). For, as scholars from Emile Durkheim to Karl Marx and Hannah Arendt have long understood, belonging to some unit beyond the singular self whose endeavor lasts beyond the here and now is critical to the social condition. And estrangement from this not only deadens the soul but evacuates everyday life.

> There are *obāsan* [old women] who go to the convenience store because they're lonely. Hearing the cashier thank them when they are handed their change is the only human contact they have in the day. There are children who have no place to play with other humans in days spent commuting between school, cram school, and home. There are mothers who have no one to help them shoulder the responsibilities of child raising. In Japan there are a lot of people who are somehow lonely. We've slipped into a big darkness [*kurayami*] of loneliness. And, in just an instant, this darkness has transformed Japan. (Website for Chiiki no cha no ma, Nīgata-shi. www .sawayakazaidan.or.jp/ibasyo/case/04koushinetsu/uchinojikka.html)

Japan is in trouble today, chiiki no cha no ma (a "regional living room") announces on its website. But the reason is not economic decline or a sinking birthrate. Rather it's loneliness. The infrequency with which humans bump up against one another or help one another out. Whether for the old woman living alone, the child over-regimented by school, or the mother struggling with raising her child or children, loneliness has become generic. A "darkness" in the social fiber: a crimp and crisis in the home (in the Bachelardian sense of sheltering the spirit and nourishing the imagination). "Darkness has transformed Japan" in that something basically human seems amiss. Something missing from basic living, as in what Butler has identified as the precariousness of social life. "Precariousness implies living socially, that is, the fact that one's life is always in some sense in the hands of the other. . . . It is not that we are born and then later become precarious, but rather that precariousness is coextensive with birth itself (birth is, by definition, precarious), which means that it matters whether or not that this infant survives, and that its survival is dependent on what we might call a social network of hands" (2009, 14). Where does one turn to for a "social network of hands" in an era of increasing self-responsibility (*jiko sekinin*) and the retreat of those institutions and networks—like the workplace, family, neighborhood—that once were more relied upon for anchoring relationality, positionality, and care? Recognition of the problem alone is insufficient. What chīki no cha no ma offers instead is something more active: a way to sense (out of) precariousness by staging human contact. This is an ethics of the social premised on the logic and need for mutual touch: a social premised on the shared condition of precariousness where people come together on the basis not of identity but responsibility. And less responsibility to and for oneself ("self-sustainability" and "aging in place") than an ethics of life geared to one another, even strangers, thus creating a new "we."

> Who then is included in the "we" that I seem to be, or to be a part of? And for which "we" am I finally responsible? This is not the same as the question: to which "we" do I belong? If I identify a community of belonging on the basis of nation, territory, language, or culture, and if I then base my sense of responsibility on that community, I implicitly hold to the view that I am responsible only for those who are recognizably like me in some way. But what are the implicit frames of recognizability in play when I "recognize" someone as "like" me? . . . What is our responsibility toward those we do not know? . . . Perhaps we belong to them in a different way, and our responsibility to them does not in fact rely on the apprehension of ready-made similitudes. (Butler 2009, 35–36)

Chiiki no cha no ma defines itself as a space for mutual human contact, a *fureai ibasho* (using the word *ibasho* much discussed in chapter 2; *fureai* means mutual contact or touch): "Children, the elderly, middle-aged people, we can get energized [*genki o moratte*] by exchanging smiles. In an ibasho with no divisions, this is power. Starting with ourselves, let's build such an ibasho. From a long time ago [*mukashi kara*], this is what we've done: we've built ibasho and come to inhabit them." A nationwide movement that currently has establishments all over the country, *chiiki no cha no ma* refers to the room in a traditional home (often in the countryside, *chiiki*) where Japanese tea is made and served (*cha no ma*) to guests. The aim is to refurbish but remake the referent as chiiki no cha no ma are intended to be homey without being family homes. The two I visited in fact had been empty homes that got reclaimed as a new kind of drop-in or hangout center where membership is fluid and open rather than bounded or pinned down (by family or private ownership). What NALC does in terms of time—offering a way of providing and calculating care work outside that of wage labor and capitalist productivity—chiiki no cha no ma does in terms of space—offering a homelike space for contact and companionship outside of family or kin. Quite pointedly, in fact, there are rules (or anti-rules) designed to purposely remap the kind of sociality fostered here. For example, in the chīki no cha no ma I visited in Niigata City (on the Sea of Japan, two and a half hours from Tokyo on the bullet train), the rules were both posted on a wall and written on the handout I was immediately given upon entering.

In the *genkan* [entrance] enter your name in the registry and pay your fee by yourself

When people enter, don't stare or ask "hey, who's that?!"

No one is to wear an apron outside the kitchen

There's no clear distinction between those caring and those being cared for

This is not a *nakama kurabu* [friendship clique]

Don't talk about people in their absence

Use a paper cup here and put your name on it

There's no set program; spend time here as you like

Come and leave whenever you want

Ask for help in those things you can't do; but let's help each other in what we are able to

Those who can help out with cleaning, raking, dish washing, do so

Uchi no jikka—"my home," using the term for natal home—is the name of the chiiki no cha no ma in Niigata. It was started in 2003 by Kawada Keiko, who earlier founded a volunteer care service in Nīgata (called Magokoro herupā, Heartfelt Helper) when faced with what was the overwhelming chore of tending to her husband's parents all alone.[2] "When nothing exists, start it yourself," she cheerfully recalls about that venture. Realizing how lonely she found so many of those using Magokoro herupā, Kawada then launched her local chīki no cha no ma out of an abandoned house. Essentially a drop-in center, Uchi no jikka is open from 10 AM to 3 PM every day and welcomes any and everyone to, basically, hang out: drinking tea, playing cards, talking to one another, eating lunch. Entrance is 300 yen (US$3.20) as is lunch; staying overnight (which requires a reservation) costs 2,000 yen (US$21). The day I visited in June 2010, the air was muggy and still—much like what I found inside this older house, down a side road, in a quiet neighborhood. Stepping into the *genkan* and removing my shoes, I entered the main eighteen-mat room. Doors opened to the outside, with a row of low tables and cushions, and tatami mats on the floor, it effused both calm and energy. A flurry of notices filled an entire wall.

That day, eighteen people visited: a mix of men and women, mostly middle-aged and elderly but including a young woman with Down's syndrome (who was being tended by those at her table) and another woman in her twenties who introduced herself as a Chinese migrant who had just settled in the area. Everyone seemed comfortable and engaged; one man rushed over to give me a paper cup (returning later to make sure I hadn't lost it) and another invited me to play cards. At lunchtime we sat wherever we wanted to and fussed over the food prepared by two preassigned participants who rotate by the day. Some lingered; some jumped immediately up. But everyone seemed to be comfortable and "lightly passing the time." One retired man in his sixties told me he came here about three days a week, traveling on a bus from his home thirty minutes away. A woman in her late fifties confided that, though she shared a nice home with her husband close by, she preferred the atmosphere here (because her husband didn't accompany her?) and came almost every day.

Another man, possibly seventy years old, recounted the accident that, years ago, had stopped him from working and had rendered him basically useless: a condition that confounded his doctors, lawyers, and family alike. Distressed and feeling abandoned, he was told about Uchi no jikka and Kawada who, in his words, brought him back to life again. Calling her his *"kokoro no sensei"* (heart teacher), the man started crying. So did Kawada, standing next to him, who took over the story: "Well, he lives in a neighborhood with a tofu vendor who makes the most amazing tofu in all of Niigata. So he brings this to us every day. Every day he feeds us delicious tofu and we appreciate what he does for us. Everyone has something they're special in you know. Everyone. And here we recognize that." Recognition and acceptance (shōnin)—the very hole in human (un)relatedness that agonized Amamiya more than anything as a furītā. And what she, in her work as an activist, tries—along with advocating for furītā unions, reforming the law for *haken* (dispatch) work, and organizing precariat May Days (on the themes of "freedom and survival")[3]—to humanly foster in those suffering hardship in life (*ikizurasa*). It was she who, at the "stop suicide" event I attended, commended the woman for coming out during the question and answer session, "seeing" her in the precariousness (of being socially withdrawn, depressed, and suicidal) that she admitted to having shared once herself. Recognition is at once personal and generic here; the woman becomes both a singularity that stands alone and a part that stands alongside the multitude of those suffering the "hardship of life" (in Loft+One that night and the country as a whole these days).

The same is true at Uchi no jikka, where anyone can enter and everyone belongs. Membership is open rather than contingent, depending on neither workplace, family, nor even geographical proximity (as in residence in a certain neighborhood). This also makes for a sociality that is unbounded by commitment or time. Rather than a community per se, it is more a watering hole—a space where people come and go and are expected only to behave humanly once there. This is a far cry from the principles of hierarchy and differentiation that Nakane Chie—in her canonical text on Japanese society, *Tate shakai no ningen kankei* (Human Relations in a Vertical Society, 1967), which was written at the height of postwar Fordism—outlined as being at the core of social relationality in the Japanese company, family, and nation. In this ontology of the social, hierarchical difference structures all relationships (older brother and younger brother; teacher and student; senior and junior colleague); indeed, without it, people don't know how to behave toward one another, Nakane wrote. At Uchi no jikka, by contrast, the operative term is not *relationship* but *connectedness* (*tsunagari*), which is post-identitarian and premised on mutuality and care. This is a zone of "mutual contact" (fureai) where everyone is to give and receive ("everyone should help to the degree that they can"), no one should be identified by even an apron (no apron wearers outside the kitchen), and all are to be infused by "a human energy" that is rejuvenating (*hito no chikara ni yotte hito wa genki ni narerumono*).[4]

On the evening of the day I visited Uchi no jikka, I was witness to how electric this connective charge could get. The small house throbbed with energy—filled to the rafters with lively chatter and convivial sociality—on what was its monthly festive night: two hours for eating, drinking, and talking (the charge is 1,000 yen [US$10.60] for beer, *obentō*, and side dishes). Over seventy people gathered, many apparently to learn more about the operation of Uchi no jikka: social workers, local officials, persons involved in care work, students (some taking classes that Kawada teaches at the local community college). As three of these visitors told me, Uchi no jikka has become legendary so there is much interest in learning how to duplicate or link up with Kawada's efforts. One, a prefectural office worker, was in the middle of establishing a chīki no cha no ma in her own ward that summer. And another woman, working with local homeless, hoped to build alliances and share information about the worsening conditions she was finding among the jobless and working poor in Nīgata. But this was not an occasion for only those here to observe. Regulars visited as well and a number I had seen earlier in the day were back this evening, intermingling with the others. The man who had lost his job and found life rekindled here sat at a table, drinking beer and eating sushi. And when his turn came for self-introductions, the ritual seemed important to him. Standing up and speaking to the room, he chose his words carefully: "I am Yonezawa Hiroshi. I come here every day. And tonight I am wearing the *happi* coat I once wore as a sake vendor." Standing proud in his blue happi coat, dressed as the worker he'd stopped being long ago, Yonezawa embraced the applause from the room. He was accepted here at Uchi no jikka, just as was I when, upon introducing myself as there to learn how this "mutual contact zone" works in practice, people urged me on with nods of the head and hearty claps at the end.

A potential—as in a reserve, a reservoir, a cushion—is what I understand the activist Yuasa Makoto to mean by the word *tame*. Whether money in the bank, academic credentials, family, or home ownership, tame are (material, social, personal) reserves that can be drawn on in hard times and get stockpiled for the future. But, with the downturn in the economy and the rise in job and life insecuritization, such reserves are drying up for more Japanese every day. This constitutes precarity to Yuasa: scarcity of tame. For not only does this make life hard in the here and now, it crimps one's ability to imagine any outside or possibility beyond: what José Munoz (borrowing Ernst Bloch) calls a there and then and also and what I, following them, call hope. As Yuasa explained to me, tame has value more in being saved than getting spent in the expediency of the moment. It generates "energy," this excess beyond present need that exists, as a potentiality, within the present ("a certain mode of nonbeing that is eminent, a thing that is present but not actually existing in the present tense" [Munoz 2009, 9]). A human reserve whose potential, for something there and then, energizes and adheres to the here and now. This would seem to be the formula for Uchi no jikka. Like, but even more than, NALC—where, alongside a "storehouse for the future," donating care time gives volunteers something meaningful to do right now—Uchi no jikka operates less as a service provider than a zone of possibility. One can come here, for help and companionship, anytime. This is the tame it creates: a reserve for human connection. Serving those who feel lonely or uninvolved, Uchi no jikka constructs a space for belonging. A space that draws energy ("light") from the potential within the human need for others, and the loneliness of lacking that ("darkness"), in contemporary Japan.

Ibasho as Human Time

"As Japan has modernized, places to gather like those that once existed have disappeared across the country—including in urban centers like Niigata. Old people have become lonely—and it's not just old people. Chiiki no cha no ma is one strategy for resolving this. Anyone can gather here to drink tea and eat together"
—(from Uchi no jikka website: www.sawayakazaidan.or.jp/ibasyo
/case/04koushinetsu/uchinojikka.html)

One of the names given such newly constructed, openly flexible "meeting places" is ibasho: a word I introduced in chapter 3, which basically means a space where one feels comfortable and at home. This word too has become something of a catchword of the times as in lacking ibasho (ibasho ga nai): what I heard constantly in the circuit of media and public discourse about the state of de-sociality plaguing Japan today. People feel disconnected (ibasho ga nai), I was told time and time again when doing fieldwork on this project during the summers between 2008 and 2010. But when I asked people where or what their own ibasoho was—a standard question I included in interview and conversation—most answered positively with replies that ranged from family, work, and friendship groups (university clubs, for example) to "wherever I am," "whenever I'm buying a book," or "in the morning when watering the plants." The question struck her as odd though, a friend finally pointed out. For "ibasho" is more commonly used in the negative: a referent to less the presence than absence of human connection and security in a relationless society. Almost everyone, she continued, has some place or space where living feels right. Or they have the memory, the fragment, the occasional sake with friends or character toy that goes everywhere on a cell phone or purse strap. But the problem is how troubled and scarce the zone(s) of comfort have become. And how panicky and insecure so many feel more and more or all the time. Ibasho (ga nai) indexes this. A state of not-ness: not feeling quite right, not sufficiently secure, noticeably not human. A slippage from a time when things were (remembered or fantasized to be) better. When home meant social security—the stable job, steady income, middle-class lifestyle, a place in society, and a future—through one's kids. Which makes "home" today seem, well, not (ibasho ga nai).

Certainly, this existential, social dis-ease (of panic, depression, and deadness in Berardi's terms) is not experienced by everyone in Japan today. But signs are that it is common enough. And it is this wound in the soul that practices like NALC, Uchi no jikka, neighborhood night patrols, Moyai, "stop suicide" events, and Kowaremono no saiten have sprung up in response to. A response to, and from, a precariousness that, increasingly shared, also becomes a source for a new commonwealth (Hardt and Negri 2009) of people and life. Such endeavors draw upon a potential in the present conditions of twenty-first-century Japan: what is at once a pain in, and a protest (of sorts) against, the insufficiency of the social state to sustain life for its citizens. And out of this human discomfiture—and the response to not simply endure it but to change the conditions of everyday living—we can see the germs of an emergent sociality: one based not on exclusive belonging or normative rules but on mutual caregiving and open acceptance. This is a biopolitics from below, spurred by a shared sense, and conditions, of precariousness. Advocating for a modicum of basic human life for anyone regardless of their place, or identity, within relations of (re)productivity, property, and wealth.

I return here again to Munoz (2009) and the radically utopic potential he sees in the very condition of exclusion from normative belonging.[5] Distinguishing between what he calls "queer time" and "straight time," Munoz aligns these two temporalities—and social spatialities—as a materialist critique of the present. Rather than exiting the social or acceding to marginality or death, those who are queered by heteronormativity are uniquely positioned to advocate for change: forcing the lines and lives of who and what gets included to be remapped, resisting "no future"—or future altogether (Furuichi 2011)—for those insufficiently (re)productive or refusing to futuristically (re)produce. It is a reterritorialization of the social, the soul on strike. Using Munoz's example of queer versus straight time, I propose a similar distinction between what could be called care or human time versus productive or capitalist time (and family-corporate time within it). When those who are excluded by the rubric of (re)productivity—the elderly, the precariat, unemployed, hikikomori, NEET—refuse to simply withdraw. When, instead of not participating in the social (the de-sociality that Miyamoto Michiko noted of Japanese youths), the social gets redefined and redeployed. When those who have found hardship in life "throw up" (hakidasu) their pain or reconstrue the "pus" of their disabilities as "broken people." And then go on to make spaces and times, within the present and the everyday where not only they, but diverse others, can find connection and belonging.

Turning the notness of ibasho into a positive: a place to touch and sense others (fureai ibasho). This is the descriptor of Uchi no jikka, making "watering holes" (tamariba) to "lightly pass time" (in patchwork, learning local history, sharing a meal to which everyone takes turns bringing the pickles)—as is the format, and name, of another chīki no cha no ma I visited on the outskirts of Tokyo in July 2010.[6] Uchi no jikka builds on, and out of, the edges of the precarious everyday, a form of social recorporeality, human survival.

The Soul on Strike

I end with two final stories. One starts out with a boy so panicked by the pressure, and his failure, to academically perform that he had bald spots from pulling his hair out at age five. This is Suzuki, the young man, now in his mid-thirties, I wrote about in chapter 4. Growing up lonely, bullied, and chastised by his parents for being a poor student, Suzuki was essentially a hikikomori: someone who withdrew into himself, though, in his case, he managed to move away from home after high school and finish his university degree. After graduating, Suzuki spent a long period basically isolated and unemployed but immersed in reading. Just as video games had given him a fantasy world to escape into as a child, now it became books—on psychology, social work, child abuse, object-relations theory—that opened his soul as a young adult. No longer convinced that he was to blame for the rejection by others that traumatized him growing up, Suzuki started reimagining his horizons of possibility. Reimagining a world where belonging and worthiness did not depend unilaterally on performance in school, money in the bank, or a wife and kids of his own, Suzuki started building a life where he refused to discount himself, and others like him, as "losers." When I first met him, in the summer of 2008, Suzuki had just made a documentary film of Kowaremono and was working as a social worker for the *Niigata chiiki wakamono sapōto sutē-shon* (Niigata Regional Young People's Support Station),[7] directing support groups for hikikomori and their parents. Two years later, when I was back in Nīgata, Suzuki took me to his most recent venture: another new zone straddling the precarious everyday where socially withdrawn youths and economically depressed elderly meet up for mutual assistance.

Nuttari yori dokoro (Nuttari Place) sits in a renovated shop in what is the depressed "old town" (*shitamachi*) section of town. Youths have fled because there are no jobs and the scattered old people who live there have few resources or stores for shopping. Next to the port, the neighborhood of Nuttari is filled with abandoned storefronts: rows of wooden structures that were once filled with markets, brothels, workshops, and bars. Funded for three years by an NPO run by Suzuki called a *bansōsha* (literally, someone who runs alongside a bicyclist to give support; Suzuki's is named *Wakē shu ra*), Nuttari yori dokoro consists of two rooms. In the front a shop sells fresh vegetables at a cheap price to the (elderly) residents of Nuttari; a plaque calls this "vegetable village" (*yasai mura*). In the back the open space is subdivided into four areas: a workspace, an area with a table and chairs to sit down, a café that serves drinks and lunch at lunchtime (with plans to convert at night to a bar), and a corner for hanging out. The sign here reads "*ibasho supēsu*" (space for ibasho). Here is where those hikikomori involved in the venture gather: to learn skills, do some work, get socialized, and start reintegrating into a world outside the rooms many of them have been living in (alone) for up to years.

The day I visit Nuttari yori dokoro eight are present: all males between the ages of eighteen and thirty-five who are sorting through clothing donated from neighbors for a recycling bazaar that will be held on the premises the next month. As the staff member who oversees their training tells me, activities vary by day and the schedule is pretty loose. But, for those who show up and for the duration of time they are there, the objective is to get them doing something they stick to and to communicate with other humans: building the café, arranging or selling the vegetables in the shop, learning about computers (one of them is an expert and teaches the others), doing minor labor (for 500 yen an hour [US$5.31]) for local merchants or house-bound elderly (delivering groceries, scrubbing toilets, making lunch, doing household repairs).

The day I visit things are pretty slow. The guys seem to be tired, and only three elderly from the neighborhood pop in for their veggies. But the very idea is extraordinary: a meeting place for two different contingencies who—due to quite different circumstances—rarely meet other humans at all. By putting them in contact with one another, the hope is that the two will help one another out: the elderly (deficient in resources and company) and the hikikomori (impoverished in human wherewithal). A potentiality in a precarious present deployed toward a not-yet future that draws upon, by reworking, the past: the village (mura), the local region (chiiki), the family tea room (cha no ma), the hang-out (tamariba), the natal home (uchi no jikka), the homey space (ibasho). A conference on volunteerism I attended in the summer of 2010 in Tokyo labeled the activities represented there harappa. Literally this means grassy fields but here it meant something metaphoric: the fields left untilled to keep the potential for future crops (or something else) alive. Grassy fields in the idiom of sociality. Cultivating fields on, and out of, the edges of society: the handicapped, the elderly, the homeless, the poor, the un- and underemployed, the socially withdrawn, the suicidal, the broken people.[8] Harappa captures Nuttari yori dokoro. The attempt to make a field—for life and human connection—out of the very precariousness of the socially displaced. Such fields, grassy if marginal, need to be cultivated. And, when they are, they "spin hope."

The second, and last, story comes from one of the interviews I did with college students in the summer of 2010. In all the interviews, the final question I asked was how they saw the future of Japan. One woman answered, as related above, that the future seemed dark. What with an economic recession and low birthrate, the vitality of the nation is at risk. She proposed a governmental response: additional support to families so they can raise children "naturally." A reinscription of the principle of reproductive futurism with futurity, and national brightness, (still) linked to the heteronormative family working hard—now with increased state support—to (re)produce.

But another young woman gave a different answer. Reflecting on something she couldn't quite name, she started to speak, then she paused. "It's something just ordinary, banal, no big deal." But, actually, for her, it stood out. So, she continued. One night, recently, she was walking home from the train station and it had started to rain. She lives in a Tokyo suburb with her parents: a "bedtown community" that sprang up in the prosperity of postwar times where men, and increasingly women, commute long hours to and from the city for work. There's little sense of community here, she pointed out; no one knows their neighbors or greets one another on the street. Everyone moves about in anonymity, including herself. But walking home she encountered someone coming the other way. No one she knew, a woman a bit older than herself, getting drenched in the rain because she'd forgotten (or didn't have) an umbrella. And to this stranger, she spontaneously gave the extra umbrella she was carrying. A gift with no expectation it would be returned. It was a gesture with no agenda — and the refusal not to act because of this.

The act deeply affected her because it was so atypical, for her or anyone, in Japan (or at least Tokyo) these days. Sharing humanness, alongside precariousness, in the zone of the ordinary everyday. "This," she said — not giving it a name or definition — "is what Japan needs more of in the future."

Not more babies, more families, more national growth, more competitive achievements. But more attention paid — by the state, social expenditures, and people themselves — to sustaining one another in life rather than allocating responsibility to the self ("self-sustainability") and dismissing, or discounting, those who can't make it: the disposable laborers, disappearing elderly, human waste. Not sacrificing (more and more of) life to the encroachment of capital that produces wealth for the "winners" but insecurity for "losers" — an increasing majority: a "social reproduction of affluence that rests on a foundation of starvation" (Bakker, Gill, DiMuzio 2003). Instead, there needs to be a revaluing of life as wealth of a different kind, based on the humanness of a shared precariousness and shared efforts to do something about it.

This would lead to a new "we," a radical reconfiguring of home, a rekindling of hope, and a reterritorialization of the social — the soul on strike in precarious Japan.

SEVEN. IN THE MUD

The Rhythms of Crisis

As soon as I touched down at Narita—almost three months after the Great East Japan Earthquake on March 11, 2011—something felt off. After passing the turnoff for passengers in transit, the hall was empty. I breezed through customs as if the only one there. And when retrieving my luggage, the carousal seemed bare. This in an airport renowned for its traffic, for a hustle and bustle befitting one of the most global and visited countries in the world. But in early June, visitors had become scarce. And most of those on my own flight were headed to China.

Was it a sign of crisis, of something out of sync in the flows? But when I went to fetch my limousine bus, normalcy prevailed. Buses lined up just as they always did. And the attendant checking tickets ordered me to stand in the correct direction even though I was the only one in line. Such a pattern

I saw repeatedly in these early stages of post 3/11 Japan: the hydraulics of life pinched in various directions, attempts to (re)claim order by structures and rituals already in place, and new alliances—and dangers—in efforts made to survive.

Such was the case in an outing I joined with a local citizen's group to plant sunflowers in Fukushima shortly after arriving. Knowing I was eager to volunteer up north, an acquaintance invited me to participate in what was intended to be "one wheel in an exchange to help in the recovery and restoration of Fukushima." Concocted almost overnight in the spirit of so much of the do-it-yourself (DIY) relief efforts sprouting up all over Japan (and beyond), this one was to build a partnership (*kōryū*) between citizens in Kunitachi, Tokyo, and the cities of Sakagawa and Shirakawa in Fukushima. Sunflowers help absorb radiation from the soil. But they also, as the organizer Arashiyama Kōzaburō, a well-known essayist now retired in his seventies, told us, were the first flower to emerge after the Second World War and, fast-growing and strong, symbolize new life. It was in one of the cities we were visiting (Sukagawa), that a farmer, upon learning that the cabbage growing in his fields was too toxic to be sold, had committed suicide in April. And, already, farmers in the region had embarked upon a "brightening the region with sunflowers" initiative: a plan designed to cultivate the now dubious fields with a plant that would help dispel the "bad rumors" associated with radioactive Fukushima. Our mission, as symbolic as real, was to give support and assistance to this initiative: plant some seeds and return, in August, to see the renaissance of the soil—six-feet tall, bright sunflowers, the fruit of a citizens' "exchange project."

We started off early one Sunday morning in a cute aqua van parked outside Kunitachi train station. Upon boarding and settling down, the nineteen of us listened to the organizer's greetings, read our itineraries, then passed the mobile mike back and forth for "self-introductions." In short, a typical group outing (including the *omiyage* of local treats purchased in Fukushima we were given when disembarking the bus later that night). The drive proved longer than anything else that day. Three hours up, even longer back due to traffic—but we took frequent pit stops and passed snacks (and beer, when coming back). Meeting up with two separate point people in the local administration in the two cities, we listened to their accounts of the devastation. No tsunami had hit here, but the earthquake had killed nine people, left one still missing, and forced two thousand into evacuation shelters, our partner in Sukagawa told us. He hadn't been out of his work uniform for three months and been forced to greet Children's Day (May 5) this year not with the flying fish banners of *koinobori* but the blue flapping tarp on house roofs hit by the earthquake. Both here, and in Shirakawa, we then planted our seeds—digging small holes and covering them with dirt in the long troughs circumventing two fields. About a half an hour in one place, a bit longer in the other, and cell-phone cameras flashing the whole time. Tending to our "tight schedule" we also made two quick touristy stops: one to a famous peony garden and the other to Shirakawa castle to see evidence of where the earthquake had struck.

All in all, it was an outing at once quirky and heartfelt. What was, or could have been, an ordinary excursion of local citizens (of which neighborhoods typically have a number during the year) became something else: a partnership of support for the citizens of Fukushima Prefecture, stretching one circle of sociality to help another and enfolding relief—for those up north—into the (no-longer-quite) mundane and normal everywhere else. Much in the outburst of volunteerism, relief efforts, contributions—of money, food, blankets, sanitary napkins—that poured out from Japanese of all walks of life to those affected by the disaster in Tōhoku assumed a pattern something like this. I encountered student groups, small businesses, groups of mothers or housewives, companies, local wards, university departments, clubs of all sorts, radio stations, restaurants, small shops, and large department stores that organized collectively to volunteer or donate support. For example, a student at Ochanomizu University in Tokyo told me that the spring activity of her club (*bukatsu*) had been making a unique onion pastry ("onion sweets") that they sold along with a pamphlet of recipes that also included information about radiation, growing onions, and farmers affected by 3/11 in Fukushima. All proceeds were donated to relief.

Another group of students at Seika University in Kyoto ran a spring camp at their university during Golden Week, the first week of May, to give kids stuck in Fukushima the opportunity to breathe fresh air. When I meet up with them in July, they are working hard on their plans and fund raising for a follow-up camp (*Waku waku camp*); it is to last all of August and accommodate twenty children. The three students I speak with are a bit breathless with planning and admit they have no prior experience in anything like this at all. Motivated "to do something," they throw themselves into an endeavor that unfolds as it goes along. This feels less about hope in the Blochian sense—investing in a not-yet-future (a nuclear-safe Japan) by addressing what is missing in the here and now (children safe from nuclear danger)—than a gesture to do something, anything in the moment. The aim, as worded in the fund-drive poster, is to do "just a little" for the many children in Fukushima who can't leave the affected area. An effort—to protect a few kids for a few days by reterritorializing their temporary existence—in which they solicit the "support" (*shien*) and "connection" (*tsunagari*) of "everyone." It's not making Japan safe precisely, but it is taking a few endangered kids to a safe(r) place. Something "everyone" can and should do together.

The words *everyone, support,* and *connection* recycle in a grammar of affinity during this period immediately following 3/11. An action of doing something; an affect of enduring; a collective "we" treading a precariousness newly shared. As a friend wrote in her blog on April 12, 2011: "We're only getting negative news about the dangers of radiation. Our spirits are dark. There isn't anything to do but endure this uneasiness together" (*Keredomo, minna de fuan ni taenakereba naranainodeshō*). The word she uses to describe the bodily, psychic state of Japan in this moment, when aftershocks continue (as they do throughout the summer) and the earth, still shaking, stays sodden in mud, is *landsick* (*gesenbyō*)—the sickness one has readjusting to land after being on sea for a long time. "Big aftershocks continue. It's been a month. Despite the fact that the cherry blossoms have come out and brightened things, we're still landsick." A sickness of equilibrium: the balance of earth and water is out of sync, producing a nation suffering from vertigo.

I see much in the way of compassion during the six weeks I am in Japan the first summer post-3/11. Many reach out, give assistance, and show solidarity. And, for some, these acts are melded into the familiar and the everyday. One of my fellow seatmates on the sunflower excursion told me about the volunteer tourism he was planning for later that summer. A *sarariman* who worked hard and would only take a week vacation, he'd decided that this year it would be to Tōhoku with his family and four others to volunteer. Winking, he added that they would drink and play at night but do some volunteer work during the day. "What could be better?" Hoping to capitalize on just this desire, Japan Railways (best-known as simply JR, the national railways) devised a summer campaign for a package deal on the bullet train up north that included overnight stays at local hot springs.

Even without a stint of volunteering added in, a trip north would signal support of the local economy so dependent upon what was now its flagging tourism and agriculture business.

It was the promotion of moral consumerism—much like buying a T-shirt at Gap with a portion of the profits going to AIDS relief in South Africa. Such was the case when friends deliberately ordered sake from Miyagi Prefecture when drinking in Shibuya one night. Gestures of alliance—from the banal and everyday to the much more strenuous and profound (such as the volunteering some Japanese did continually and closeup) were commonplace. So were the signs of togetherness: of being in this crisis together and of facing and fighting it as "one unit." The Japaneseness of the country in crisis reasserted and reclaimed. Banners posted everywhere read: *Nihon tōitsu* (Japan, as one unit), *Nippon ganbarō!* (Hang in there, Japan!). And as a friend put it when I asked about reconstruction (*fukkō*, one of the buzzwords of the moment along with *fukkyū*, recovery or repair), "don't worry Anne-chan, we won't lose [*makenaiyo*]," as if I imagined Japan would sink into the ocean.

But what does "not losing" mean in this context, who does it include, and with what stakes and rubric of "togetherness"? Certainly, the "we" here is the Japanese, as evidenced by the fact that—much reported on in the news and by so many I spoke to—foreigners left the country immediately after the crisis (called "fly-jin" as in flying-away *gaijin*). Many Japanese, from shop clerks to train attendants, thanked me for being in Japan at all this summer and particularly for volunteering up north when I did so. But what, for a foreigner, is optional, becomes more mandatory for the "Japanese." Charges of disloyalty and selfishness—captured by the new buzzword *hikokumin* (non-citizenly)—got waged against those leaving the country or even the region (outside those mandated to do so by the government in the evacuation zones in a thirty kilometer range of the Fukushima Daiichi Nuclear Plant). Staying close to home and sticking it out became a badge of loyalty and trust (but also a matter of sheer livelihood for some).

By contrast, exhibiting too much concern about one's own safety or that of one's family triggered suspicion. Mothers who'd left homes in Sendai (in Miyagi Prefecture) for temporary shelters in Kyoto to protect their kids recounted to me the ostracism they felt from neighbors back home. And, for those who stayed but tried other tactics for self-protection from radiation—sending homemade lunchboxes to school so children could avoid the school lunch, for example — faced discrimination as well. In the case of the former, a child pleaded with her mother to allow her to eat the school lunch along with everyone else, as if the danger of group expulsion was worse than that of radiation. And a mother, sending *obentō* to school with her child, told her circle of mother friends that her reason for doing so was simply that she had more time on her hands now since she'd lost hours at work (due, needless to say, to the crisis) (Yamane 2011).

Cutbacks and Protests

When the Great East Japan Earthquake struck Japan's northeast coast on March 11, it was felt for hundreds of miles. The largest earthquake in the country's recorded history, it jolted the ground in shocks, then aftershocks, that vibrated for months. People stayed jittery; nervous systems on alert. But the water was the real killer; the tsunami waves, cresting over forty feet high, pummeled the coastline, churning what had been solid — houses, boats, gas stands, and bodies of humans, horses, cattle, and dogs — into grotesque carcasses or worse. Minutes of pounding left unbearable devastation, not the least of which was spewing radiation from Fukushima's nuclear reactors whose breakwaters proved laughably breakable — the fault not of nature but humans who'd ignored safety precautions and routine drills for years in the interests of saving money and making more profits for its owner, the Tokyo Electric Power Company (TEPCO). In the end close to 20,000 were reported missing or dead; almost 350,000 displaced; endless businesses, fields, and livestock destroyed; trillions of yen in property damaged; and the effects and threat to life due to radiation exposure remains an everyday, if, elusive and incalculable threat two years later.

The events of 3/11 triggered a crisis of unimaginable intensity. Beyond those it killed, it has made life, for so many, even less safe than it was before: precarity intensified. It has also thrown into relief aspects of life that were precarious already: the fact, for example, that so many of the workers in the Fukushima nuclear plants were, both before and after 3/11, part of the precariat — disposable workers for whom the safety of other Japanese (as in cleaning up and containing the spread and exposure of radiation) are now so intimately intertwined. News reports on precarious employment (dispatch, contract) are much more common these days, and the precariat have assumed greater recognition and sympathy in the general public eye. Sensibilities of Japanese across the country have also been newly raised to the politics of the "nuclear village" (*genshiryoku mura*), to the location of so many nuclear reactors in the region of Tōhoku where—because of its depressed economy and aging population—residents had accepted the dangers in order to acquire revenues and jobs. Sentiments against nuclear energy and the nuclear industry have soared. So has disgust and suspicion against the owners of the nuclear plants as well as the government for their collusion of interests and for their mismanagement of safety regulations, clean up, and the withholding of (and lying about) information regarding radiation exposure. People who have never protested before or rallied against the government or corporate interest have done so now. A protest in September 2011 drew sixty thousand, many of them mothers brought there out of concern for their children. This was the banner given the entire protest in fact, "to protect the safety of our children." It was something that everyone and anyone could rally under, even if—as many of these newly marching mothers told a colleague who interviewed them (David Slater who has been actively involved in both relief and research post-3/11)—their protest wasn't for politics but for life. As if being an activist for life isn't political.

No one feels safe anymore (which means not just the precariat). And just as more people are giving public voice to their own fears and dissatisfactions, more are making common cause with those of others. As someone I met on the sunflower excursion put it: "we need to create a society where those who suffer are taken care of by us all." In his own case, an engineer for Hitachi, he was working furiously long days to build alternative energy sources to replace Japan's depleted nuclear power. By the end of the summer only thirty-four of fifty-four nuclear plants were operating nationwide; by May 2012 the number had fallen to zero. In a country that had been the third largest producer of nuclear energy worldwide and had relied on it for 30 percent of its own power, the majority of Japanese—along with this Hitachi worker—now say they are against nuclear energy and endorse a policy of working toward becoming a nuclear-free country (*datsugenpatsu*), the stance Germany adopted following Japan's crisis. What this might mean for the industrial viability, economic wealth, and everyday ("modern") lifestyles of Japanese in the future—the possibility of its "third-worlding"—is much debated.

A foreshadowing of such cutbacks came in the aftermath of 3/11 when, after initial blackouts even in Tokyo, citizens were asked to undergo *setsuden* (conservation of energy consumption). This entailed a massive turning down of electricity (everything from city lights and escalators to hand driers in public toilets and ACs everywhere). Businesses and companies changed operating hours to conserve power; workers adopted a new dress code of "cool biz" with open-necked Okinawan shirts instead of button-up suits; and citizens conserved in every way imaginable, including purchasing an array of gadgets such as ice packs worn as neck wraps and spray bottles with instant "ice." Everyone sweated, and talked about it, in this conservation of power and resensing of the everyday. And, by the end of summer, the goal of 15 percent power reduction had been not only met but exceeded. It was a sign of collective will and disciplined spirits; Japan was fighting back.

But setsuden also caused deaths by heat exhaustion, and under the moral imperative of collective *ganbaru*—working hard together—the risks of some individuals were also sanctioned or ignored. The elderly and refugees in evacuation shelters were particularly at risk with little (or no) AC relief. And, according to a news story midsummer, precariat workers in the Daiichi Nuclear Reactor found themselves working longer hours and taking fewer breaks because they felt so driven to restore safety to the nation. This despite the fact that, suited up head to toe in protective gear and laboring without fans in unbearable heat, sweat would start impairing their vision after only a few minutes at work.

Safety and security for whom precisely, and whose responsibility does this become?

Ocean and Death

Flows disrupted, energy restrained. But it is not only leaking radiation and power shortage that draw attention this summer. It is also the enormity of the death and devastation up north: wreckage on an unimaginable scale thrown up by a sea that savaged the coastline with such intensity it took countless lives and livelihoods in a flash. The scenes of destruction that continually replay in the mass media—of entire towns wiped out, miles of coastline reduced to rubble, houses and cars thrown for miles, fishing boats stuck in rice fields—resemble a warzone. Everything looks dead, and this is without showing the bodies (or body parts) of all the living creatures that got killed. Death gets reported less visually through pictures than through statistics (reported daily in the papers in the three categories of dead, missing, and displaced) and through stories: of those who survived, the horrors they endured, what they know (and don't know) of those who didn't make it, and how those displaced (in evacuation shelters and elsewhere) struggle with the reminder of so much loss. These stories—circulating everywhere—have an aesthetic, a rhythm all their own. On the television, I listen to countless tales, told episodically with temporality uprooted and edges left raw, of lives suspended, families and familiarities torn asunder.

One story, around the hundredth-day anniversary of the crisis (a special day in the Buddhist cycle of departed souls), involves a middle-aged woman whose husband is missing. If she claimed him dead, the woman could start drawing compensation. But she is not ready to do this. Instead she waits and goes to the municipal office daily to check on the new names of reported dead. Meanwhile she talks to her husband for long stretches every day. As the news program shows, she visits his truck—the place where she last saw him alive—and sits in his seat, stroking the dashboard and recounting what has happened to their town, and their house, since the event. So and so survived, so and so did not, this is how we're managing. But it's hard to keep going without him, she utters to the steering wheel at last. When are you coming back?

In the background, we see scenes of the ocean, the culprit, now chastened and calm. It laps against a beach strewn with rubbish and disorder: a sickening site at once familiar and forlorn. There's always a return, at some point, to the sea in this storytelling of tsunami and death. This is the case quite literally in a story I am told by Ueda, a retired man in Tokyo who, ever since the crisis, has been going up to Iwate on the weekends to offer relief. The first time there, just days after the tsunami, he met an *obāchan* (old woman) walking up and down the beach who was thinking of throwing herself in to join her husband who had been swept away in the waves. There are many stories of mainly women attempting to drown themselves to reunite with those claimed by the tsunami. This is the reason Ueda returns every weekend to Iwate himself—to the obāsan on the beach. He's trying to keep her alive and has succeeded so far by telling her that, if she dies, there will be no one to give her husband *kuyō* (service for the dead): no one to pray for his spirit as it makes its way to the other side. A reason for living becomes staying alive to service the dead. But another survivor Ueda speaks to is tormented by the fact that since his grandmother's body was never found, he fears that the family can't do proper memorial rites. Her spirit is trapped in the ocean, liminally at sea. Every night he dreams about her and every morning wonders why he is still alive. Ueda says mental health issues are plaguing survivors of 3/11, and suicide is now the leading cause of death among them.

Rescue and Mud

But death is not the only plotline in these stories—of a raging sea that battered the land and took so much away. There is also the life and death that remains on shore in the mud, in ground still soaked in water and zones once of living transformed now into mush. The tsunami rendered the entire northeast coastline a cesspool of waste: dead remains and dying life entwined—animals, humans, boats, cars, oil, houses, vegetation, and belongings. And before even the thought of reconstruction, there is the chore of cleaning up (getting rid of the dead): a massive job given the scope and degree of the damage. The government responded much more forcefully than it did following the Kobe earthquake on January 17, 1995 (killing 6,434 people), when its slow and mismanaged response became a symptom of Japan's failure of national leadership. This time it called out the Self-Defense Forces (SDF) almost immediately (rather than relegating them to peripheral cleanup as it had in the Kobe case) and, in their biggest mission since 1945, 100,000 troops were sent out—almost half the entire force. In their response the SDF searched for bodies and life, reconnected power lines and cleared travel routes, moved survivors into evacuation shelters and provided food and supplies to those who stayed in place, and tended to the dangers mounting at the Fukushima nuclear reactors. They also did extensive cleanup, razing the ruins of what was unsalvageable and hauling off tons and tons of debris.

In its recovery and rescue campaign, the SDF of Japan were also given assistance from foreign countries—another contrast from the Kobe earthquake when their presumed inability to communicate in Japanese became a rationale for initially declining assistance from other countries (including the United States). This time, offers of help from outside were accepted and, of these, *Tomodachi sakusen* (Operation Friend) conducted (as inconspicuously as possible) by the U.S. Armed Forces was the largest and most recognized. ("It was great," Ueda told me.) Launched the day after the earthquake and lasting until May 4, it cost US$90 million and involved 24,000 U.S. service members, 189 aircraft, and 24 naval ships.

Besides all the official (domestic and foreign) relief efforts that converged on Tōhoku overnight, so did a slew of NGOs, volunteers, and private cleanup operations (employing precariat workers in a business that, as rumor had it, eventually got taken over by the yakuza, the Japanese mafia). Much of this initial relief work involved mud—wading through it, shoveling out debris, navigating the sludge for signs of life and valuable remains. But while the outpouring of relief and volunteerism from all over Japan and beyond was staggering, not everyone was eager to go up north into the mud itself to help out. I spoke with many in Tokyo who didn't go because, as one woman put it, she couldn't stand to see or feel the death up close, the death that was promiscuously perverse in its origins and trapped in a mud that was exuding an unbearable stench—what I was warned about before going there myself. But when I went in July with a global NGO outfit called Peace Boat, I found the experience almost organically transfixing.

Like many relief operations, Peace Boat targeted one locale; this was Ishinomaki in Miyagi Prefecture on the coast—a town of sixty thousand where 40 percent of households sustained major damage and four thousand were dead or missing. Choosing the short-term option (two days, three nights instead of the longer trips conducted in one-week blocks) for which I had to bring all my own food, bottled water, and sleeping and work gear (a job that took me literally days to prepare for in Tokyo), I head out on an overnight bus from Shinjuku. There are sixty of us in the two-bus caravan, mostly youths in their twenties and thirties, including college students, housewives, people in-between jobs, and many of them part of the precariat. After arriving at our temporary home base (a converted fashion school) with porta potties, a couple faucets, and racks of drying rubber (rubber boots, gloves, raingear) outside, we store our gear in our gender-segregated dorms and dress to get going. By 7:30 AM we are lined up in our *han* (groups) to do morning exercises. And an hour later, after driving through the wreckage of the city, which none of the visuals from the TV or newspaper has remotely prepared me for, we're into the belly of the disaster itself: Ishinomaki's downtown area with its jagged lines of fragments still standing—shops, statues, street signs—next to boats in the middle of parking lots and buildings crumpled into a waste dump.

Our job is to tackle the waste dump. But little is said about the overall aims other than that we're there to help and be respectful of those who have incurred so much loss in Ishinomaki. Stress is placed on the immediacy of the action and on the ethics of care. (We're told to greet everyone we see, to be mindful of not getting hurt or overdoing things as that would be a bigger burden for the locals, and to run up the hill if another earth-quake and resulting tsunami hits while we're there — a distinct possibility our head leader tells us matter-of-factly.) Our focus, in other words, turns to the mud. And, after gathering our equipment — wheelbarrows, shovels, buckets, bags — my team heads to the street where we've been assigned to shovel mud from the rain ditches (*sokkō sōji*). Suited up in rubber from goggles to boots (and with masks on our faces, helmets on our heads, and rain pants taped shut to the tops of our boots), our bodies quickly become hot and spent by the work — removing the cement blocks in the street, dig-ging out the sludge in the ditches, and replacing the blocks. The labor is hard, the mud heavy, and we all push ourselves for hours.

But our rhythms — of shoveling, schlepping into wheelbarrow, greet-ing the few residents walking by — bounce off one another, generating an energy that mediate and mitigate the mud. A mud that oozes everywhere: standing in pools, smeared against buildings, encased in the ruins of what had become this downtown. Slimey, inky, riddled with particles — some decipherable (like a child's toy) but most not — and pungent with a smell that hasn't left me yet, the mud fills our senses. It also feeds a sensuality — a social sensuality — so powerful to some in this operation that they stay on for weeks, or return, time and time again. In the evening, when we assemble to share our objectives in coming and our reflections from the first day, a number say that helping out just felt like the right thing to do: "we're all Japanese and this is something I could do." Some add that the work feels good, and a number say they haven't felt so alive in years. One woman in her early thirties admits that she's a loner and being a volunteer staff member now gives her contact with others, a community. And a man in his mid-twenties, just returning from abroad, says Japan had been dead when he left but it is now stirring again. "This time I won't leave. We young people are going to remake Japan."

When my team returns the next day and our assignment is to remove the mud-infested things (*mono dashi*) inside someone's home, the owner — a man in his seventies — joins us, supplying us drinks and telling us his story of survival and loss during our breaks. He thanks us repeatedly for laboring so hard to empty the house that soon will be gone. Apparently this is a job — picking through his belongings by hand to find anything of value (photos, certificates, prized dishes) — that the SDF cleanup crews can't perform. But, in truth, we salvage almost nothing. The slog inside his house is almost unidentifiable: everything has dissolved into mud, which makes our own work digging out and depositing as trash on the curb treacherous. But in working together with the man who has lost so much, in our rubber suits, hot beyond belief, slipping in the disgust of the mud, there is a pain collectively, if not equally, shared. A relationship—of sorts—produced through the willingness to enter the mud and touch the traces of life but also death that we find there. As Talal Asad notes about a sociality formed in pain: "as a social relationship pain is more than an experience. It is part of what creates the conditions of action and experience" (2003, 85).

But what kind of action is this? While tremendously moving, the work we do moves little in fact. Ten of us working hard for six hours barely manage to clear one floor of a tiny house. What we retrieve seems scant: maybe two boxes worth of photos, certificates, a few cups and plates. A bulldozer razing the house would have been far more efficient. But that wouldn't allow for recovery of anything "precious." And there would be no human touch. This would seem the point as much, if not more, than anything else in this relief work: just being there, alongside those who have suffered so much, and giving recognition—and respect—to the dead.

The woman who is my group leader can't articulate the reasons she's come here. Maybe thirty, married to a Nigerian, she tells me her job is in "night service": probably working in a bar or club. She's a part of the precariat. But ever since the crisis, she's been working as a volunteer staff in the Tokyo office of Peace Boat: almost nonstop it seems and as much, if not more, than the hours at her part-time job. Her husband's visa has run out so he's in Japan illegally now. Their life is risky, but "this—," she says, gesturing to the razed landscape we're passing on the way to our worksite in the bus. The sentence goes unfinished. Completed not by words but by action, by her body that moves once we arrive at the mud with an energy and resolve that stays remarkably strong. An action in the moment, circumscribed by the immediacy of the here and now, the life and death indeterminacy of the "crisis ordinariness" (Berlant 2011) of muddy relief work. This woman is the one who helps me when I stumble. She's also the one who washes the last of the rubber gloves at the end of the day. And as we leave on the bus, she tells me she'll be back next week for another two days.

Waving from the parking lot are the skeleton staff who stay put in Ishinomaki. The head leader bows to the bus showing us a panda figure buzz cut into his hair. This youngish man assuming leadership of a relief operation is probably a precariat like the woman beside me. Is this the new post-3/11 generation of Japanese young people, I wonder? Ones who defy, or transform, what I've heard so repeatedly (pre-3/11) of the de-social, un-involved, apolitical Japanese youths? Or is this something that existed already in the conditions of life—and temporality of living—that I've been tracking in this book of precarious Japan? Action taken on the part of taking care not only of oneself but also of others, even strangers: those with whom one shares the condition of ontological vulnerability. Precariousness as establishing human relations and as a means of calibrating what is precious in life.

Radiation and Washing Memories

When I talk with Ueda, the man who is going up every weekend to Iwate to talk the obāsan on the beach into staying alive, he tells me that what is hard for the survivors is their inability to see a future. They have no reason to keep living because they can't see anything ahead of them (*saki ga mienai*). What he means is that the routines and relationships that grounded normalcy have been so broken that time seems literally to have stopped: the situation Jonathan Lear described for the Crow Nation upon losing their right to hunt buffalo (see chapter 4). In his book *Radical Hope* (2006), Lear writes that it is not only a way of life that is lost but also one's subjectivity: the ability to see, or know, oneself in the face of radical change and, in this case as well as that of 3/11, utter devastation and death.

One response to such loss is not to merely mourn all that and those who have died or to move resolutely forward with plans for reconstruction but to stay awhile with the pain and uncertainty. To sit with it, hold it, sometimes for others, those too distraught to do much about it themselves. Not closure but something quite different, giving a space and time for not-closure, respecting the dead but also sensing the precariousness of the in-between when attachment to others includes those both living and dead.

I feel the sense of precarity immediately on the third volunteer trip I take to Fukushima Prefecture later that summer. Hearing they have a volunteer shortage (and calling ahead to make sure they'll take a foreigner), I head close to the evacuation zone where the "contaminated beef problem"—high levels of cesium radiation detected in cattle fed hay left outside after the nuclear reactors exploded—breaks the very day I arrive in mid-July. In this place (Haruno machi)—emptied of children, mothers pushing baby strollers, almost anyone on a bike or moving around outside—

much of the talk centers on animals. Stranded dogs, recovered horses, abandoned cattle. In the municipal office where I go to sign in the walls are covered with information: lists of missing and dead, instructions on how to claim damages and compensation (and to claim death for bodies not yet found), directions for volunteers. There's also a shrine to the dead and a wall of pictures of missing dogs. Outside a digital dosimeter posts the daily cesium levels.

The day I show up to volunteer, there are fifty-five of us (the numbers and where we're from are posted on a board; one hundred is ideal, we're told). This is an older group than the Peace Boat operation: mainly men, some retired, none local. At the instructional meeting we're assigned to one of four activities, and mine involves recovery of images. Trooping to a building close by in our boots and donning masks and gloves in the entrance hall, we enter a room with a long table where we'll soon be working in silence. Given retrieved photos from tsunami-battered homes such as the one my team had emptied in Ishinomaki, we are to "clean" these (*kirei ni suru*) as best we can. "Be respectful," our team leader urges us as if these photos are a form of life itself. But that's all in the way of instruction for a task we're to pick up as we go along. It all feels very Buddhist. The room quiets down and our team leader turns the radio on to *enka* (a popular form of melancholic music).

Dusting off dirt with a toothbrush, we dab—with wet towels and wipies—to recover the semblance of a group outing or face. Sometimes we discard photos that show too little promise; the man sitting next to me—breathing like Darth Vader through his mask—gestures to the trash bag when he feels I'm wasting my effort. Otherwise, the rubbing and wiping stay steady. A room full of small movements. Laboring cocooned under our masks, intimate—but not—with those whose images we are trying to save. We hang the finished photos on clotheslines draped throughout the room. During one of the breaks, a volunteer says he is haunted by the image of a young girl in one of the photos, is she alive or dead? And another, one of a group of men in their thirties (who have been given a week off from their company to volunteer), says he finds the work disturbing. He prefers shoveling debris.

As I later learn, this activity of washing images to preserve "memory things" (*omoide no mono*) has become a nationwide effort: it is done not only onsite, where the tsunami hit, but also "outsourced" to volunteers, many of them schoolchildren, laboring throughout the country. It is done, as a gift of sorts, to the victims of the tsunami, almost always by strangers. In the bulletin put out by the municipal office, it informs residents about "taking home your memory things!" As it describes, these are "things that have been gathered from the rubble by the SDF, police, and firefighters, and their dirt carefully removed, one piece by one piece, by the hands of volunteers." They are assembled weekly at the municipal office—on clotheslines, in boxes, in newly assembled photo albums—for victims to come and inspect. But, "when confirming ownership of memory things," one needs to show a driver's license or some kind of proof of identity (*hon-nin kakunin*)—a problem, I'm told, for some who have lost everything, including any form of self-identification (not only from home but from files that have been washed away in municipal offices as well). Not only are bodies of dead missing, so are the records of existence for some who have survived. Things out of place, identities disappeared.

The cleaning itself is an arduous task, painstakingly slow, and rarely produces a truly clean image. Most results are fragments; edges rubbed off revealing traces at best: one face out of a group of three, a mother holding empty air. They resemble what Tim Ingold describes about drawing, a visual art that sketches rather than projects images in what he calls "wayfaring," "breaking a path through a terrain and leaving a trace, at once in the imagination and on the ground, in a manner very similar to what happens as one walks along in a world of earth and sky" (2011, 178). Drawing is at odds with a representational art like oil painting where the logic tends toward totalization: "its aim is to wrap things up, to enframe, and thereby to enforce a kind of closure" (179). By contrast, the aim of drawing, as Ingold puts it, "is always to prise an opening, to find a way through." Anti-totalizing, drawing involves more a process than a structure: an act, and action of "gathering," which is "more analogous, perhaps, to sewing and weaving than to shooting arrows at a target" (178).

This seems an apt description for the activity of washing memory things: the effort made to prise an opening (out of death and destruction) and leave a trace at once in the imagination and on the ground. The results are hardly representational in that they don't fully capture an image from the past. They're snippets of memory that have both weathered and been transformed by the tsunami, with traces of the water now part of the image—water-logged photos with the frame rubbed clean. And they emerge as an act of gathering. In the room where I work that day in Fukushima, alongside eight others in the morning and twenty by the afternoon, we're assembling parts of people's lives. People we don't know, nor do we know whether they survived and, even if so, will ever want, see, or claim the images getting cleaned. But we "clean" nonetheless. A "we" of strangers, gathering together and gathering with the dead, to sew and weave whatever this is in a gesture where the act is as important as the thing we produce.

The day I clean photos, no one local is part of our team. I'm told that those hit hardest by the crisis are subsumed by other chores or just the toil of getting through the day. In this town, close to the evacuation zone and the Daiichi nuclear reactor with its radiation now leaking into the air, earth, and water of the environment where people once made their lives/livelihoods, life itself feels removed of the frame (Ingold 2011, 220). The train lines have been washed out, the streets are empty, and any produce still growing (or cattle slaughtered, fish pulled from the sea) is now suspect. Those in evacuation shelters are getting moved out to temporary housing and starting to claim compensation. But jobs are scarce: a situation of socioeconomic precarity that preceded 3/11 in this region of the country overly populated by elderly (even more so than Japan at large), one of the reasons that so many who died were elderly. One of the pressing issues facing the country, as well as each of these regions hit the hardest by the crisis, is whether—or to what degree—to rebuild. It is a question of resources: how to pay for not merely reconstruction but, even before that, cleanup (as well as where to deposit the radiated soil—the newspapers report that school playgrounds in Fukushima are getting covered with a layer of fresh soil yet piles of radiated soil are left onsite given that no one else in Japan is willing to take it). But, it is a matter also of viability, which means security of and for life: security of employment, security from nuclear exposure, security from the danger of future (natural and nuclear) disaster.

Hope

In his first public speech following Japan's Great East Earthquake on 3/11, Emperor Akihito asked Japanese citizens to remain hopeful and calm and to help one another out. The theme of hope (kibō) reverberated throughout the country. But hope had already been much in public discourse where, primarily in the negative, it registered as a catchword of the times. If hope is the capacity to imagine a horizon of expectation beyond the here and now, something about the moment and the way Japanese were living it out had sapped the collective imagination about tomorrow. But in the early days following 3/11, a number of voices claimed hope's return.

Murakami Ryū, the novelist and public personality mentioned earlier for his book *Kibō no kuni no ekusodasu* (2002), wrote a commentary titled "Amid Shortages, a Surplus of Hope" that circulated widely; a friend even posted it on her blog. Noting how the Japanese have been adept at organizing collectively in the face of great adversity in the past, he praised their response to the crisis now: of orderliness, civility (no looting), sacrificial efforts made by workers in the nuclear plants (such as the "kamikaze fifty" who first went in). "Our way of life has been threatened by the crisis," he admitted, and the government and utility companies have failed to adequately respond. And yet, as he continued: "for all we've lost, hope is in fact one thing we Japanese have regained. The great earthquake and tsunami have robbed us of many lives and resources. But we who were so intoxicated with our own prosperity have once again planted the seed of hope" (*New York Times*, March 16, 2011, 17).

Similarly, Azuma Hiroshi, a professor of philosophy, the leading figure in *otaku* (nerd-fan) studies, and author of *Otaku: Japan's Database Animals* (2011), adopted a hopeful rhetoric in a commentary published six days after the earthquake (both his and Murakami's articles were originally published on the op-ed page in the *New York Times*, then republished in Japanese following that).[1] Already he noticed a radical turnabout in something akin to the public imagination or collective spirit. This contrasted to how little pride the Japanese had felt in their country ever since Japan's defeat in the Second World War but particularly in the last two decades, a period marked by the bursting of the bubble economy, tumultuous turnover in leadership, the Kobe earthquake of 1995, and the incompetent response of the government: "Only recently the Japanese people and government were seen as indecisive and selfish, muddled with complaints and bickering. But now, they are boldly trying to defend the nation together as if they were a changed people. To borrow an expression from the younger generation here, the Japanese people seem to have completely transformed their *kyara* [character]" (March 16, 2011, 17). Admitting that this seeming transformation in the early days following 3/11 could lead to nationalism, Azuma said that he "nonetheless wish[es] to see a ray of hope in this phenomenon."

In both cases, Azuma and Murakami sensed something in the early aftermath of 3/11 they referred to as *hope*. The sense of a turn, or return, to a collective working together; a willingness to see beyond the singular, atomized self; a spirit of belonging to and in a state of becoming alive (again). This view was widely shared: seeing hope, and hoping for hope, as the affect and effect of 3/11. It was as if natural disaster had shocked people out of their "social disaster" (*shakai saigai*) of the relationless society, aging demographic, and a social fabric where communities collapse and lose ties—as one reader writing into a newspaper put it. This view alone was hopeful. That jolted by the tremors underfoot, pounded by the waves of water pouring over land, and sickened by the radiation now spewing out from nuclear reactors melting down, Japanese people responded with traits of "character" that indexed a renewed bond both to each other and to Japan. As Rebecca Solnit (2009) has written about the surging of community that can arise in the face of disaster, there was much talk of this in post-disaster Japan. People were showing a (re)commitment to life with others. I felt it too: a retired man in Tokyo taking weekly trips to Iwate to keep an obāsan from joining her dead husband in the ocean; precariat youth becoming the new reserves of volunteer relief work(ers) in Ishinomaki.

Belonging became the new buzzword: belonging to one another, to Japan, to a homeland transformed by mud and radiation. References to connectedness (*tsunagari*) and bonds (*kizuna*) gushed everywhere—from a rise in marriage applications to surveys pronouncing its new importance to a majority of Japanese. On January 1, 2012, the banner phrase coined for the New Year was "*en no jidai*"—an era for relationships using the same word *en* as in *muen shakai* (or relationless society). But, for all the euphoria (and nationalism) surrounding togetherness, it also was very much of the moment: a "we-ness" brokered in an emergency not entirely or equally shared. Produced out of the immediacy of crisis, people certainly came together to conserve energy (setsuden) in the cities, send or deliver supplies up north, shovel mud or visit evacuation shelters in disaster zones, wash recovered pictures all over the country. There was a gathering of life and death; a wayfaring through the muddiness, quite literally, of debris. But what of the next step, of the life beyond destruction and death, and of the time beyond when time stopped for those that it did? What of a time of new forms of precarity and the continuance of the old?

Genda Yūji, the founder of "hope studies" (*kibōgaku*) at Tokyo Univer-

sity's Institute of Social Science, traveled to Tōhoku one month following the crisis. Accompanying Uno Shigeki, a political scientist and fellow
member of the hopology faculty, they went to Kamaishi in Iwate Prefecture where Uno had been conducting research on the ideology of hope
for five years. "Hope has disappeared," the mayor said when they called,
distraught over his inability to do anything to save the many who died. In
a region already struggling with economic decline and an aging population, Kamaishi was hit hard; 888 dead, 156 missing, 154 missing treated as
dead (in a population of 39,578 in 2010). When asked if there was anything
they could do, the mayor told the professors to just come up and show
their faces (*"tonikaku kao o dashite mitara"*), as if presence alone — sharing
and sensing the pain — would be something. But when they went, Genda
took along calendars, knowing how important time is in the construction of hope. Because thinking about the future — thinking oneself into
the future (tomorrow, then the next week, on a calendar) — becomes "the
energy for action" (*Asahi Shimbun*, July 23, 2012, 13). Genda distributed
calendars among victims as both a symbol and method of hope. A vision
of living into the future that demands action and energy now: Genda's
(quite Blochian) notion of hope.

In a newspaper article four months after the crisis on how to revive hope
in the stricken areas, Uno and Genda also speak of the action demanded
by the state — in managing cleanup, reconstruction, the nuclear accident
and industry. They emphasize that the work of moving forward and rebuilding needs to be a collaboration between the local and national government just as between the victims in Tōhoku and citizens (helping out)
all over Japan. Noting how popular the mention of hope became across
the world after Obama introduced it in his political campaigning, they express wariness about the politics of hope; it's dangerous to think that hope
is something that a politician (or anyone) can give. Hope shouldn't be top-
down — or pronounced in the name of a collective Japan that exerts pressures and exclusions all its own. Rather, it should come from going to the
scene itself and hearing from those victimized. "Go up and give support,
like giving a calendar," Genda advises. As he and Uno see it, this — the
social ecology of hope — stems from a relationship; what I call an ethics of
care built from a precariousness ontologically shared if differentially distributed (Butler 2009). Not just personal — based on the efforts of volunteers working alone or in NPOS — but also between the local and national
government: working together to make not only Tōhoku but the entire

country livable (as in secure for employment, from nuclear fallout, toward hopeful horizons).

In this, both Genda and Uno express frustration with the national government that is getting acted out by individuals only vested in their own interests and politics. And here they wish that some of the young people so energetically volunteering would turn now to politics and become the politicians leading Japan into its future. The old structures—of politics, family, authority—need to change and loosen up: become "loose relationality" (*yuruyakana kizuna*) rather than "strong relationality" (*tsuyoi kizuna*) in Genda's terminology. Their final message is clear; what happened in the north is a disaster and problem not just for northerners but for all of Japan. Just as the activist Yuasa Makoto sees "net café refugees" (working poor) as symptomatic of a "refugeeization" plaguing the entire country, Uno and Genda link the future and hope of Tōhoku to that of Japan itself: "Hope is not just a matter of individual by individual of those hit by the disaster; it's a matter for all of Japan. If things go well in the stricken areas, things will go well in Japan too. But Japan's future can be seen perhaps in whether or not we can make the stricken areas into a region where people can have hope" (*Asahi Shimbun*, July 23, 2011, 11).

But what constitutes hope, as a vision for the future, can radically differ. In Tokyo protests against the nuclear industry exploded. Starting almost immediately and sparked by shock and disgust over TEPCO's mismanagement of its nuclear reactors and the government's collusion in lack of oversight and safety precautions, they spread to other cities (Osaka, Kyoto). In April hundreds of mainly youths in their twenties protested in Yūenji; by June thousands joined the multisited protests all over the city, including older, middle-aged, working and non-working Japanese; by September as many as sixty thousand demonstrated in protests organized around "save our children" (*kodomo o mamorō*) and notable for the mothers and labor organizations that showed up. Enraged about the dangers unleashed by the meltdowns at the Fukushima Daiichi nuclear reactor, protesters clamored for a nuclear-free (or safe) future Japan, which, for most, meant shutting down all current reactors until or unless precautions could be sufficiently guaranteed. By the end of summer, only thirty-four out of fifty-four reactors were still running. And nine months later, on May 6, 2012, the last reactor shut down, making Japan nuclear free for the first time in decades. Though two reactors (the Ōi reactors in Fukui Prefecture) were restarted two months later in July, Japan remains today relatively nuclear-free, if precariously un- and underpowered.

Up north, by contrast, views regarding TEPCO and the nuclear industry that brought jobs and revenues to (what was otherwise) an economically depressed region have been more guarded. As Kainuma Hiroshi, author of *Fukushimaron* (Fukushima theory, 2011), notes, the nuclear power plants were an "effective local developmental tool" that sutured local governments to the industry. And for the people of Fukushima, the nuclear power plant constituted their social environment, their relations of being and belonging: not something on television but their friends, exclassmates, coworkers, acquaintances. The battle over nuclear energy isn't their business. The deeper issue, writes Kainuma, is the structure of the center and periphery. These nuclear power plants generated energy for Tokyo, not Tōhoku, and Tōhoku is structurally positioned—in the political economy of the nation—as what Akasaka Norio has called Tokyo's colony (*Asahi Shimbun*, September 10, 2011). As he predicts, reconstruction in Tōhoku will be carried out by big companies in Tokyo returning the profits and revenues once again to the colonizer. As for people in Fukushima, one-third say they would leave if they could, fearful of being able to find jobs, rebuild their homes, reconstitute life of any kind in the stricken areas. And, of course, there is the radiation—not, curiously enough, something I heard local people talking much about when I visited there myself in July.

Ritual and Contamination

Instead, when stopping in at the municipal tourist office when I saw it open on the empty streets of Haramachi, the staff was eager to tell me about the upcoming *nomaoi* festival: a regional festival in late July that, dating back a thousand years, recreates a battle scene with four hundred mounted samurai in traditional Japanese armor with long swords and ancestral flagstaffs who ride across fields on their horses. Though Haramachi wouldn't be having it this year because of the crisis, it was being held by Minami Sōma next door: something local officials hoped would draw in tourists from the rest of the country. Introduced to the "scribe" of the festival when he came into the office and then taken to the municipal office to interview local officials (something the young Japanese woman

I was traveling with wanted to do for the DIY relief she was organizing as part of the NPO she'd started virtually the day after 3/11), we were told about the "hope" that was riding on this event. A traditional ritual, a ritual from the past, seen as a means (a method of hope) to engineer revenues and life for those staying in Fukushima, now a stricken area within kilometers of the evacuation zone.

When two women, a mother and daughter, who had crafted clay figurines of a nomaoi festival displayed at the municipal tourist office, befriended us and offered to drive us the twenty kilometers to Minami Sōma (no rental cars were available because of the surge of relief and cleanup workers) so we could visit a temple there now housing an evacuation shelter for horses, they shifted the conversation when we asked about radiation. As for the protests in Tokyo, it seemed an alien concept—a reaction I'd had from my team leader with Peace Boat as well. Riding in the bus to the stricken area, she'd wondered what kind of action was protest: "why not come here and shovel mud instead?" And, on their side, few protesters I joined up with in Tokyo had volunteered up north—a division of labor or differential cartography (relief versus protest) of hope? In Fukushima attention seemed more geared to treating the disaster and devastation one could see (unlike the invisibility of radiation) on the ground. But even this was hard to take in. When we ask the two women befriending us if we could drive to the beach, they graciously agree. But the scene there—of mile after mile of rubble, shards of mismatched ruins, boats on top of houses, hotels ghostly bare—seems too much and the two stay inside the car. Just as the man whose home we helped clean of mud in Ishinomaki told us he was glad there was no electricity after 3/11 because seeing the image on the television would have been too much to bear.

Hope is collective action, in my paraphrase of Genda, not just a feel good togetherness: "we Japanese as one." It is a working partnership recovering, relieving, reconstructing the stricken area, moving it—and Japan—forward, cultivating hope. Such a practice is riddled with difficulties, needless to say. Just one is in the radiation endangering all of the country, but particularly Tōhoku—a region that, as ground zero of the nuclear accident, is seen as the source of a contamination associated with everything coming from there. If safety from nuclear exposure is an issue facing all of Japan, how does this get navigated on the ground when some people live closer and rely—for their jobs, livelihood, place of residence—on literally the land so contaminated now? In the politics of "from Fukushima" consumption, showing solidarity with the region abuts against seeking safety for oneself (and one's family). One food home-delivery service in Tokyo reported in September that customers of the service were exhibiting two tendencies; one was to avoid any food produced in the Tōhoku region, the other was to actively support it. The first group was younger (mainly between twenty and forty), and the other group was older (fifty and above) (*Asahi Shimbun*, September 23, 2011).

Even rituals, those summer festivals whose cyclical repetition would symbolize hopefulness this year, got tainted by radiation. In Kyoto controversy ensued when the decision to use trees torn down in the tsunami in a traditional bonfire event (*Gozan no okuribi*) was then overturned due to fear the wood had been contaminated (even though it came from two hundred kilometers away from the Daiichi nuclear plant). Similarly, a "support reconstruction" charity fireworks festival held in Aichi prefecture cancelled their plans to use made-in-Fukushima fireworks when citizens complained they "might spread radiation from the sky" (*Asahi Shimbun*, September 21, 2011).

Precarity and the Future

On the first-year anniversary of 3/11, a Japanese friend of mine wrote to me.

> News about Japan's Great East Earthquake is reported on television every day. We are surprised again at the degree of the damage. And we're angry again at how little progress is being made. The problems we face are huge. It's a new problem for us; and how to resolve them is totally unknown. I feel we're already too late. Politically, the parties only fight between themselves. What is happening to Japan? I feel very uneasy. Is there any future for children? One year has passed.
>
> Even if all I feel is precariousness, there's nothing to be done. All we can do is pray and give assistance. But nothing is progressing. I wonder what will happen to us?

What has happened to the sense of a new era of belonging to a newly re-energized and collectivized Japan now—at this stage of post-3/11? In a letter by a reader published in *Asahi Shimbun* in August just four months after the disaster, a fifty-eight-year-old man wrote that reconstruction needs to be a reconstruction not only of businesses and towns in Tōhoku but also of the Japanese social structure. What he describes is a transformation of soul to relieve the "disaster" of communities where ties between people have frayed and old people die all alone. What is needed, he says, is a plan for (re)connection (*musubu keikaku*) on a human level. A blueprint for ways that people can regain a sense of identity and meaning in life (*ikigai*) away from mere accumulation, competition, and wealth. A plan for making Japan a place where people share and are connected to each other: what he calls "an economy of people" (*Asahi Shimbun*, August 1, 2011). This is also what I've been calling—and tracking—throughout this book as *ibasho*: a space where one feels comfortable and at home. But can ibasho be effected through a plan, *mandated*—as the term would seem to imply—by the state or a statelike body? Is this where precariousness can or will be handled? Perhaps not, as my friend suggests with her worries about politics and the squabbling and ineffectiveness of national leaders— a complaint I hear time and time again these days.

In the distrust that has emerged, and spread, among an ever-wider contingency of citizens against the national government and its collusion with the nuclear industry that has put the lives and safety of people at risk (as many are inclined to see it these days), there has been remarkable push back at the local level: municipalities that are refusing to allow their nuclear reactors to restart without beefed up safety precautions (if then). The mayor of Osaka, Hashimoto Tōru, is one such maverick. Young (in his late thirties) and the son of a yakuza mafioso, he resisted pressure from Tokyo to restart the nearby nuclear reactors in Ōi (that restarted anyway in July 2012), earning him populist praise. He represents a new, youthful kind of politician, as does the new mayor of Yubari, a once prosperous mining town in Hokkaido that went bankrupt in 2007. Having been assigned to advise the town for a year when working in Tokyo's social welfare department, Suzuki Naomichi was then asked to run for mayor by a group of citizens sensing the need for radical change. He won at the age of thirty-one, becoming the youngest mayor in the history of the town. These are signs of change—and promoting flexibility and change—in the political culture of postwar Japan. But the very reliance on local initiative and peoples' movements today signals a crisis of indecisiveness and uncertainty in the national leadership that makes many people uneasy, just like my friend. And this uneasiness could lead people into accepting something much more totalitarian on the part of their political leaders, even their young leaders.

Hashimoto Tōru, the new mayor of Osaka, has stated that once politicians get their seat after election, it means that they are given carte blanche to practice even dictatorship.

My own sense is that things are still in the mud. And that is not altogether bad as long as people can stay with the uncertainty for awhile and give both the lives that have been lost and the changes brewing in the current landscape (tapping into that resurge of sociality and channeling it to structural transformations that would turn the tide on the socioeconomic inequities, trends toward insecuritization and precaritization of pre-3/11 Japan, and gross negligence of corporations like TEPCO) the time needed to prevent mere repetition of the past. Stay with the present, precarious as it is, and face the pain but also the pleasures of working together in the mud.

As mentioned earlier, a recent book getting attention these days is by a young Japanese in his twenties proclaiming that those in his generation are quite happy, much happier, in fact, than any other generation, with a satisfaction of life approaching 87 percent. Despite all the indications of a society and economy in decline—low birthrate, an aging population, precarious employment, diminishing resources—young people are content because they live, and act, in the present. In his book *Zetsubō no kuni no kōfuku na wakamonotachi* (Happy youth in a country of despair, 2011), written after the crisis, Furuichi Noritoshi disputes that many of his generation have truly fallen victim to poverty. Poverty is twenty years in the future for his generation with baby boomer parents who worked and saved enough to keep their children materially comfortable. Youths only require two things, he writes: acceptance from others (*shōnin*) (which they can easily get on the Internet with social media) and enough money to buy street chic clothes at UniQlo (doable by living at home and working even a part-time job).

This presentist living, content in the here and now at a basic level of social and material subsistence, Furuichi calls happiness. Today's youths are not driven by the aspirational normativity of the competitive society of the family-corporate system of Japan, Inc., nor are they driven by social justice, the ethics of care, or politics of precarity of such figures like Yuasa Makoto and Amamiya Karin that I've filled my book with. Furuichi doesn't claim that his relationship to the world is one of hope nor is he interested, for the time being at least, in a temporality of the future. And if he ever goes out to volunteer or join an antinuclear protest, he says it's more like a consumer choice; he could just as easily watch a home drama on TV. Having fun (*tanoshii*) in the moment is what matters.

This too then is part of the mud. For if Furuichi is at all right about his generation (one decade younger than those in their thirties like Amamiya and Yuasa), they represent a generation disenchanted from the past but not invested in the future. This does not make them necessarily alienated, withdrawn, or enervated—as their critics so often pronounce. But whatever this is, it is part of the mix of the becoming that is post-3/11 Japan. There are some youths shoveling mud in Ishinomaki, others are becoming mayors of towns, and still others are happy to live with their parents and hang out online with their friends.

Is a temporality of the forever-present precarious?

With people still living in temporary housing, decisions to be made about reconstruction, a nuclear industry to dismantle or figure out how to live with, and security and precarity of all the old(er) types still at bay, the present is soon not the present anymore. If not the future (or no future), what is it? Who can live (securely) in it? And with what kinds of "economies of people" (a "we" that includes and excludes whom)?

I leave these questions dangling over a post-3/11 Japan that still, for the time being, is precarious, just like everywhere today.

NOTES

CHAPTER 1. PAIN OF LIFE

1. Japanese names are written last name first.

2. N.H.K. ni yōkoso translates as "Welcome to the N.H.K." NHK is the national broadcasting system in Japan. But in the story the main protagonist, who is suffering from delusions, thinks this stands for Nippon hikikomori kyōkai or the Japanese Hikikomori Association.

3. Manga are comic books, while anime are animated videos or cartoons. Takimoto Tatsuhiko, the author, published the novel in 2002 with Kadokawa shoten. The manga version, also published by Kadokawa, was serialized in its manga magazine *Shōnen Ace* between June 2004 and June 2007. The television anime, broadcast in twenty-four episodes, was televised by Gonzo between July and December 2006. There are English versions of the novel, comic book, and animated cartoon.

4. This is somewhat of a new usage by Yuasa, which he takes from words like *tamekomu* (to hoard or save up) and *tameiki* (to sigh).

5. Pierre Bourdieu (1998) is one of the first scholars said to have used the word.

6. Named after Henry Ford, who started the Ford automobile plants in Dearborn, Michigan, in 1915, Fordism refers to a social and economic system of industrial mass production. Unique to the United States until the end of the Second World War, Fordism spread and was exported to other countries in Europe, Latin America, Japan, and East Asia in postwar times. Based on Taylorization, production was broken down into discrete steps to make it more rational and efficient. Also, under the model introduced by Ford, workers were paid a sufficiently decent wage so they could purchase the objects they were producing for their own consumption (such as a Model-T Ford). Due to a number of factors, including the oil shock in 1973 and increased international competition of consumption goods, Fordist production started shifting to post-Fordism in the 1970s characterized by more just-in-time production (or "lean production"), flexible labor, and outsourcing (see Harvey 2007).

7. According to Guy Standing (2011, 9–10), the precariat (workers in precarious employment) lack seven forms of labor-related security: 1) labor market security (adequate income-earning opportunities), 2) employment security (protection against arbitrary firing), 3) job security (the ability to advance), 4) work security (protection against accidents), 5) skill reproduction security (the opportunity to acquire and advance skills), 6) income security (adequate income), and 7) representation security (access to a collective voice in the labor market).

8. *Embracing Defeat: Japan in the Wake of World War II* is the title of John Dower's (1999) excellent history about Japan's defeat in the Second World War and its subsequent reconstruction under Allied (mainly American) occupation.

9. By May 2012 the decision had been made never to reopen the four nuclear reactors in Fukushima. The number of nuclear reactors in the country is thus tallied now to be fifty, not fifty-four, that is, fifty now pending reopening.

10. There is an emergent body of scholarship on the affect/sensing/embodiment /everydayness of precarity/survival/raw life/abandonment. My own work has been deeply informed and influenced by this scholarship, and particularly that by fellow anthropologists on: ordinary affects and precarity's forms (Stewart 2007, 2012), life in zones of social abandonment (Biehl 2005), affective space and phantomic existence (Navaro-Yasmin 2012), raw life and the hope/ugliness of social forms (Ross 2010), existential reciprocity and living on the margins (Lucht 2012), the uneven distribution of well-being (Jackson 2011), social suffering and pain (Das 1997), care and debt amidst unequal social arrangements (Han 2012), the chronicity of pain in a pastoral clinic (Garcia 2010), ethics and volunteerism (Muehlebach 2012), exhaustion, endurance, and a social otherwise (Povinelli 2011), and queerness, precarity, and fabulousity (Manalansan, talk given at Feminist Theory Workshop, Duke, March 23, 2013).

11. Japanese names are written in Chinese ideograms (*kanji*) that can be read in different ways.

CHAPTER 2. FROM LIFELONG TO LIQUID JAPAN

1. Mass culture also picked up the theme of the three sacred imperial regalia in its commercial slogans for desirable consumer goods: the three *S*'s of the late 1950s and

early 1960s (*senpūki, sentakuki*, and *suihanki*—electric fan, washing machine, and electric rice cooker), the three C's of the mid-1960s (*kā, kūrā*, and *karā terebi*—car, air conditioner, and color television), and the three J's of the early 1970s (*jueri, jetto*, and *jūtaku*—jewels, overseas vacation, and private house) (Kelly 1993, 195).

2. *Furītā* comes from coupling the English word "free" with *arubaito*, a Japanese transliteration of the German word used to denote work.

3. They, along with the work they performed, were called "*pūtarō*" instead (Slater 2009).

4. Protecting the long-term employment contracts for their regular workers has been a hallmark of Japanese companies since the 1960s, of course. But this policy also developed alongside a flexibility of the employment system that was arguably more advanced than in other developed countries. Given that (core) workers were hired into a company rather than a specific job meant that they could be reassigned to other tasks or other offices (*haichitenkan*) or even loaned to another company (*shukkō*) where they might eventually be reassigned. Companies adopted other strategies as well to cope with the fluctuations of the market. When demand declined, they would reduce overtime and stop midterm career recruitment. Next they would adjust employment internally, cut back on new recruits, and stop renewing contracts for irregular workers. Laying off regular workers or inducing them into early retirement came only as last resorts (Chatani 2008).

5. With this new policy, workers were now divided into three categories: 1) those with long-term accumulation ability, 2) those highly skilled, and 3) flexible workers (*jūnan koyō*) (Amamiya and Kayano 2008).

6. The term was coined by Yamada Masahiro (1999) in reference to youngish adults who live even into their forties or fifties at home, eating mother's cooking and spending whatever disposable income they make on a pampered lifestyle of boutique cafés, travel overseas, and indulgent hobbies.

7. According to a survey done by the Ministry of Health and Labor in 2007. These figures, however, are higher than what many part-time and temporary workers get; in Hokkaido, for example, the minimum wage remains 660 yen an hour ($7).

8. According to another survey done by the Ministry of Health, Labor, and Welfare in 2007, this one on homelessness (Matsumoto 2008).

9. Temporary or dispatch work (*haken*) has steadily increased since the mid-1980s. Initially 95 percent of temp workers were women; this had gone down to 80 percent by the end of the 1990s. Female temp workers are relatively young (average age is thirty-three) compared to men (average age is thirty-eight), and 64 percent of female temp workers are single and continue to receive financial support from their parents; 71 percent of registered temp workers had contracts for less than three months in 1999, but more than two-thirds remain with the same employer for more than one year. Temp workers receive lower overall compensation than do part-time workers (more the purview of married women), though they may receive a higher hourly wage; 66 percent have health care coverage (33 percent of part-time workers do). Two-thirds of temp workers have access to employment insurance and pension insurance, but few receive bonus payments (28.8 percent), lump-sum retirement

payments (15.4 percent), or private enterprise annuities (9.6 percent) (Gottfried 2009).

10. Although unemployment is actually higher for males than for females.

11. In contrast to 81 percent in the United States, 82 percent in the United Kingdom, and 86 percent in France.

12. Women constitute 6.9 percent of business managers, 12.6 percent of lawyers, and 17.2 percent of doctors.

13. Benefits included air tickets back to Brazil, cash payments of $3,000 for unemployed workers of Japanese descent, and $2,000 for each family member, upon the proviso that they won't (and can't) return to Japan until economic and employment conditions improve (Masters 2009).

14. Since the initiation of its bilateral economic agreements with the Philippines and Indonesia to bring over nurses and nursing care workers in 2008, a total of 998 have entered Japan. In 2009 virtually none passed the exam and in July 2010 the media announced the departure of 33: 11 after failing the exam and 22 in frustration over the slim prospects they had of succeeding (*Yomiuri Shimbun* July 9, 2010:1).

15. Uninsured citizens can access the health system by either paying 100 percent of the expenses out of pocket or by paying the outstanding premiums and thus attaining temporary insurance.

16. *Otoko ohitorisama dō* (The Way of a Gentleman Alone) is the title of Ueno's 2009 book, which she says was written in response to readers asking her to make this book, for men—unlike the first one, which was directed more toward women.

17. For this, and other reasons, the elderly spend considerable time in hospitals. This is where 78 percent of them die (13 percent die at home and 2 percent in old-age facilities), and the average length of stay, whether at time of death or for other hospitalizations, is 36.4 days (in contrast to only 3.3 days in the United States).

18. Lecture by Matsushita Hiro at Temple University of Japan on June 18, 2010.

19. Every Tuesday there is a drop-in consultancy (*sōdanshitsu*) service, staffed by volunteers, where anyone can attain advice on how to find jobs and housing and help in applying for welfare.

20. Only 2 percent of children are born outside of wedlock in Japan, though the figure is rising.

21. This is a reference to a story about the "disappearing elderly" that appeared in July 2010 when a number of elderly, particularly centenarians, were found not to have been reported dead in the records of municipal offices. I discuss this in chapter 5.

22. Vuvuzelas were the plastic horns much the rage in South Africa (and as much in Japan, for some reason) during the 2010 World Cup.

CHAPTER 3. ORDINARY REFUGEEISM

1. One in three workers is irregularly employed, 49 percent of young workers (between the ages of fifteen and twenty-four), and 53 percent of all women. The trend is also increasingly toward irregularization; 33,930 new regular workers joined the workforce in 2007 (compared to 34,880 in 1990), and 17,260 new irregular workers

in 2007 (an increase from 8,810 in 1990). The average annual salary of irrregular workers in 2007 was 2,000,000 yen (2,400,000 yen is a subsistence wage, according to the government [US$21,243 versus US$25,491]). While health insurance is mandated, irregular workers increasingly don't pay into it and are not made to do so by their employers (73.2 percent of those who sleep in net cafés are not on it). Irregular workers are not covered by unemployment insurance in which payment is down nationwide as well (in 1982, 59.5 percent of unemployed received unemployment benefits, but in 2006 only 21.6 percent of the unemployed received benefits). *Shakai hoken* (social insurance) is a safety net for workers, but it can only be withdrawn if workers have paid into it. *Seikatsu hojo* is welfare; about 26 percent of the population receives it in some form: 44.3 percent to households with elderly, 7.8 percent to single mothers, 22.8 percent to households with sick, 11.6 percent to households with disabled. It is also true that welfare applications are often refused and many hesitate to apply, out of ignorance of the system or embarrassment. Further, one needs to have a residence in order to receive welfare, so those who are homeless are particularly vulnerable (Matsumoto 2008; Yuasa 2008a).

2. This seems to be a pattern of the homeless all over the world. See, for example, Hőjdestrand (2009) about homelessness ("and humanness") in post-socialist Russia.

3. This is a point Lawrence Grossberg (2005) has also made about the United States and the "war" it has made against American kids.

4. According to Guy Standing (2011), the precariat is not precisely a class because of the nomadic, flexible, and transient form of work they do. To him, precariat workers are more a "class in the making" who need to activate not as old-style unions did but with different kinds of alliances and politics.

5. Published in 2007 as *Wākingu pua: nihon o mushibamu yamai* (NHK Special Documentary; Working Poor: The Sickness Undermining Japan).

6. The title of one of Amamiya's books is *Ikisasero! Nanminka suru wakamonotachi* (Let Us Live! The Refugeeization of Youth) (2007).

7. For more on the subject of *tame* and how differential distributions of human "reserves" is reorganizing Japanese social life and the lives of Japanese, see Yuasa 2008c.

8. Hatoyama Yukio was a short-term prime minister in office for only nine months: from September 16, 2009 to June 2, 2010. But his election as a member of the progressive Democratic Party of Japan (Minshutō) signaled the displacement of the long-entrenched, and far more politically conservative, Liberal Democratic Party (LDP) that had held power since 1955.

9. Shibuya is a central hub — and train station — in Tokyo known as a hip youth center, but also one where (in the station and adjacent city parks) many homeless sleep.

10. The Self-Defense Forces are known as *jieitai*. Under Article 9 of Japan's so-called peace constitution, Japan is not allowed to arm itself except for self-defense nor to expend more than 1 percent of its GNP on such self-defense.

11. I have paraphrased rather than quoted Yuasa directly here.

12. Koizumi Jun'ichirō was prime minister for three terms between 2001 and 2006.

13. Harvey is using here the term originally introduced by Marx of primitive (or

original) accumulation, which included the commodification and privatization of land forcefully taken from peasants. Neoliberalism produces a different type of accumulation of dispossession that has four features, according to Harvey (2007): 1) a new order of privatization and commodification (spread now to domains once considered off-limits such as water and social welfare), 2) the highly predatory and speculative waves of financialization since the 1980s, 3) the management and manipulation of crises such as the U.S. bail out of Mexico (which we certainly have seen a lot of since 2008), and 4) state redistributions (how the state has cut back on expenditures for prisons, for example, which is now a thriving, heavily privatized, industry).

14. When first renting an apartment in Japan, a deposit as well as "key" money is required, which may come to an equivalent of six months' rent.

15. Akagi means college here. But, up until the recession and labor cutbacks in the 1990s, high school graduates could secure stable, long-term employment upon graduation as well. Akagi is also referring here to the relatively short window of time graduates, at whatever level, have for finding secure (regular) employment in Japan. For college students, the job-hunting process (*shūkatsu*) starts junior year. By the end of this time, students expect to have found a steady job. I have been told that two years is about the limit that young people feel they are given for finding this steady, long-term job upon graduation. After that time, their job options narrow considerably.

16. Akagi uses the word *ryūdōka* in a double sense here: acknowledging its usage to reference the new "flexible" labor force, he also finds the social circumstances in which this new labor class actually lives to be not "flexible" (or mobile) enough.

17. For this account, and commentary, on what was called the "*Akihabara musabetsu tero jiken*" (Akihabara indiscriminate terrorist attack), I relied primarily on a special issue of the journal *Rosujene* (Lost Generation) from 2008.

18. The word *fuman* suggests something more active than *fuan*.

19. Though her focus seems to be on Japanese citizens who are suffering hardship in life rather than non-Japanese migrants.

20. Amamiya writes mainly political essays and books on current conditions; her very first book, however, was a novel. She writes a column in the local homeless newspaper (*The Big Issue Japan*), but she also writes scholarly books, often in collaboration with a professor (she also writes in collaboration with Yuasa Makoto). A commanding public speaker who dresses in goth, Amamiya also appears widely in activist events—everything from indie May Day parades (which she has co-organized) and street demonstrations to speaking events on suicide, youth, the precariat, furītā unions, and proletariat literature. She also publishes "diaries" of what she does throughout the year. See, for example, Amamiya 2009.

21. Deregulation of laws restricting and protecting temporary workers started in 1985 with the Workers Dispatching Law that lifted the ban (imposed after the war) on temporary agency work for sixteen occupations. On December 10, 1996, this list was expanded by cabinet order to twenty-six job categories (which included computer operators, secretarial work, stenographers, and new media). In 1999 there was

a major revision of the Worker Dispatching Law: now practically all job areas were opened to temp agency employment with, as one concession made to unions, a one-year time limit on the use of agency temp contracts in formerly restricted occupations (Gottfried 2009).

22. *Dankai junior*: children of the baby-boomer (*dankai*) generation who came of age in the postwar era of hard work and miraculous economic growth. These "boomer juniors" were generally born in the 1970s (like Amamiya, who was born in 1975).

23. Born Chihara Koji in 1974 (part of the "dankai junior" generation, born one year earlier than Amamiya), he is an actor and comedian (performing with his brother as part of the comedy duo Chihara kyōdai—the Brothers Chihara).

24. *Tōjisha* is what social withdrawees tend to call themselves; it literally translates as "the person in question."

CHAPTER 4. HOME AND HOPE

1. And, in emphasizing temporality, I differ from Bachelard whose topoanalysis of the home is much more rooted in space.

2. The first "lost decade" was during the 1990s. The second I am referring to here is the first decade of the twenty-first century.

3. Japanese students say studying abroad tends to penalize, rather than reward, them upon entering the job market in Japan because "promotions tend to go to those who attend the same Japanese schools as their bosses" (cited in Harden 2010). Thus it seems less a case of (not) having the funds than seeing study abroad as a liability that keeps students away.

4. Abélès argues that, since the seventeenth century and "the generalization of ideas about the social contract and civil status, an interrogation about 'living together' [*l'etre ensemble*] has been at the center of political philosophy, as a focal reflection on the conditions of being together, on the means to put into place a harmonious society" (2006, 10–11). Today there has been a radical transformation in the political realm to a preoccupation now not on convivance "but a preoccupation with living and surviving—what I refer to as survival—at the heart of political action" (11).

5. See chapter 2.

6. Protests (often but not always related to labor) have certainly taken place, most notably those by Shirōto no ran in Yūenji that take on a *matsuri* (festival) or indie feel with music and cosplay. And the indie May Day parades thematized around "freedom and survival" (in which Amamiya has been involved) have joined up with transnational May Days elsewhere. But participation in and impact of these precariat and youth protests remain relatively low. See Mori 2009, however, who argues that the very shape of street politics is changing today.

7. Tokyo Disneyland was built in 1983—and quickly became the most profitable Disneyland in the world. See Yoshimi 2000.

8. Citing the demographer Nick Eberstadt and his findings about declining fertility in Japan, from which the article is drawn: "Japan is evolving into a type of so-

ciety whose contours and workings have only been contemplated in science fiction" (Eberstadt 2012, 30).

9. Because renting one's own apartment requires a substantial outlay of money—six months' "key" money as well as a deposit of several months' rent—young people often remain at home with parents until they get married. With marriage getting later—or not happening at all—some are staying ever longer with parents; one study reports 70 percent of unmarried males between the ages of twenty-one and thirty-four and 80 percent females of the same age range (Furuichi 2011).

10. UniQlo is a chain of low-cost but cool fashion. One has recently opened up in New York City.

11. For an interesting novel, made into a movie, about a Japanese teenager who "produces" another (kinder) version of herself by texting a former classmate to give her hints on how to ward off bullying (earlier, the protagonist had done nothing when her classmate was being bullied and now wants to help her in the new school where she'd heard the girl was getting bullied again), see Mado 2007. The main actress (Maeda Atsuko) was formerly one of the "AKB48" (Akihabara 48).

12. *Otaku* would be akin to the perverse in Freud's terminology.

13. Sachiko's father recently died at the age of ninety-one. Though more of a scholarly type (fluent in English from having attended college in the United States, he worked for the government during the war as a code breaker) he became a *sararī-man*, working for an import-export firm and then, at his wife's insistence, left to work in her business. Never much good at the work, however, he was seen as weak and a failure by his wife.

14. This is standard fare at *kissaten* (coffee shops) but also considered to be comfort food of sorts.

15. The entrance fee was 1,500 yen (US$16), and though we waited (in a waiting room one floor below) only an hour to go in, the wait can be much longer.

16. Actually, this cartoon is still broadcast on TV along with a serialized manga in children's magazines and a host of *Anpanman* figures (characters made of curry bread, white bread, rice balls and—as the arch enemy—bacteria) that sell in the stores.

17. Paro was designed by Japan's National Institute of Advanced Industrial Science and Technology (AIST).

18. According to its designer, the name *tamagotchi* comes from *tamago* (for egg) and *watch*.

19. *Bentō* is a boxed lunch bought, in this case, at a convenience store.

20. Part of the duo Kirin, which has subsequently split up. Tamura is very much a celebrity today and works as both an entertainer and an actor. I contacted him to do an interview for this book, but the charge was too exorbitant for me to pay.

21. The cover of the book is made to look like a piece of cardboard with a bite taken out.

22. The typical pattern of sararīman, particularly before the economic decline, was to work long hours during the day then go out drinking together in places like hostess clubs on company expense at night (Allison 1994).

23. I thank Claudia Koontz for this insight.

24. Munoz is arguing against the pragmatic approach for inclusion in straight society by such pro–gay marriage advocates as Evan Wolfson. Wolfson's assimilationist politics wind up being "homonormative" and, in that, exclusionary, for not all queers have the resources or capital to join the capitalist culture of (family) life in the twenty-first-century United States. At the other end of the spectrum, Munoz is also taking a position against such antirelationality queers as Leo Bersani and Lee Edelman.

25. This is his real name.

CHAPTER 5. THE SOCIAL BODY—IN LIFE AND DEATH

1. Miyazaki Prefecture is on the eastern coast of the island of Kyūshū.

2. For those that want to give, 500 yen an hour (US$5.31) is what is suggested. As I was told, "Japanese don't like to receive something for nothing." Users also pay all transportation fees for the volunteers giving them care labor.

3. I adopt this word from Ehrenreich and Hochschild (2002, 8), who use it to describe the globalization of care work today being driven by a "care deficit" in the Global North (as more women join the work force, they need others to replace them as caretakers of children and elderly at home) and supplied by migrants from the Global South who, driven by poverty, leave their own families and homes behind to become the nannies, domestic workers, and elderly care providers of others.

4. According to Abélès, convivance has been the center of political philosophy since the seventeenth century.

5. This is the "Akiba musabetsu terojiken" when, on June 7, 2007, Katō Tomohiko, a twenty-three-year-old haken (dispatch) worker plowed his rented truck into a crowded crossing in Akihabara, then jumped out to stab more victims, leaving seven dead. See chapter 2.

6. Several prefectures also banned it by labeling the book "harmful to youth," and today the book is sold with a paper wrapper concealing the cover, with a warning that it is not to be sold to anyone under eighteen years of age.

7. Carried out first in 2009, Toshikoshi haken mura (Dispatch Worker's New Year Village), it was repeated in 2010 when, as I have heard, the volunteers outnumbered those receiving help. Even when called a political event staged for the media, haken mura has been considered a brilliant ploy largely attributed to Yuasa.

8. Yuasa kept this position after Hatoyama left office in June 2010 (but had departed by the summer of 2012). Officially these are two positions stitched together: naikakufusanyo kinkyūkoyō taisaku honbu kinkyū shien team: jimukyokucho. Roughly translated as Consultant to the Cabinet Minister's Emergency Task Force Addressing (Counter-)measures regarding Employment and head of the Secretariat for the Advising Team on Poverty. I thank David Slater for tracking this down.

9. Article 25 of the constitution guarantees all Japanese citizens the right to a healthy and culturally basic existence.

10. And after he leaves and has handed the microphone over to Tsukino Kōji who is the moderator, he calls in on his cell phone a half an hour later to add the contact

information of help desks for women suffering discrimination at work and domestic abuse. Tsukino took the call on his own cell phone in front of the audience.

11. I adopt this phrase from my colleague Diane Nelson (1999).

12. But someone I interviewed who works with NEET, trying to assimilate them into the work force, had a different opinion of a job in a convenience store. According to him, such employment can be relatively stable and even desirable: a fairly decent way to get by these days.

13. See chapter 4.

14. Directed by Sono Shion, the film was released in 2005.

15. Most of the members of Kowaremono have jobs of one sort or another: Tsukino works as a security guard, Suzuki as a social worker, Kacco as an editor. Of the four I speak with during the interview, two live at home with their mothers.

16. This phrase is commonly used by activists and scholars of labor these days: for example, Amamiya Karin tends to call *furītā* "disposable workers" and Yamada Masahiro (2003, 18), translating from Euro-American scholars, speaks of "disposable life" (*tsukaisuteteno jinsei*).

17. In the case of the seventeen-year-old boy, the family was reported to be "strained." The mother was a single mother who worked and struggled hard to make ends meet while raising two children. It seems that the father was uninvolved in the family and didn't contribute, in any sense, to the upbringing of the children. It was to send her children to a school in a better district that the children were living alone in an apartment that she visited when she could—as she had the night she was killed.

18. This is the argument made for basic income as well (see Weeks 2011, Standing 2009).

19. There have been multiple policies implemented (or initiated) to assist, and encourage, working parents. Though most are targeted at women (such as the law for maternity leave in 1991 and endless reforms to it that now extend to small and medium-sized companies as well as to contract and part-time workers), others—like the New Angel Plan—are geared more to gender equity (The Basic Act for Gender-Equal Society established in June 1999, and revised twice later that year, and the Equal Employment Opportunity Law, first established in 1986, revised in 1997 and again in 2006 when measures protecting men from discrimination were implemented as well) (Kimoto 2008).

20. Yamada Masahiro, the sociologist who authored *Kibō kakusa shakai* as well as endless other books about the family, youths, labor, and contemporary times in Japan, has also coauthored (along with Shirakawa Tōko) a study of *konkatsu* (2008). In addition, the two also came out with something of a how-to manual obviously geared to the commercial marketplace promoting the practice.

CHAPTER 6. CULTIVATING FIELDS FROM THE EDGES

1. See Muehlebach (2012) for a discussion of how the Italian state actively incorporates and promotes volunteerism from its non- and post-waged citizens like the retired.

2. A book (Yokokawa 2004) has been written about Kawada and her various grassroots efforts at care service, caregiving, and community building.

3. For an account of all the multifarious activities, events, and activism Amamiya either participated in or sponsored herself in the year 2008, see Amamiya 2008.

4. Quotes are taken from handouts I received at Uchi no jikka; this information is also repeated on its website (www.sawayakazaidan.or.jp/ibasyo/case/04koushinetsu/uchinojikka.html).

5. In advocating for a post-work society engineered by, in part, a policy of basic income, Kathi Weeks (2011) advocates for what she calls a "utopic demand."

6. In Saitama-ken, Sayama-shi, on the outskirts of Tokyo, its full name is *Tamariba sekireitei*, (*tamariba* = hang out center; *sekirei* = the name of a bird in the area; *tei* = garden). It is operated by Numazaki Chieko in the nearly 200-year-old house she has inherited from her parents. Funded by an annual bazaar that makes it entirely self-sustaining, the *tamariba* hosts a weekly gathering open to anyone. The one I attend starts with a lecture on local history given by the head of the museum near-by followed by a lunch of *onigiri* (rice balls) and pickles (brought by the eldest one there, a 91-year-old woman). About twenty people drop by on any given week: a mixture of middle aged and elderly.

7. *Niigata chiiki wakamono sapōto sutēshon* is a subsidiary of the government-sponsored Hello Work that offers classes, counseling, and training to young people struggling to find work.

8. This was the Japanese Volunteer Academic Conference of 2010 held on June 26 and 27 at Meiji Gakuin University, Shirogane Campus. Also known as the Shirogane Mass Harappa Meeting (*Shirogane harappa taikai*), its descriptor was "cultivating fields, spinning hope on the edges of Tokyo" (*harappa o umidasu: tōkyō no ejji de kibō o tsumugu*).

CHAPTER 7. IN THE MUD

1. Murakami's op-ed was titled "Amid Shortages, a Surplus of Hope" and Azuma's, "For a Change, Proud to be Japanese" (published on March 16 in the *New York Times*). Afterward, Azuma released the Japanese original on his own blogsite (entitled "Azuma Hiroki no kajō genron: hatena hinan ban [Azuma Hiroki's Spiral Discourse: Evacuation to Hatena version] http://d/hatena.ne.jp/hazuma/20110322. Murakami released his Japanese version on *Time Out Japan* under the title: "*Kiki teki jōkyō no naka no kibō: gaikokujin kara kandō no koe zokuzoku*, Murakami Ryu's Contributed Essay to *The New York Times*."

REFERENCES

Abélès, Marc. 2010. *The Politics of Survival*. Translated by Julie Kleinman. Durham, NC: Duke University Press.

Agamben, Giorgio. 1998. *Homer Sacer: Sovereign Power and Bare Life*. Translated by Daniel Heller-Roazen. Stanford, CA: Stanford University Press.

Akagi, Tomohiro. 2007. "Kibō wa sensō: Maruyama Masao" o hippatakitai 31 sai fu-rītā" [Hope is War: From a Thirty-One-Year-Old Furītā, I'd Like to Slap Maru-yama Masao]. *Ronza*, 1 January, 53–59.

———. 2009. "Katō yōgisha o azawarau shikaku ga watashitachi ni arunoka?" [Do we have the qualifications to sneer at the suspect Kato?]. In *Akibadōrimajiken o dō yomuka?* [How Do We Read the Akiba Terrorist Attack?], edited by Yosensha MOOK henshūbuhen, 22–24. Tokyo: Yosensha MOOK henshūbuhen.

Allison, Anne. 1994. *Nightwork: Sexuality, Pleasure, and Corporate Masculinity in a Tokyo Hostess Club*. Chicago: University of Chicago Press.

———. 2000. *Permitted and Prohibited Desires: Mothers, Comics, and Censorship in Japan*. Berkeley: University of California Press.

————. 2006. *Millennial Monsters: Japanese Toys and the Global Imagination*. Berkeley: University of California Press.

Amamiya, Karin. 2007. *Ikisasero! Nanminkasuru wamonotachi* [Survive! The Refugeeization of Young People]. Tokyo: Ōtashuppan.

————. 2008. *Amamiya Karin Tōsō* [Amamiya Karin's Battle Diary]. Tokyo: Shūeisha.

————. 2009. *Amamiya Karin no "seizon kakumei" nikki* [Amamiya Karin's Diary of the "Survival Revolution"]. Tokyo: Shūeisha.

Amamiya, Karin, and Kayama Rika. 2008. *Ikinuku koto* [Survival]. Tokyo: Nanatsu-mori.

Amamiya, Karin, and Kayano Toshihito. 2008. *"Ikizurasa" nitsuite: hinkon, aidentitī, nashyonarizumu* [Concerning "Hardship of Life": Poverty, identity, nationalism]. Tokyo: Kobunsha shinsho.

Anderson, Benedict. 1983. *Imagined Communities: Reflections on the Origins and Spread of Nationalism*. London: Verso.

Appadurai, Arjun. 2006. *Fear of Small Numbers: An Essay on the Geography of Anger*. Durham, NC: Duke University Press.

————. 2007. "Hope and Democracy." *Public Culture* 19, no. 1: 29–34.

Arai, Andrea G. 2003. "Killing Kids: Recession and Survival in Twenty-first Japan." *Postcolonial Studies* 6, no. 3: 367–79.

Arendt, Hannah. (1951) 1986. *The Origins of Totalitarianism*. San Diego, New York, London: A Harvest Book, Harcourt, Inc.

Arnold, Dennis, and Joseph R. Bongiovi. 2011. "Precarious, Informalizing, and Casualizing Labor: Concepts and Definitions." Paper prepared for the workshop Precarious Work in Asia, Chung-Ang University, Seoul, South Korea, July 19–20.

Asad, Talal. 2003. *Formations of the Secular: Christianity, Islam, Modernity*. Stanford: Stanford University Press.

————. 2007. *On Suicide Bombing*. New York: Columbia University Press.

————. 2011. "Thinking about the Secular Body, Pain, and Liberal Politics." *Cultural Anthropology* 26 (4): 657–75.

Asada, Akira. 1989. "Infantile Capitalism and Japan's Postmodernism: A Fairy Tale." In *Postmodernism and Japan*, edited by Masao Miyoshi and H. D. Harootunian, 273–78. Durham, NC: Duke University Press.

Asahi Shimbun. 2007. "Rosujienereshōn; samayō 2000mannin" [Lost Generation: 200,000 Wanderers]. Tokyo: Asahi shimbunsha.

————. 2010. "Hōmuresu 'ore mo saigo wa muroku hotoku ka?'" [A Homeless Person Asks: "Will I Too Be an Unrecorded Buddha at the End?"]. August 31: 1.

————. 2011. "Seiji jibyō: Karenda ni kizameru ashita o wakamono, josei 'tsunagari' kitai" [Political News Commentary: Marking Tomorrow in a Calendar; Women and Youth Expect "Connections.] July 23: 11.

————. 2011. "Kozoku no kuni dai 3 bu 3/11 kara: Shinsai, shi itamu miuchi nashi" [Series Nation of Isolation From Families Part 3: Scenes from 3/11: Disaster, No Relatives to Mourn Death]. July 24, 2011: 1.

————. 2011. "Saiyūshūshō Sato Toshirō-san 'Higashi nihon fukkō keikaku shian' zenbun – Nippon mae e teigen ronbun shū" [Full Text of Grand Award Winner Sato Toshiro's "Proposal for Reconstruction of Eastern Japan": Proposal Article Collection "Japan Move Forward"] August 1: B20.

———. 2011. "Shinsai kara hantoshi Tōhoku yo - "Tōhoku gaku" o teishō suru minzoku no gakusha, Akasaka Norio-san" [Six Months Since Disaster in Tohoku: Folklorist Akasaka Norio Advocates "Tohokuology"]. September 10: 15.

———. 2011. "Tsukinu hōshanō fuan - Shokuzai takuhai, tsuzuku mosaku - Kuni yori kibishī jishu kijun e" [Never Ending Radiation Anxiety, Continual Trial at Food Delivery Industry: Voluntary Standards Stricter than National.] September 23, 2011: 3.

———. 2011. "Fukushima no hanabi chūshi, Kawamata chōchō ni shazai – Aichi Nisshin shichō 'Shinrō kaketa'" [Fukushima Fireworks Not Used, Nisshin City Mayor Apologizes to Kawamata Town Mayor "Caused a Lot of Stress"]. September 23: 38.

———. 2011. Fukushima Dai'ichi genpatsu no jiko shūsoku o sengen, Noda shushō "Reion teishi joutai o kakunin," kokusai kōyaku dōri nen'nai ni [PM Noda Declares Fukushima Dai'ichi Power Plant is Stable, Keeping the International Pledge: "Cold shutdown is Confirmed"]. December 15, 2011: 1.

Azuma, Hiroki. 2011. *Otaku: Japan's Database Animals*, trans. Jonathan E. Abel and Shion Kono. Mineapolis, Londo: University of Minnesota Press.

———. "For a Change, Proud to be Japanese." *The New York Times*, March 16, 2011: A35.

———. 2011. Azuma hiroki no kajō genron: hatena hinan ban [Azuma Hiroki's Spiral Discourse: Evacuation to Hatena Version]. http://hatena.ne.jp/hazuma /20110322. Posted March 22.

Bachelard, Gaston. 1964. *The Poetics of Space*. New York: Beacon Press.

Bakker, Isabella, Stephen Gill, and Tim DiMuzio. 2003. "Introduction to Part IV: Human In/Security on a Universal Scale." In *Power, Production, and Social Reproduction*, edited by Isabella Bakker and Stephen Gill, 163–68. New York: Palgrave MacMillan.

Bauman, Zygmunt. 2004. *Wasted Lives: Modernity and Its Outcasts*. Cambridge, UK: Polity Press.

Berardi, Franco "Bifo." 2009. *The Soul at Work: From Alienation to Autonomy*. Translated by Francesca Cadel and Giuseppina Mecchia. Cambridge, MA: Semiotext(e).

Berlant, Lauren. 2004. "Compassion (and Withholding)." In *Compassion: The Culture and Politics of an Emotion*, edited by Lauren Berlant. New York: Routledge.

———. 2011. *Cruel Optimism*. Durham, NC: Duke University Press.

Biehl, João. 2005. *Vita: Life in a Zone of Social Abandonment*. Berkeley: University of California Press.

Bloch, Ernst. 1986. *The Principle of Hope, Vol. One*. Translated by Neville Plaice, Stephen Plaice, and Paul Knight. Cambridge, MA: MIT Press.

———. 2000 (1923). *The Spirit of Utopia*. Stanford, CA: Stanford University Press.

Bourdieu, Pierre. 1998. "La precarité est aujourd'hui partout." In *Contre-feux*, 95–101. Paris: LiberRaison d'agir.

Brodie, Janine. 2003. "Globalization, In/Security, and the Paradoxes of the Social." In *Power, Production, and Social Reproduction*, edited by Isabella Bakker and Stephen Gill, 47–65. New York: Palgrave MacMillan.

Butler, Judith. 2009. *Frames of War: When Is Life Grievable?* New York: Verso.

Castel, Robert. 2003. *From Manual Workers to Wage Laborers: Transformation of the Social Question*. Translated by Richard Boyd. New Brunswick, NJ: Transaction Publishers.

Chatani, Kazutoshi. 2008. "From Corporate-Centered Security to Flexicurity in Japan." Employment Sector, Employment Working Paper No. 17, International Labor Office. Geneva, Switzerland.

Chihara, Jyunia. 2007. *14sai* [Fourteen years old]. Tokyo: Kōbunsha.

Das, Veena. 1997. "Language and Body: Transactions in the Construction of Pain." In *Social Suffering*, edited by Arthur Kleinman, Veena Das, and Margaret Lock. Berkeley, Los Angeles, London: Univesrity of California Press: 67–92.

Desjarlais, Robert. 1997. *Shelter Blues: Sanity and Selfhood among the Homeless*. Philadelphia: University of Pennsylvania Press.

Doi, Takeo. (1971) 2001. *"Amae" no kōzō*. Tokyo: Kōbundō.

Douglas, Mary. (1966) 2002. *Purity and Danger: An Analysis of the Concept of Pollution and Danger*. London: Routledge.

Douthat, Ross. 2012. "Japan: The Incredible Shrinking Country." *New York Times*, Sunday Review, April 28.

Dower, John W. 1999. *Embracing Defeat: Japan in the Wake of World War II*. New York: W. W. Norton.

Driscoll, Mark. 2007. "Debt and Denunciation in Post-Bubble Japan: On the Two Freeters." *Cultural Critique* 65 (winter): 164–87.

Eberstadt, Nicolas. 2012. "Japan Shrinks." *Wilson Quarterly* 36, no. 2 (spring): 30–37.

Economist Intelligence Unit. 2011. *From Silver to Gold: The Implications of Japan's Ageing Population*. GE Imagination at Work in co-operation with the Economist Intelligence Unit. http://newsroom.gehealthcare.com/_uploads/assets/silver-to -gold.pdf.

Edelman, Lee. 2004. *No Future: Queer Theory and Death Drive*. Durham, NC: Duke University Press.

Ehrenreich, Barbara, and Arlie Russell Hochschild. 2002. "Introduction." In *Global Woman: Nannies, Maids, and Sex Workers in the New Economy*, edited by Barbara Ehrenreich and Arlie Russell Hochschild, 1–13. New York: Holt.

Fackler, Martin. 2010. "Japan Goes from Dynamic to Disheartened: Asian Giant's Retrenchment Offers a Warning to the West." *New York Times*, October 17.

———. 2011. "Japan May Declare Control Over Damaged Reactors, but Skeptics Demure." *New York Times*, December 15, A6, A11.

Fassin, Didier. 2008. "The Humanitarian Politics of Testimony: Subjectification through Trauma in Israeli-Palestinian Conflict." *Cultural Anthropology* 23, no. 3: 531–58.

Ferguson, James. 2006. *Global Shadows: Africa in the Neoliberal World Order*. Durham, NC: Duke University Press.

Fingleton, Eamonn. 2012. "The Myth of Japan's Failure." *New York Times*, Sunday Review, January 8.

Foucault, Michel. 1998. *The History of Sexuality, Vol. 1: The Will to Knowledge*. London: Penguin.

———. 2003. *"Society Must Be Defended": Lectures at the Collège de France 1975–76*. New York: Picador.

———. 2008. *The Birth of Biopolitics: Lectures at the Collège de France 1978–79*. New York: Palgrave Macmillan.

Fukuyama, Francis. 1995. *Trust: The Social Virtues and the Creation of Prosperity*. New York: Free Press.

Furuichi, Noritoshi. 2011. *Zetsubō no kuni no kōfukuna wakmonotachi* (Happy Youth in a Country of Despair). Tokyo: Kodansha.

Galbraith, Patrick. 2009. *The Otaku Encyclopedia: An Insider's Guide to the Subculture of Cool*. Tokyo: Kodansha International.

Garcia, Angela. 2010. *The Pastoral Clinic: Addiction and Dispossession along the Rio Grande*. Berkeley: University of California Press.

Genda, Yūji. 2005. *A Nagging Sense of Job Insecurity: The New Reality Facing Japanese Youth*. Translated by Jean Connell Hoff. Tokyo: International House of Japan.

———. 2006. *Kibōgaku* [Hope Studies]. Tokyo: Chuokoron shinsho.

Genda, Yūji, and Uno Shigeki, eds. 2009. *Kibōgaku 4: Kibō no hajimaru: ryūdōkasuru no sekai de* [Hope studies vol. 4: The Start of Hope: In a World that has Become Flexibilized]. Tokyo: Tokyo daigaku shuppankai.

Gottfried, Heidi. 2000. "Compromising Positions: Emergent Neo-Fordisms and Embedded Gender Contracts." *British Journal of Sociology* 51, no. 2 (June): 235–59.

———. 2009. "Japan: The Reproductive Bargain and the Making of Precarious Employment." In *Gender and the Contours of Precarious Employment*, edited by Leah F. Vosko, Martha MacDonald, and Iain Campbell, 76–91. London: Routledge.

Grossberg, Lawrence. 2005. *Caught in the Crossfire: Kids, Politics, and America's Future*. Boulder, CO: Paradigm Publishers.

Hage, Ghassan. 2003. *Against Paranoid Nationalism: Searching for Hope in a Shrinking Society*. Annandale: Merlin Press.

Hakuhōdō seikatsu sōgō. 2005. *10dai no zenbu* [Everything about Teenagers]. Tokyo: Hakuhōdō seikatsu sōgō.

Han, Clara. 2012. *Life in Debt: Times of Care and Violence in Neoliberal Chile*. Berkeley: University of California Press.

Harden, Blaine. 2010. "Once Drawn to U.S. Universities, More Japanese Staying Home." *Washington Post*, April 11.

Hardt, Michael. 2011. "For Love or Money." *Cultural Anthropology* 26 (4): 678–9.

Hardt, Michael, and Antonio Negri. 2004. *Multitude: War and Democracy in the Age of Empire*. New York: Penguin Press.

———. 2009. *Commonweath*. Cambridge: Harvard University Press.

Harootunian, H. D. 1989. "Visible Discourses/Invisible Ideologies." In *Postmodernism and Japan*, edited by Masao Miyoshi and H. D. Harootunian, 63–92. Durham, NC: Duke University Press.

Harvey, David. 2007. *A Brief History of Neoliberalism*. New York: Oxford University Press.

Hochschild, Arlie Russell. 2002. "Love and Gold." In *Global Woman: Nannies, Maids, and Sex Workers in the New Economy*, edited by Barbara Ehrenreich and Arlie R. Hochschild, 15–38. New York: Holt.

Hoffman, Danny. 2011. "Violence, Just in Time: War and Work in Contemporary West Africa." *Cultural Anthropology* 26, no. 1: 34–58.

Höjdestrand, Tova. 2009. *Needed by Nobody: Homelessness and Humanness in Post-Socialist Russia*. Ithaca, NY: Cornell University Press.

Honda, Tōru. 2005. *Denpa otoko* [Radio-wave man]. Tokyo: Miobukkusu.

———. 2007. *Jisatsu suru nara, hikikomore: Mondai darake no gakkō kara mi o mamoru ō* [If You're Going to Commit Suicide, Withdraw: Ways to Protect Oneself from Problem-Filled Schools]. Tokyo: Kobunsha shoten.

Ingold, Tim. 2012. *Being Alive: Essays on Movement, Knowledge and Description*. London, New York: Routledge Press.

Ivy, Marilyn. 1995. *Discourses of the Vanishing: Modernity, Phantasm, Japan*. Chicago: University of Chicago Press.

Iwabuchi, Kōichi. 2002. *Recentering Globalization: Popular Culture and Japanese Transnationalism*. Chicago: University of Chicago Press.

Iwata, Masami. 2007. *Gendai no hinkon: wakkingu pua/hommuresu/seikatsuhogō* [Poverty today: Working poor/homeless/welfare]. Tokyo: Chikuma shoten.

Jackson, Michael. 2011. *Life Within Limits: Well-being in a World of Want*. Durham, NC: Duke University Press.

Joseph, Miranda. 2002. *Against the Romance of Community*. Minneapolis: University of Minnesota Press.

Kainuma, Hiroshi. 2011. *Fukushimaron: genshiryoku mura wa naze umareta noka* [Theory of Fukushima: Why Was the Nuclear Village Born?]. Tokyo: Seidosha.

Kalleberg, Arne L. 2009. "Precarious Work, Insecure Workers: Employment Relations in Transition." *American Sociological Review* 74 (February): 1–22.

———. 2011. *Good Jobs, Bad Jobs: The Rise of Polarized and Precarious Employment Systems in the United States, 1970s to 2000s*. New York: Russell Sage Foundation.

Kaneko, Sachiko. 2006. "Japan's 'Socially Withdrawn Youths' and Time Constraints in Japanese Society." *Time and Society* 15, nos. 2/3: 233–49.

Katsuno, Hirofumi. 2011. "The Robot's Heart: Tinkering with Humanity and Intimacy in Robot-Building." *Japanese Studies* 31, no. 1: 93–109.

Kelly, William W. 1993. "Finding a Place in Metropolitan Japan: Ideologies, Institutions, and Everyday Life." In *Postwar Japan as History*, edited by Andrew Gordon, 189–238. Berkeley: University of California Press.

Kimoto, Kimiko. 2008. "Kazoku, jenda. kaisō" [Gender, Family, Class]. In *Koyōryū-dōka no naka no kazoku* [The Family Within Flexible Labor], edited by Funabashi Keiko and Miyamoto Michiko, 33–54. Tokyo: Minerubua shoten.

Kleinman, Arthur. 2010. "Caregiving: The Divided Meaning of Being Human and the Divided Self of the Caregiver." In *Rethinking the Human*, edited by Michelle

Molina and Donald K. Swearer, 17–29. Cambridge, MA: Center for the Study of World Religions, Harvard Divinity School.

Kobayashi, Akako and Yamane, Yūsa. 2011. "Mienai 'teki' to tatakau haha" [Fighting Mothers and Invisible Enemies]. *Asahi Shimbun Weekly AERA*, Jun 27, 2011: 10–15.

Koselleck, Reinhart. 1985. *Futures Past: On the Semantics of Historical Time*. Cambridge, MA: MIT Press.

Lazzarato, Maurizio. 2004. "The Political Form of Coordination." *Transversal*. Accessed from http://eipcp.net/transversal/0707/lazzarato/en on December 23, 2007.

Lear, Jonathan. 2006. *Radical Hope: Ethics in the Face of Cultural Devastation*. Cambridge, MA: Harvard University Press.

Lefebvre, Henri. 2004. *Rhythmanalysis: Space, Time, and Everyday Life*. New York: Continuum.

Lucht, Hans. 2012. *Darkness Before Daybreak: African Migrants Living on the Margins*. Berkeley: University of California Press.

Mado, Kaori. 2007. *Ashita no watashi no tsukurikata* [Making the Me of Tomorrow]. Tokyo: Kōdansha.

Makino, Tomio. 2008. "'Kakusa shakai' ni dō tachimukauka" [How to Confront "a Differential Society"], in *Kakusa to hinkon ga wakaru 20kō* [Twenty Cases to Understand Difference and Poverty], eds., Makino Toshio and Murakami Eigo. Tokyo: Akashi shoten: 214–227.

Marx, Karl. 1978. *Capital*. In *The Marx-Engels Reader*, vol. 1. 2nd ed. Edited by Robert C. Tucker, 294–438. New York: W. W. Norton.

Massey, Doreen. 1995. *Space, Place, and Gender*. Minneapolis: University of Minnesota Press.

Masters, Coco. 2009. "Japan to Immigrants: Thanks but You Can Go Home Now." *Time* in partnership with CNN, April 20.

Masuda, Akitoshi. 2008. *Kyō, tōmuresu natta: 15nin no sararīman tenraku jinsei* [Today, I Became Homeless: The Lives of 15 Salarymen Who Have Fallen Down]. Tokyo: Saizusha.

Matsumoto, Ichirō. 2008. Hinkon, tei to shakai shotoku mondai to shakai fukushi—kakusa kakudai no saki ni arumono [Social Welfare and the Problem of Low Income and Poverty—The Point of a Widening Gap], in *Kakusa to hinkon ga wakaru 20kō* [Twenty Cases to Understand Difference and Poverty], eds., Makino Toshio and Murakami Eigo. Tokyo: Akashi shoten: 53–65.

Mazzarella, William. 2009. "Affect: What Is It Good For?" In *Enchantments of Modernity: Empire, Nation, Globalization*, edited by Saurabh Dube, 291–309. London: Routledge.

Miyamoto, Michiko. 2008. "Koyōryūdōka no shit ade no kazokukeisei" [The Formation of Family under the Flexibilization of Labor.] In *Koyōryūdōka no naka no kazoku* [The Family Inside the Flexibilization of Labor], edited by Funabashi Keiko and Miyamoto Michiko. Tokyo: Minerubua shobō.

Miyamoto, Tarō. 2008. *Jiyū e no toi #2: Shakai hoshō—sekyuritē no kōzō tankan*

[Question for Freedom #2: Social Security—Structural Turn-About in Security].
Toyko: Iwanami shoten.

Miyazaki, Hirokazu. 2004. *The Method of Hope: Anthropology, Philosophy, and Fijian Knowledge*. Stanford, CA: Stanford University Press.

———. 2010. "The Temporality of No Hope." In *Ethnographies of Neoliberalism*, edited by Carol Greenhouse, 238–66. Philadelphia: University of Pennsylvania Press.

Mizushima, Hiroaki. 2007. *Netto kafue nanmin to hinkon Nippon* [Net Café Refugees and Poverty in Japan]. Tokyo: Nihon terebi hōsō kabushiki kaisha.

Molé, Noelle J. 2012. *Labor Disorders in Neoliberal Italy: Mobbing, Well-being, and the Workplace*. Bloomington: Indiana University Press.

Mori, Yoshitaka. 2009. *Sutorīto no shisō: tenkanki to shite no 1990-nendai* [Theories of Street: 1990s as Turning Point]. Tokyo: Nippon hōsō shuppan kyōkai.

Muehlebach, Andrea. 2012. *The Moral Neoliberal: Welfare and Citizenship in Italy*. Chicago, London: The University of Chicago Press.

Munoz, José Esteban. 2009. *Cruising Utopia: The Then and There of Queer Futurity*. Durham, NC: Duke University Press.

Murakami, Ryū. 2002. *Kibō no kuni no ekosodasu* [The Exodus of a Country With Hope]. Tokyo: Bunshun Bunko.

———. 2003. *Kyōseichū*. Tokyo: Kōdansha Bunko.

Murakami, Ryū. 2011. "Amid Shortages, a Surplus of Hope." *The New York Times*, March 16: A35.

———. 2011. "Kiki teki jōkyō no naka no kibō: Gaikokujin kara kandō no koe zokuzoku, Murakami Ryū no nyūyōku taimuzu e no kikōbun" [Hope in the Devastating Situation: Foreigners Voice Deep Emotion, Murakami Ryū's Contributed Essay to the *New York Times*]. *Time Out Japan*, March.

Nakane, Chie. 1967. *Tate shakai no ningen kankei* [Human Relations in a Vertical Society]. Tokyo: Kodansha.

Navaro-Yasmin, Yael. 2012. *The Make-Believe Space: Affective Geography in a Postwar Polity*. Durham, NC: Duke University Press.

Neilson, Brett and Ned Rossiter. 2008. "Precarity as a Political Concept, or Fordism as Exception." *Theory, Culture & Society* 25 (7–8): 51–72.

Nelson, Diane. 1999. *A Finger in the Wound: Body Politics in Quincentennial Guatemala*. Berkeley: University of California Press.

Ngai, Pun. 2004. *Made in China: Women Factory Workers in a Global Workplace*. Durham, NC: Duke University Press.

NHK Muen shakai purojekuto. 2010. *Muen shakai: muenshi sanman-nisennin no shōgeki* [Relationless Society: The Shock of 32,000 Relationless Deaths]. Tokyo: Bungei shunjū.

NHK Special Documentary. 2007. *Wakkingu pua: Nihon o mushibamu yamai* [Working Poor: The Sickness Undermining Japan]. Tokyo: Poplar Press.

Nihon Kodomo Sosshyaru Wāku Kyōkai. 2005. *Kazoku ni shite hoshi koto. Shite hoshikunaikoto: futōko. hikikomori taikensha kara no messejji* [Things to Wish For, and Not to Wish For, in Families: Messages from Those who Have Experienced Refusal to Go to School and Social Withdrawal]. Tokyo: Nihon kodomo sosshyaru wāku kyōkai.

OECD. 2012. "Social Spending after the Crisis": Social Expenditure (SOCX) Data Update 2012. http://www/oecd.org/els/soc/OECD(2012)_Social spending after the crisis_ (downloaded 3/26/2013).

Ong, Aihwa. 2006. Neoliberalism as Exception: Mutations in Citizenship and Sovereignty. Durham, NC: Duke University Press.

Ozawa-de-Silva, Chikako. 2010. "Shared Death: Self, Sociality and Internet Group Suicide in Japan." Transcultural Psychiatry 47, no. 3: 392–418.

Piot, Charlie. 2010. Nostalgia for the Future. Chicago: University of Chicago Press.

Polanyi, Karl. (1944) 2001. The Great Transformation: The Political and Economic Origins of our Time. Boston, Beacon Press.

Povinelli, Elizabeth A. 2011. Economies of Abandonment: Social Belonging and Endurance in Late Liberalism. Durham, NC: Duke University Press.

Redfield, Peter. 2013. Life in Crisis: the Ethical Journey of Doctors Without Borders. Berkeley: University of California Press.

Roberson, James E. and Nobue Suzuki. 2003. Men and Masculinities in Contemporary Japan: Dislocating the Salaryman Doxa. London and New York: RoutledgeCurzon.

Roberts, Glenda S. 2005. "Balancing Work and Life: Whose Work? Whose Life? Whose Balance?" Asian Perspective 29, no. 1: 175–211.

Rose, Nikolas. 2001. "The Politics of Life Itself." Theory, Culture, and Society 18, no. 1: 1–30.

Ross, Fiona C. 2010. Raw Life, New Hope: Decency, Housing and Everyday Life in a Post-Apartheid Community. Claremont, South Africa: University of Cape Town.

Rosujiene [Lost Generation]. 2008. Special issue on "Akihabara musabetsu tero jiken, 'teki' wa daredatta no ka?" [Who Was the Enemy in the Akihabara Indiscriminate Terrorist Attack?]

Sannomiya, Chikako and Miyake, Reiko. 2011. "Fukushima to tōkyō haha no shōgen: ko o mamoreru no wa watashishikanai" [Testimonials of Fukushima and Tokyo Mothers; It is Only Me Who Can Protect my Child]. Asahi Shimbun Weekly AERA, June 27: 28–30.

Shimizu, Masahiro. 2008. "Hōmuresu chūgakusei" sono ato: mo hitotsu nakaseru monogatari [After "Homeless Middle School Student": One More Story to Make You Cry]. Tokyo: Koara Bukkusu.

Shimizu, Yoshiko. 2009. Kaigo utsu: onechan, nande shinjyattano [Caregiving depression: Older Sister, What Made You Die?]. Tokyo: Bukkumansha.

Silver, Beverly. 2003. Forces of Labor: Workers' Movements and Globalization Since 1870. Cambridge: Cambridge University Press.

Slater, David H. 2009. "The Making of Japan's New Working Class: 'Freeters' and the Progression from Middle School to the Labor Market." In Social Class in Contemporary Japan: Structures, Socialization, and Strategies, edited by Ishida Hiroshi and David H. Slater, 103–115. New York: Routledge.

Solnit, Rebecca. 2009. A Paradise Built in Hell: The Extraordinary Communities That Arise in Disaster. New York: Viking.

Standing, Guy. 2011. *The Precariat: The New Dangerous Class*. New York: Bloomsbury Academic.

Stewart, Kathleen. 2007. *Ordinary Affects*. Durham, NC: Duke University Press.

———. 2012. "Precarity's Forms." *Cultural Anthropology* 27 (2): 518–525.

Suzuki, Wataru. 2007. "Problems on Labor, Health and Support for Being Independent for Homeless People" Nihon rōdō kenkyū zasshi. No. 563: 61–74.

Tabuchi, Hiroko. 2010. "For Some in Japan, Home Is a Tiny Plastic Bunk." *New York Times*, January 1. http://www.nytimes.com/2010/01/02/business/global/02capsule.html.

———. 2011. "Japan's Premier Says Nuclear Crisis Is Over, but Critics Say He's Premature." *New York Times*, December 17, A8.

Tachibanaki, Toshiaki. 2008. "Intorodakushyon—kakusakara hinkon e" [Introduction—From Difference to Poverty]. In *Kakusa to hinkon: 20 kō* [Difference and Poverty: 20 Cases], edited by Makino Tomio and Murakami Eigo, 8–18. Tokyo: Akashi Shoten.

Takahara, Motoaki. 2006. *Fuantei nashyonarizumu no jidai* [The Era of Unsafe Nationalism]. Tokyo: Yōsensha.

Takeda, Hiroko. 2008. "Structural Reform of the Family and the Neoliberalization of Everyday Life in Japan." *New Political Economy* 13, no. 2 (June): 153–72.

Tamura, Hiroshi. 2007. *Hōmuresu chūgakusei*. Tokyo: Wani Books.

Tsukino, Kōji. 2004. *Ie no naka no hōmuresu*. Nīgata nippō jigyōsha.

Tsurumi, Wataru. 1993. *Kanzen jisatsu manyuaru* [The Complete Manual of Suicide]. Tokyo: Futa shuppan saizu.

———. 1994. *Bokutachi no "kanzen jisatsu manyuaru"* [Our Complete Suicide Manual]. Tokyo: Futa shuppan saizu.

Uchi no jikka. 2011. www.sawayakazaidan.or.jp/ibasyo/case/04koushinetsu/uchinojikka.html.

Ueno, Chizuko. 2007. *Ohitorisama no rōgo* [Aging Alone]. Tokyo: Hōken.

———. 2009. *Otoko ohitorisama dō* [The path of a gentleman alone]. Tokyo: Hōken.

Vogel, Ezra F. 1979. *Japan as Number One: Lessons for America*. Cambridge, MA: Harvard University Press.

Waldby, Catherine, and Robert Mitchell. 2006. *Tissue Economies: Blood, Organs, and Cell Lines in Late Capitalism*. Durham, NC: Duke University Press.

Weeks, Kathi. 2011. *The Problem with Work: Marxism, Feminism, Anti-Work Politics, and Post-Work Imaginaries*. Durham, NC: Duke University Press.

Yamada, Masahiro. 1999. *Parasaito shinguru no jidai* [Era of parasite single]. Tokyo: Chikuma shobō.

———. 2001. *Kazokutoiu risuku* [Family Risk]. Tokyo: Keiso Shobō.

———. 2003. *Kibō kakusa shakai: "makegumi" no zetsubōkan ga Nihon o hikisaku* [A differential hope society: The despair of being a "loser" that is tearing Japan apart]. Tokyo: Chikuma Shobō.

Yamada, Masahiro, and Shirakawa Tōko. 2008. *"Konkatsu" jidai* [The Age of the "Marriage Market"]. Tokyo: Discover.

Yardley, Jim. 2010. "India Asks, Should Food Be a Right for the Poor?" *New York Times*, August 8.

Yoda, Tomiko. 2006. "The Rise and Fall of Maternal Society: Gender, Labor, and Capital in Contemporary Japan." In *Japan After Japan: Social and Cultural Life from the Recessionary 1990s to the Present*, edited by Tomiko Yoda and Harry Harootunian. Durham, N.C.: Duke University Press: 239 – 274.

Yokokawa, Kazuo. 2004. *Sono te wa inochizuna: Hitori de yaranai kaigō, hitori demo ī rōgō* [With These Hands, a Lifeline: Care That Can't Be Done Alone, Good Aging Even Alone]. Tokyo: Tarōjirōsha edītasu.

Yomiuri Shimbun. 2010. "Kōkoku: shakai zentai de "kosodate" o oenshite ikō !" [Public Announcement: Let's Help To Raise Children Altogether as a Society!]. June 14: 12.

———. 2011. "'Nihon de kangoshi' dan'nen zokuzoku- hi nado e kikoku 33 nin— kanji ya yōgo nankai na shaken" [More People Give Up on Being a Nurse in Japan—Thirty-Three Returned to Philippines and Indonesia: Difficult Kanji and Technical Terms, Difficult Exam]. July 9, 2011: 1.

Yosensha MOOK henshūbuhen. 2008. *Akibadōrimajiken o dō yomu ka?* [How Do We Read the Akiba Terrorist Attack?]. Tokyo: Yosensha MOOK henshūbuhen.

Yoshimi, Shunya. 2000. "Consuming 'America': From Symbol to System." in *Consumption in Asia: Lifestyles and Identities*, ed. Chua Beng-Huat. London, New York: Routledge Press: 202–224.

Yuasa, Makoto. 2008a. *Hanhinkon: "Suberidai shakai" kara no dasshutsu* [Reverse Poverty: Escape from a "sliding down society"]. Tokyo: Iwanami shinsho.

———. 2008b. "Kakusa to hinkon o nakusu tame ni watashitachi ni dekirukoto" [What We Can Do to Get Rid of Poverty and Difference]. In *Kakusa to hinkon: 20 kō* [Difference and Poverty: 20 Cases], edited by Makino Tomio and Murakami Eigo, 242-53. Tokyo: Akashi.

———. 2008c. *"Ikizurasa" no rinkai: "tame" no aru shakai e* [The criticality of the "Hardship of Life": Toward a Society of "Reserves"]. Tokyo: Junposha.

———. 2009. *Hinkon shūrai* [Invasion of Poverty]. Tokyo: Sansui shoten.

INDEX

Abélès, Marc, 84, 128, 160–61, 213n4, 215n4
Adachi, Mariko, 99–100
affect: (lack of) compassion others, 146–47;
  epistemology of, 138–39; global labor related to, 99–100; holding onto mother's
  bones and, 158–59; in memorialization,
  147–48; panic and depression linked to, 15,
  30, 40, 101, 114, 129, 131, 132–33, 141–42, 145,
  155, 175; in postwar work/leisure, 26–28;
  social and de-social, 70; touch and, 103–8.
  See also *ikizurasa*; senses; souls
age: of *hikikomori*, 3, 74; life expectancy,
  35–36, 39–40, 148; poverty rates and, 5; retirement, compared, 36. See also children;
  elderly people; youth
AIBO (Sony), 102

aidagara: communal value of, 25, 27. See also
  human relationships
Aiko (Kowaremono performer), 130, 131,
  153, 156
Akagi, Tomohiro, 59–61, 64, 212nn15–16
Akiba musabetsu tero jiken (indiscriminate
  terrorist attack), 63–64
alienation of the soul (annihilation of the
  spirit, *seishintekina ikizurasa*): circumstances of, 129; concept of, 15–16; lack of
  recognition underlying, 67–68, 70–71;
  ordinariness of, 69. See also pain; social
  withdrawal; "the soul on strike"
amae. See dependency
Amamiya, Karin: as advocate for *furītā*, 29,
  65–67, 82, 154–55, 212n20, 216n16; on anni-

Amamiya, Karin (*continued*)
hilation of the spirit, 67–68, 70–71; background of, 64–65, 131, 138, 167–68; belonging and right-wing, 61–62; as "boomer junior," 67, 213n22; Butler's concept of precarity/precariousness compared with, 65–66; *Ikisasero!*, 154–55, 211n6; on *ikizurasa*, 15, 16, 65; on precariat, 46; protest involvement of, 213n6; on recognition (*shōnin*), 65–68, 172; on "refugeed," 47; stop-suicide and, 132, 135

Angel Plans (1994 and 1996), 164, 217n19

animals, missing after earthquake, 194. *See also* pets

Anpanman characters, 98–99, 214n16

Appadurai, Arjun, 62

Arendt, Hannah, 53, 168

art, utopic potential of, 80–81. *See also* film and documentaries; literature; performance

Aruitemo aruitemo (Still Walking, film), 148

Asad, Talal, 192

Asada, Akira, 27–28

Asahi Shimbun (periodical): on *himote* fad, 96; on missing elderly, 40, 147, 148–49, 158; on post-3/11 reconstruction, 203–4; on precarious workers, 122; reproductive futurism in, 162–63; on social withdrawal, 19; on son's holding onto mother's bones, 159

@home (café), 97–98

atomic bombs, 7–8, 12, 156. *See also* nuclear energy and industry

Aum Shinrikyō (cult), 30

autonomist school (*operaismo*), 69

Azuma, Hiroshi, 197–98

Bachelard, Gaston, 77–78, 81, 91–92, 168, 213n1

Basic Act for Gender-Equal Society (1999), 217n19

Battle Royale (film), 143

Baumann, Zygmunt, 149

belonging: assistance in rebuilding, 56–58; human necessity of, 55, 168–69; loss of, 47–48, 119–20; post-3/11 discourse on, 198–99; postwar costs of, 118; relationship to violence and hope, 61–62; of *sararīman* (company man), 23. *See also* connectedness; disbelonging; family; human relationships; "my-home-ism"

Berardi, Franco "Bifo": on cognitariat, 15–16, 54, 84, 141; on home and soul, 157; on panic, depression, and anxiety, 142, 155; on precariat, 91; "soul at work," 129

Berlant, Lauren: on cruel optimism, 85; on feeling for an-other, 146; on my-home-ism, 33–34; on place and normalcy, 47–48, 61

The Big Issue Japan (newspaper), 212n20

binbō (poor), 137. *See also* poverty; working poor

biopolitics of everyday life, 128–29

biopower, 34, 37, 39

Bloch, Ernst: Genda's Blochian notion of hope, 91–92; on hope, 79, 173, 183, 199; on temporality of not-yet- vs. no-longer-conscious, 79–81, 83

Bokutachi no kanzen jisatsu manyuaru (Tsurumi), 134–35

Bourdieu, Pierre, 85, 207n5

Buddhist traditions, 147–48, 151

bullet trains, 124

bullying (*ijime*): as game of sociality, 70; increase in, 71; media on, 94, 214n11; school-refusal (*futōko*) due to, 73; stories of, 93–95, 118–19, 138

busjacker incident (2000), 73

Butler, Judith: on grievability, 55; on precarity and precariousness, 13–14, 15, 58, 65–66, 105–6, 169

cafés: cats (for touch), 107–8. *See also* maid cafés; net café dwellers

Cahn, Edgar, 126

capitalism: care and human time vs., 176–79; characteristics of, 83–84; cognitariat's work in, 15–16, 54, 84, 141; collective depression under, 129; currencies of value in, 166–67; human leftovers in, 149–51; infantile vs. mature, 27–28; normalcy tied to, 59; social corporeality of, 155–56; time and labor in, 126; work and post-work, 69. *See also* neoliberalism

capsule hotels, 49, 87

care and caregiving: changing political economy of, 100–101; costs of, 36–38; current attention to childcare, 163–64; deficit in,

denizens: Standing's use of term, 53–54

Denmark: workers' security in, 1–2

Densha otoko (Train Man, novel), 95–96

dependency (*amae*): hikikomori linked to, 74; in home and work, 26–28; longing for, 68; neoliberal rejection of, 28–29. *See also* independence

Desjarlais, Robert, 134

disbelonging: beginning at home, 85; disaster as intervening against, 197–98; in everyday life, 167–70; extent of, 53, 174–75; in homelessness, 149–50; as key problem for precariat, 65. *See also* belonging; *muen shakai*

disease: anorexia, 94–95; dementia, 103–4, 105–6; nonproductivity as, 155–56; panic and depression, 15, 30, 40, 101, 114, 129, 131, 132–33, 141–42, 145, 155, 175. *See also* death; pain

Disneyland (Tokyo), 85, 213n7

dispatch worker. *See* temporary or dispatch work

displaced persons, 53

Doi, Takeo, 27

Dower, John, 208n8

Durkheim, Emile, 168

earthquakes: future likelihood, 12–13; Kobe (1995), 19, 30, 189, 197. *See also* Great East Japan Earthquake

Eberstadt, Nick, 213–14n8

economic recession (1991–): beginning of, 6, 29–30; happiness claimed in the face of, 89–91, 205–6; life expectations in the aftermath of, 144–45; malaise due to, 82–85; as only one factor in poverty, 52; U.S. media coverage of, 86–87; as warning for others, 85–86; youth blamed for, 30, 139–40. *See also* capitalism; flexibilization; neoliberalism

economy: impact due to health care costs, 36–38; "miracle" (1970s and 1980s), 5, 10–11, 25–26; postwar growth, 7, 22, 24–25; structural reform in, 30–34. *See also* capitalism; economic recession; neoliberalism; social economy

Edelman, Lee, 23–24, 48, 163, 215n24

education: academic credentializing and, 68, 76, 140; mothers' role as *kyōiku mama*, 16, 24, 26, 118–19; workers penalized for

studying abroad, 82, 213n3. *See also* school system

Ehrenreich, Barbara, 215n3

elderly people: advice books for, 36, 210n16; alternative to loneliness (see *chiiki no cha no ma*); concerns about being a burden, 125, 152–53; family's refusal to claim belongings or body of, 151–52; *hikikomoris'* interaction with, 177–78; holding onto bones of, 158–59; life expectancy vs. healthy life expectancy for, 39–40, 210n17; "missing," 40–41, 147–53, 158–59; night patrol checks on, 165; number of, 35–36; pension funds and, 30, 32, 35–36; post-3/11 risks for, 187; poverty rate for, 5; solitary, lonely deaths of, 1–2, 20, 126–27, 148–52. *See also* care and caregiving

employment. *See* work

enterprise society: derided today by "new era Japanese management style," 29; gender roles in, 22–23. *See also* Japan, Inc.; Japanese management style

Equal Employment Opportunity Law (1986), 217n19

ethics: of care in post-3/11 cleanup, 190–91, 199–200; of healing, 134; of sociality (see *chiiki no cha no ma*). *See also* human relationships

EuroMayDays, 69

everyday life: anguish of, 2–3; assistance in rebuilding, 56–58; attention to, 127–28; biopolitics of, 128–29; breakdown of, 1–2, 113–15, 120, 142–43, 193; disbelonging in, 167–70; effects of insecuritization of labor, 81–82; energy conservation (*setsuden*) in, 186–87; life satisfaction decline, 40; post-3/11 rhythms of, 180–85; radical recalibrations of, 115–17, 193; relational changes in, 8; security in context of, 160–65; sensing a new, 139–43; sharing precarity of, 179. *See also* family; good life; pain; precarity; survival

Fackler, Martin, 86

family: breakdown and crises in, 30–31, 81–82, 113–15, 120; changing "function" of, 152–53; children's allowance (*kodomo teate*) proposed for, 162, 163; datafication and demise of, 106; decline of safety net (*tame*),

5–6; decreased size, 24; de facto welfare institution, 37–39, 40, 42; disinterest in and loss of, 147–52, 158–59; duty and affect toward, 103–6; factor in assessing a "good life," 144, 145; hometime beyond, 117–21; logic of, in crisis, 150–51; modern fable of survival, 2, 108–12; post-postwar role questioned, 157–59; postwar role of, 22–23, 25; sustainability of, 159–60; violence within, 4, 43–44, 97, 158, 216n17; wounds caused by, 155–57. *See also* everyday life

family-corporate system (*kazoku kigyō kan kankei*): collapse of, 28–30, 137; current precarity compared with, 84–85; dependency, performance, and affect in, 26–28; dynamics of, 10–11, 23–25; hope- and homelessness in context of, 45–46; labor and soul relationship in, 16; moral community in, 150; nostalgia for, 99; social corporeality of, 155–56; students' rejection of, 144, 145. *See also* "my-home-ism"; social reproduction

FBI *chōnōryoku sōsa kan* (television show), 111

film and documentaries, topics: breakdown of everydayness, 113–15, 120; bullying, 94, 214n11; dystopic inferno, 143; family and Obon, 148; *hikikomori*, 120–21; homelessness, 2, 110–12; Kowaremono performance group, 153, 177; mother's abandonment, 104–5; net café refugees, 43–47, 73; *otaku* ("geek"), 96; relationlessness, 152–53; suicide, 134–35. *See also specific titles*

Fingleton, Eamonn, 86

flexibilization (*ryūdōka*): concept, 7–8, 118; of daily sociality, 81–82; of labor force, 28–29, 46–47, 60, 64–65, 212n16; precarity of, 83–84

flexicurity, 10

food: abandoned child's search for, 109; comfort foods, 1, 214n14; local space for purchase, 177; mother and, 96–100, 109, 114; post-3/11 delivery requests, 203; preparation and meanings of, 97, 106–7; television characters made from, 98–99, 214n16. *See also* net café dwellers

Fordism: defined, 208n6; in Japan, 28, 172; in U.S., 6–7

Foucault, Michel, 34, 37

Fujita (profile for NHK special on lonely death), 150–52, 168

Fukusaku, Kinji, 143

fukushi ginkō. *See* welfare bank

Fukushima Daiichi Nuclear Plant and disaster (2011): abandoned souls in aftermath of, 152; crisis of, 18, 185–87; decision to never restart, 208n9; dismantling and cleanup process ("cold shutdown"), 11–13; disposable workers of, 8–9, 185–86; jobs in (post-3/11), 19, 187; ocean and death in context, 187–89; precariousness in aftermath, 66–67; safety concerns and, 184–85; summarized, 7. *See also* Great East Japan Earthquake; radiation

Fukushima Prefecture: post-earthquake support for, 181–84; symbols of hope in, 201–3; washing images of photos retrieved from tsunami, 194–96

Fukuyama, Francis, 27

fuman (dissatisfied) and *fuan* (uneasy), 63, 212n18

fureai ibasho. *See chiiki no cha no ma*

furītā: advocacy on behalf of, 29, 65–69, 82, 154–55, 212n20, 216n16; concept, 28–29; difficulties in getting married, 33–34; etymology, 209n2; exclusion and lack of recognition felt by, 65–68, 167–68; "hope is war" article by, 59–61, 212nn15–16; lack of hope among, 88; maid cafés patronized by, 98; as precarious social deformation, 31; stories of, 64–65, 131; suicides of, 66. *See also* irregular (*hiseikikoyō*) employment; temporary or dispatch work; youth

Furuichi, Noritoshi: everyday enjoyment of, 145; Genda compared with, 92; on happiness, 89–91, 205–6; WORK: *Zetsubō no kuni no kōfuku na wakamonotachi* (Happy youth in a country of despair), 89–91, 205–6

futurist hopes: collapse of, 128–29, 164; daydreams fueled by, 79–81; decline among youth, 82–88, 178; difficulty for earthquake survivors, 193–96; exit from or withdrawal within (national) home, 85–88; flatness in/ as, 88–91; parental cultivation of, 92–93; possibilities glimpsed in film, 115; postwar beliefs, 6, 23–24, 139; radical recalibrations of, 115–17, 193; in sharing precarity, 179. *See also* reproductive futurism

Galbraith, Patrick, 98
garbage (*gomi*): humans as, 149, 156
Garcia, Angela, 134
Genda, Yūji: earthquake and response to, 198–200; hope studies ("Hopology"), 83, 91–93
gender: café dwellers, 44; enterprise society, 22–23; equity laws, 217n19; *hikikomori*, 3, 74; life expectancy vs. healthy life expectancy, 39–40, 210n17; poverty rates, 5; precariat and temp workers, 9, 32, 209–10n9; unemployment, 210n10; wages, 32. *See also* men and boys; women and girls
Germany: Japan's situation compared with, 51, 61; nuclear-free energy goal of, 186
gomi (garbage): humans as, 149, 156
good life: construction of, 143–47; corporeality in, 141–42; *furītā*'s definition, 61; postwar definition, 22; shop owner's definition, 164. *See also* everyday life
Great East Japan Earthquake (2011): author's perspective on, 16–17; crisis of, 8–9, 185–87; as crossroads, 20; hope after, 196–201; *nomaoi* festival after, 201–2; ocean and death in context, 187–89; reconstruction issues after, 203–4; relief efforts after, 146, 189–93; rhythms of life in aftermath, 180–85; use of term, 7; visitors to site of, 19; washing images retrieved from tsunami, 194–96. *See also* Fukushima Daiichi Nuclear Plant and disaster
grievability of life lives: Butler on politics of social life, 14, 15; connectedness in, 55; killing others to achieve, 64; missing elderly in context of, 20, 149; playacting of, 153
Grossberg, Lawrence, 84, 211n3

Hage, Ghassan, 62
haken work. *See* temporary or dispatch work
hakidashi (venting or throwing up), 138–39
hakidasu: use of term, 138, 153, 176
Hanhinkon (Reverse Poverty; Yuasa), 55, 135
Hanhinkon netto wāku. See Reverse Poverty Network
Hanshin earthquake (Kobe, 1995), 19, 30, 189, 197
harappa: meanings of, 178
Hardt, Michael, 54
Harvey, David, 54, 211–12n13
Hashimoto, Tōru, 204–5

Hatoyama, Yukio: election of, 122–23, 211n8; health power strategy of, 38–39; removed from office, 123, 215n8; social welfare platform of, 161–62
healing (*iyashī*) boom, 102–3, 107–8
health care system: costs for elderly in, 36–38; responsibility shifted to family, 37–39, 40, 42; uninsured citizens and, 210n15, 211n1. *See also* care and caregiving; hospitals; welfare
health power strategy, 38–40
heart (*kokoro*), 101–3
Hello Work (program), 217n7
hikikomori (socially withdrawn individuals): absence of bodily touch, 106; advocates for, 119–20; as alternative lifestyle, 95–96, 130; elderly people's interaction with, 177–78; involved in making film, 120–21; non-(re)productive, 24, 155; as popular topic, 2–4, 8; possibilities for reimagining life, 176–79; radio show for, 131; as refugees at home, 71–76; stories told by, 131–32, 135, 153; *tōjisha* term for, 74, 213n24; youths' de-sociality compared with, 82, 85. *See also* social withdrawal
hikokumin (non-citizenly) person or action, 184
himote fad, 96
hinkon. See poverty
Hiroshima: atomic bomb deaths at, 7, 12. *See also* radiation
hiseikikoyō employment. *See* irregular (*hiseikikoyō*) employment
hiyatoi. See day labor
Hochschild, Arlie Russell, 215n3
Höjdestrand, Tova, 149
home (*ibasho*): alternative construction of, 97, 118–21; approach to studying, 78–79; breakdown of everydayness in, 113–15, 120; call to reconstruct, 204; daydreams sheltered in, 77–78, 81; elderly disconnected from, 150–52; health care responsibility shifted to, 37–39, 40, 42; *hikikomori* as refugees at, 71–76; homeless inside of home, 73, 85, 157; hope connected to, 33–34, 79–81; as human time, 174–76; inward turn toward, 85–88; loss of, 3–4, 47–48; "oneiric" (dream of house yet to

Indonesia: care workers from, 36, 99–100, 210n14

Ingold, Tim, 195

insecurity. *See* precarity

Institute of Social Science (Tokyo University), 92–93

Iraq: Japanese hostages in, 146–47

irregular (*hiseikikoyō*) employment: affiliation (*shozoku*) lacking for, 65; denizens in, 53; homeless conditions linked to, 44–47; material and existential insecurities of, 15–16; rates and implications of, 5–6, 29–30, 210–11n1; social context of, 66–67; structural reform's impact on, 31–34. See also *furītā*; net café dwellers; temporary or dispatch work

Italy: "mobbing" in, 83; volunteerism in, 216n1

Iwabuchi, Kōichi, 85

iyashi (healing) boom, 102–3, 107–8

Japan: center and periphery in, 201; corporate familism as blueprint for, 23–24; crisis and national identity, 46–47, 181–85; democratic system endangered, 91; inward tendencies in, 85–88; lost decades in, 29, 79, 83, 102, 213n2; nationalism in, 61–62, 65; post-3/11 cutbacks and protests in, 185–87; as refugeed from its soul, 136; relations with and attitudes toward Chinese, 139–40; securing nation vs. people of, 160–65; socioeconomic preferences in, 160; U.S. occupation (postwar), 7, 208n8. See also consumer culture; demographics; economy; family; Great East Japan Earthquake; hope; postwar period; poverty; precarity; work

Japan, Inc.: academic credentializing (*gakureki shakai*) in, 68, 76, 140; aftermath of, 128–29; current precarity compared with, 84–85; flexible laborers in, 29; strategies in, 25–26; use of term, 10–11, 21. See also family-corporate system; "my-home-ism"

Japanese government: assertions of containment of Fukushima reactors, 11–12; distrust of, 11, 13, 185, 200–201, 204–5; Gold Plans of, 37; response to economic decline, 52; "risk and individual responsibility" slogan of, 28

Japanese management style (*nihonteki keiei*):

bullet trains as exemplar of, 124; characteristics, 25–28; demise of, 28–29; hiring practices, 209n4. See also enterprise society; family-corporate system

Japanese management style, new era of (*shinjidai nihonteki keiei*): flexibilization of labor force in, 28–29, 46–47, 60, 64–65, 212n16; implementation of, 29–30; slogan, 28; *Tokyo Sonata*, 113–15, 120; traditional family unsuited for, 99–100. See also economic recession; flexibilization; neoliberalism; temporary or dispatch work

Japanese Ministry of Health, Labor, and Welfare (*Kōseirōdōshō*), 40, 47, 73–74

Japan Railways (JR), 183–84

jieitai (self-defense forces), 50–51, 61, 189, 211n10

jiko sekinin. *See* individual responsibility

jiritsu. *See* independence

Jisatsusu nara, hikikomore (Honda), 71

job-hunting process (*shūkatsu*), 60, 89, 144, 212n15. See also work

Joseph, Miranda, 150

Kacco (performer): background, 156, 216n15; on being "sick" and performing, 154; as Kowaremono member, 153; on parents, 157; on pus (*umi*), 155–56; at stop-suicide talking event, 130, 131

Kaigo utsu (Shimizu), 42

Kainuma, Hiroshi, 201

kakusa shakai (divided society): discourse on, 33, 135–36; hope differential in, 34, 87–88; trend toward, 65; youth's attitudes regarding, 88, 146

Kan, Naoto, 18, 123, 162

Kanzen jisatsu manyuaru (The Complete Manual of Suicide; Tsurumi), 132–34, 215n6

Katō, Sogen, 148

Katō, Tomohiro: Akihabara attack by, 3, 62–64, 215n5; identification with, 119, 138

Katsuno, Hirofumi, 102

Kawada, Keiko, 170–72, 173

Kayano, Toshihiko, 63, 67

kazoku kigyō kan kankei. *See* family-corporate system

Kazoku toiu risuku (Family Risk; Yamada), 31

kibō. *See* hope

Kibō kakusa shakai (Yamada), 87–88, 112
Kibō no kuni no ekusodasu (The exodus of a country with hope; Murakami), 6, 79, 95, 197
Kita Kyūshū City: starvation in, 1–2
Kleinman, Arthur, 105, 159
Kobe earthquake (1995), 19, 30, 189, 197
Koide, Hiroaki, 11–12
Koizumi, Jun'ichirō: Japanese hostages denounced by, 147; neoliberal restructuring under, 27, 31, 38, 52, 100, 111, 160; on poverty, 33; term of office, 211n12
kokoro (heart), 101–3
konbini. See convenience stores
konkatsu (marriage market), 164, 216n20
Korēda, Hirokazu, 104–5, 147–48
Kōseirōdōshō (Ministry of Health, Labor, and Welfare), 40, 47, 73–74
Kowaremono ("broken people," performance group): background, 153, 216n15; documentary on, 153, 177; founder, 131; mentioned, 175; stories of, 153–57
kūki o yomu (reading the scene), 70
Kurosawa, Kiyoshi, 113–15, 120
Kyōseichō (Murakami), 73
Kyoto: camp for kids from Fukushima in, 182–83; radiation concerns in, 203

labor. *See* work
laws: gender equity, 217n19; temp workers' protection dismantled, 67, 212–13n21
Lear, Jonathan, 115–17, 193
Liberal Democratic Party (LDP), 30, 122–23, 211n8
liquidization of work and life (*ryūdōka*). *See* flexibilization; precarity
literature: by entertainers, 110, 112; on *hikikomori*, 73; on homelessness, 2, 108–13; *otaku* ("geek") in, 95–96; poetics of radical hope in, 115–17, 193; utopic potential of, 80–81
Loft+One (club), 129, 134, 172
loneliness (*kodoku*). *See muen shakai*
love: 2-D, 96; caregiving as, 104; heart (*kokoro*) and, 101–3. *See also* family-corporate system; human relationships; "my-home-ism"

maid cafés, 97–98
mai-hōmushugi. See "my-home-ism"

Ma-kun niwa yume ga nai (Mr. Ma Doesn't Have Dreams, film), 120–21
marriage: 2-D, 96; current faddism around, 164; factor in "good life," 144, 145; gay rights advocates approaches to, 215n24; irregular work's impact on, 33–34; as nuisance (*mendōkusai*), 100–101
Marx, Karl, 166, 168, 211–12n13
May Days (Japan), 69, 213n6
memorialization: in Buddhism, 147–48; challenges of (post-3/11), 188–89. *See also* death
memory things (*omoide no mono*), 194–96
men and boys: abandonment by fathers, 108–10; advice for living alone, 210n16; as core workers, 22–23; new herbivorous man (*sōshoku danshi*), 99; postwar work and leisure interwoven, 26–28; reunion with father in *Hōmuresu chūgakusei*, 111; as *sararīman* (company man), 16, 23, 113–14, 214n22
middle class, 22, 33, 60. *See also* classism; economic recession; family-corporate system; "my-home-ism"
migrants. *See* immigrants and migrants
military. *See* self-defense forces
Minami Sōma: *nomaoi* festival in, 201–2
Miyagi Prefecture: post-3/11 cleanup in, 13, 190–92; post-3/11 jobs in, 19; unnamed elderly deaths in, 20
Miyamoto, Michiko: on de-sociality, 70–71, 81–82, 85, 139; mentioned, 33
Miyamoto, Tarō, 159–61
Miyazaki Prefecture: precarious workers in, 123–24
Mizushima, Hiroaki, 43–47, 73
Molé, Nicole J., 83
mothers: abandonment by, 41–42, 104–5; caring for and relationship with, 103–4, 105–6; children's killings of, 4, 158, 216n17; as "education mamas," 16, 24, 26, 118–19; food preparation by, 97, 98–99; holding onto bones of, 158–59; sacrificial type of, 109
Moyai (organization): author's visit to, 55–56, 136; goals, 55, 57–59; mentioned, 44; stories from drop-ins at, 49–50, 56–57. *See also* Yuasa, Makoto

mud: going into, 13, 205–6; nuclear radiation linked to, 7–9, 13; post-3/11 cleanup of, 190–93; symbols of hope juxtaposed to, 201–3; washing images and, 194–96

muen shakai (pain of social loneliness and disbelonging): alternative to (see *chīki no cha no ma*); flexibilization's effects on, 81–82; missing elderly in, 41, 149–52, 158–59; ordinariness of, 114–15, 165, 167–70; post-3/11 stories and survey of, 18–20; sensory nature of, 15; suicidal thoughts and cutting in, 63, 118–19, 131, 138; television program on, 126–27, 149, 150–51; use of term, 8. *See also* disbelonging; *furītā*; *hikikomori*; *ikizurasa*; social withdrawal; suicides

Munoz, José Esteban, 117, 120, 173, 175–76, 215n24

Murakami, Ryū: on exit and survival, 95; on *hikikomori*, 73; on hope, 6, 79, 139, 197, 198

mutual contact (*fureai*), 127, 169–70, 172–73. See also *chīki no cha no ma*

"my home" (*uchi no jikka*): use of term, 170–71. See also *chīki no cha no ma*

"my-home-ism" (*mai-hōmushugi*): concept and characteristics, 22–28; current contradictions, 157–59; new version, 39–40; pain of losing, 17, 61; persistence of ideal, 33–34; postwar context, 21–22. *See also* belonging; family-corporate system

Nagasaki: atomic bomb deaths at, 7, 12. *See also* radiation

Naitō, Daisuke, 94

Nakane, Chie, 26–27, 172

NALC. *See* Nippon Active Life Club

NEET (not in education, employment, or training) individuals: advocates for, 119–20; as hidden and nonproductive, 155; number of, 70; as "parasite singles," 30, 60, 209n6; as precarious social deformation, 31; stories about, 49–50; use of term, 8

Negri, Antonio, 54

neighborhoods. *See* community residents

neoliberalism: accumulation under, 212n13; affective labor in, 99–100; characteristics, 52–55, 83–84; everyday effects of, 4–6, 140–42; home and labor affected by, 30–34; human leftovers in, 149–51; management

style dismantled under, 28–29; politics of survival in, 12–13, 14, 58–59, 66, 84, 128, 143, 213n4; "security of life" concerns in, 159–61. *See also* capitalism; Japanese management style, new era of; precarity

net café dwellers: characteristics and context, 43–47; *hikikomori* compared with, 73; stories of, 49–50, 59; U.S. media on, 87; wages and health issues of, 210–11n1

Netto kafe nanmin (documentary), 43–47, 73

New York Times, 86–87, 197

NHK (broadcasting service): *muen shakai* special and reportage on, 126–27, 149, 150–52; poverty series on, 47

NHK ni yōkoso (Takimoto), 3, 73, 207nn2–3

Niigata: *chiika no cha no ma* in, 170–74, 176; employment rate in, 155; Kowaremono performance in, 153–54; self-help group in, 119; youth support station in, 177, 217n7

Niigata chiika wakamono sapōto sutēshon (Nīgata Regional Young People's Support Station), 177, 217n7

ningenkankei. *See* human relationships

Nippon Active Life Club (NALC): *chīki no cha no ma* compared with, 170, 174; concept underlying, 124–25; currency and value in, 166–67; stories of, 125–27

Noda, Yoshihiko, 11

nomaoi festival, 201–2

Noriko no shokutaku (Noriko's Dinner Table, film), 152–53

nuclear bombs, 7–8, 12, 156

nuclear energy and industry: attitudes toward, 8–9, 18–19; politics and shutdown of, 185–86, 200–201, 204. *See also* Fukushima Daiichi Nuclear Plant and disaster

nuclear refugees (*genpatsu nanmin*), 12

Nuttari yori dokoro (Nuttari Place), 177–78

Obama, Barack, 199

OECD (Organisation for Economic Co-operation and Development), 5, 36, 136, 160, 163

Ōhira, Masayoshi, 26

Ohitorisama (television drama), 39

ohitori-sama ("being single") fad, 39

Ohitorisama no rōgo (Aging Alone; Ueno), 39

omoide no mono (memory things), 194–96

precarity (continued)
intensified after 3/11, 8–9, 185–87, 196; memories of past and, 84–85; in multiple areas (sociality, work, life), 9–10, 65–67; post-3/11 dismay and distrust, 203–5; radical hope in moving beyond, 115–17, 193; rhythms of life in, 180–85; sensing and symptoms of, 13–16, 58; sharing and contending with, 13, 205–6; structural reform's effects on, 30–34; washing memories and staying with, 193–96. See also ikizurasa (the pain of life); muen shakai (pain of social loneliness and disbelonging); public discourse; social precarity; vulnerability

protest: anti–nuclear power, 186, 200; limits of, 213n6; volunteers' response to, 202; withdrawal as, 71, 95–96

public discourse (topics): Akiba terrorist incident, 63–64; belonging, 198–99; competitive society, 143; health power strategy, 39–40; hikikomori and social withdrawal, 2–4, 8, 73–74; hikokumin (non-citizenly) person or action, 184; home and hometime, 112–13; hope (post-3/11), 196–201; hostages in Iraq, 147; ibasho ga nai, 174–75; low birthrates, 164–65; militarism (former), 50; ocean and death, 187–89; precarity, 122–24; refugees (nanmin), 47; reproductive futurism, 162–64; sacred imperial regalia theme, 208–9n1; "security of life," 159–61; tsunagari (connectedness), 198. See also consumer culture; politics; social media

radiation: contamination from, 18; continued threat of, 185, 193, 196; mud linked to, 7–9, 13; reconstruction issues and, 203–4; stigma attached to survivors, 12; symbols of hope juxtaposed to, 201–3. See also atomic bombs; Fukushima Daiichi Nuclear Plant and disaster

recognition (shōnin): in chiiki no cha no ma, 171–72; desire for, 65–69, 152–53; effects of lack of, 70–71, 119–20, 167–68; of loss and pain, 191–93; social media for, 90–91

Recruit (temp company), 28–29

refugeeization (nanminka) and refugees (nanmin): emergence of issue, 46–47; Japan as refugeed from its soul, 136; nuclear, 12; number of, 52–53; ordinari-

ness of, 69; post-3/11 risks for, 187; social withdrawal as form of, 70–76. See also homelessness; net café dwellers; ordinary refugeeism

"regional living room." See chīki no cha no ma

reproductive futurism: alternative to, 118–21; concept, 23–24; dissolution of, 48; life expectancy rates and, 35–36; re-embrace of, 162–65. See also futurist hopes; social reproduction

reserves. See tame

resource (shigen): absence of, 140; care as "storehouse for the future" (mirai no kura) in context of, 127, 166–67, 174

responsibility (sekinin), familial, 103–6. See also individual responsibility

reterritorialization: in camp for kids from Fukushima, 182–83; of connectedness and the social, 141–42, 165, 176; human vs. capitalist temporalities in, 176–79

Reverse Poverty Network (Hanhinkon netto wāku), 44–45, 135, 136. See also Moyai; Yuasa, Makoto

Rifkin, Jeremy, 89

right-wing organizations, 61–62

Riry, Franky, 110

robotics, 101–3, 214n18

Ronza (journal), 59–61, 212nn15–16

Rosujiena (journal), 63

Russia: homelessness in, 149–50, 211n2

ryūdōka. See flexibilization

Sachiko (friend): on Japan's problems, 139–40, 142–43; parents of, 214n13; on youth crime, 97

sacred imperial regalia, 22, 208–9n1

Saika University (Kyoto), 182–83

saiten. See performance

sarin gas attacks (1995), 30

school system: alternative to, 75–76; competitiveness and bullying in, 71, 73, 93–95, 118–19, 143; economic downturn blamed on laxness in, 140; motivation for attending university, 89; refusing to go to school (futōko), 73; students' failure to excel, 62, 68, 118, 156–57, 176–77; teachers' missed days for civil disobedience (kyūshoku) in, 51. See also education

security: of life (seikatsu hoshō), 159–61; of

nation vs. people, 160–65. *See also* precarity

seikatsu hogo. *See* welfare

seishintekina ikizurasa. *See* alienation of the soul

sekinin (responsibility), familial, 103–6. *See also* individual responsibility

self (selves): credo of, 152; in defining "good life," 144, 145; oneiric, 91–93; reeducation by, 119–20. *See also* individual responsibility

Self-Defense Forces (*jieitai*), 50–51, 61, 189, 211n10

self-sustainability: concept, 39–40; elderly's perspective on, 40–41; embrace of, 152; ethics of the social vs., 169–70. *See also* independence; individual responsibility

senses: into dementia, 105–6; of disbelonging, 167–70; of new everyday, 139–43; poverty combined with, 58; precarity registered on, 14–16. *See also* affect; *chiiki no cha no ma* ("regional living room")

Serizawa, Shunsuke, 74, 106

shakai hoken (social insurance), 211n1. *See also* social security system

shi. *See* death

shigen. *See* resource

Shimizu, Yoshiko, 42

Shimizu, Yukiko, 42

Shimomura, Sanae, 41–42

shinkansen (high-speed rail system), 124

Shirakawa, Tōko, 216n20

Shirogane Mass Harappa Meeting (Volunteer Academic Conference, 2010), 178, 217n9

Shirōto no Ran ("amateur revolt"; antinuclear and social movement), 213n6

shōnin. *See* recognition

shūkatsu (job-hunting process), 60, 89, 144, 212n15. *See also* work

"sick" and "broken people": disabilities listed, 153; stories of, 153–57

Silver, Beverly, 25

Slater, David H., 29, 50, 186

social connectedness. *See* connectedness

social corporeality: of family-corporate system, 155–56; part of good life, 141–42; reanimated, 165

social economy: aging vs. aged society distinctions, 35–36; family-corporate system

and growth of, 24–25; post-bubble crises in, 30–31. *See also* economy

social insurance (*shakai hoken*), 211n1. *See also* social security system

sociality: collapse of, 70–71, 81–82, 85, 128–29, 139; competitiveness of, 69–70; conviviance in, 84, 128, 161, 213n4, 215n4; deficit of, 127; disassembled among precariat, 62–64; emergence of mutual endeavors and openness in, 175–76; pain formed in, 192–93; politics of, 58–59; remapping of, 170–71. *See also* care and caregiving; *chiiki no cha no ma*

social media: bullying in, 93–95; competitive sociality in, 69–70; *Hōmuresu chūgakusei* discussed in, 111, 112; intimacy via, 96; recognition via, 90–91; suicide dateline in, 130; touch absent in, 106. *See also* public discourse

social precarity: approach to studying, 17; components, 124; of everyday life, 1–4, 53–55; relational changes underlying, 8. *See also* precarity

social reproduction: basic income tied to, in post-work society, 69, 217n5; in capitalism, 150–51; *hikikomori*'s failure in, 24; poverty's implications for, 33–34; women's roles in, 22–28. *See also* family-corporate system; reproductive futurism

social security system: aging society's impact on, 35–38; stay-at-home mothers penalized in, 32

social welfare. *See* welfare

social withdrawal: as alternative lifestyle, 95–96, 130; due to bullying, 93–95; as form of refugeeism, 70–71; memoir of, 71–72, 74–76, 77; ordinariness of, 139; poetics of, 117–21; as popular topic, 2–4, 8. *See also* alienation of the soul; *hikikomori*; *muen shakai*

Solnit, Rebecca, 198

"the soul on strike" (spiritual void): "broken people" performance group and, 153–57; concept, 16, 18, 129, 176; missing elderly and, 147–53, 158–59; stories about, 176–79; throwing up frustration in, 135–39; *tōjisha* stories and, 131–32; youth blamed for, 139–40. *See also* alienation of the soul; suicides